COMPLETE WRITINGS

THE
OTHER VOICE
IN
EARLY MODERN
EUROPE

A Series Edited by Margaret L. King and Albert Rabil Jr.

RECENT BOOKS IN THE SERIES

Isotta Nogarola

COMPLETE WRITINGS

Letterbook,
Dialogue on Adam and Eve,
Orations

જી

Edited and Translated
by Margaret L. King and Diana Robin

THE UNIVERSITY OF CHICAGO PRESS
Chicago & London

Isotta Nogarola, 1418–66

Margaret L. King is professor of history at Brooklyn College and the Graduate Center, City University of New York.

Diana Robin is professor emerita of classics and comparative literature at the University of New Mexico.

The University of Chicago Press, Chicago 60637
The University of Chicago Press, Ltd., London
© 2004 by The University of Chicago
All rights reserved. Published 2004
Printed in the United States of America
13 12 11 10 09 08 07 06 05 04   1 2 3 4 5

ISBN: 0-226-59007-0 (cloth)
ISBN: 0-226-59008-9 (paper)

Library of Congress Cataloging-in-Publication data

Nogarola, Isotta, 1418–1466.
[Works. English. 2004]
Complete writings : letterbook, dialogue on Adam and Eve, orations / Isotta
Nogarola ; edited and translated by Margaret L. King and Diana Robin.
p. cm. — (The other voice in early modern Europe)
Includes bibliographical references (p.   ) and index.
ISBN 0-226-59007-0 (cloth : alk. paper) — ISBN 0-226-59008-9 (pbk. : alk. paper)
1. Nogarola, Isotta, 1418–1466—Translations into English.   2. Speeches,
addresses, etc., Latin (Medieval and modern)—Translations into English.
3. Women—Italy—Verona—History—Middle Ages, 500–1500—Sources.   4. Authors,
Latin (Medieval and modern)—Italy—Correspondence.   5. Nogarola, Isotta,
1418–1466—Correspondence.   6. Humanists—Italy—Correspondence.
7. Verona (Italy)—History—Sources.   8. Women—Italy—Correspondence.
I. King, Margaret L., 1947– II. Robin, Diana Maury. III. Title. IV. Series.
PA8555.N6 A25 2004
211'.6'092—dc22   2003018991

In memory of our mothers
Marie King and Helen Vass Kurtz

CONTENTS

THE OTHER VOICE IN
EARLY MODERN EUROPE:
INTRODUCTION TO THE SERIES

Margaret L. King and Albert Rabil Jr.

THE OLD VOICE AND THE OTHER VOICE

In western Europe and the United States, women are nearing equality in the professions, in business, and in politics. Most enjoy access to education, reproductive rights, and autonomy in financial affairs. Issues vital to women are on the public agenda: equal pay, child care, domestic abuse, breast cancer research, and curricular revision with an eye to the inclusion of women.

These recent achievements have their origins in things women (and some male supporters) said for the first time about six hundred years ago. Theirs is the "other voice," in contradistinction to the "first voice," the voice of the educated men who created Western culture. Coincident with a general reshaping of European culture in the period 1300–1700 (called the Renaissance or early modern period), questions of female equality and opportunity were raised that still resound and are still unresolved.

The other voice emerged against the backdrop of a three-thousand-year history of the derogation of women rooted in the civilizations related to Western culture: Hebrew, Greek, Roman, and Christian. Negative attitudes toward women inherited from these traditions pervaded the intellectual, medical, legal, religious, and social systems that developed during the European Middle Ages.

The following pages describe the traditional, overwhelmingly male views of women's nature inherited by early modern Europeans and the new tradition that the "other voice" called into being to begin to challenge reigning assumptions. This review should serve as a framework for understanding the texts published in the series "The Other Voice in Early Modern Europe." Introductions specific to each text and author follow this essay in all the volumes of the series.

TRADITIONAL VIEWS OF WOMEN, 500 B.C.E.–1500 C.E.

Embedded in the philosophical and medical theories of the ancient Greeks were perceptions of the female as inferior to the male in both mind and body. Similarly, the structure of civil legislation inherited from the ancient Romans was biased against women, and the views on women developed by Christian thinkers out of the Hebrew Bible and the Christian New Testament were negative and disabling. Literary works composed in the vernacular of ordinary people, and widely recited or read, conveyed these negative assumptions. The social networks within which most women lived—those of the family and the institutions of the Roman Catholic Church—were shaped by this negative tradition and sharply limited the areas in which women might act in and upon the world.

GREEK PHILOSOPHY AND THE FEMALE NATURE.   Greek biology assumed that women were inferior to men and defined them as merely childbearers and housekeepers. This view was authoritatively expressed in the works of the philosopher Aristotle.

Aristotle thought in dualities. He considered action superior to inaction, form (the inner design or structure of any object) superior to matter, completion to incompletion, possession to deprivation. In each of these dualities, he associated the male principle with the superior quality and the female with the inferior. "The male principle in nature," he argued, "is associated with active, formative and perfected characteristics, while the female is passive, material and deprived, desiring the male in order to become complete."[1] Men are always identified with virile qualities, such as judgment, courage, and stamina, and women with their opposites—irrationality, cowardice, and weakness.

The masculine principle was considered superior even in the womb. The man's semen, Aristotle believed, created the form of a new human creature, while the female body contributed only matter. (The existence of the ovum, and with it the other facts of human embryology, was not established until the seventeenth century.) Although the later Greek physician Galen believed there was a female component in generation, contributed by "female semen," the followers of both Aristotle and Galen saw the male role in human generation as more active and more important.

In the Aristotelian view, the male principle sought always to reproduce

---

1. Aristotle, *Physics* 1.9.192a20–24, in *The Complete Works of Aristotle*, ed. Jonathan Barnes, rev. Oxford trans., 2 vols. (Princeton, 1984), 1:328.

itself. The creation of a female was always a mistake, therefore, resulting from an imperfect act of generation. Every female born was considered a "defective" or "mutilated" male (as Aristotle's terminology has variously been translated), a "monstrosity" of nature.[2]

For Greek theorists, the biology of males and females was the key to their psychology. The female was softer and more docile, more apt to be despondent, querulous, and deceitful. Being incomplete, moreover, she craved sexual fulfillment in intercourse with a male. The male was intellectual, active, and in control of his passions.

These psychological polarities derived from the theory that the universe consisted of four elements (earth, fire, air, and water), expressed in human bodies as four "humors" (black bile, yellow bile, blood, and phlegm) considered, respectively, dry, hot, damp, and cold and corresponding to mental states ("melancholic," "choleric," "sanguine," "phlegmatic"). In this scheme the male, sharing the principles of earth and fire, was dry and hot; the female, sharing the principles of air and water, was cold and damp.

Female psychology was further affected by her dominant organ, the uterus (womb), *hystera* in Greek. The passions generated by the womb made women lustful, deceitful, talkative, irrational, indeed—when these affects were in excess—"hysterical."

Aristotle's biology also had social and political consequences. If the male principle was superior and the female inferior, then in the household, as in the state, men should rule and women must be subordinate. That hierarchy did not rule out the companionship of husband and wife, whose cooperation was necessary for the welfare of children and the preservation of property. Such mutuality supported male preeminence.

Aristotle's teacher Plato suggested a different possibility: that men and women might possess the same virtues. The setting for this proposal is the imaginary and ideal Republic that Plato sketches in a dialogue of that name. Here, for a privileged elite capable of leading wisely, all distinctions of class and wealth dissolve, as, consequently, do those of gender. Without households or property, as Plato constructs his ideal society, there is no need for the subordination of women. Women may therefore be educated to the same level as men to assume leadership. Plato's Republic remained imaginary, however. In real societies, the subordination of women remained the norm and the prescription.

The views of women inherited from the Greek philosophical tradition became the basis for medieval thought. In the thirteenth century,

---

2. Aristotle, *Generation of Animals* 2.3.737a27–28, in *The Complete Works*, 1:1144.

the supreme Scholastic philosopher Thomas Aquinas, among others, still echoed Aristotle's views of human reproduction, of male and female personalities, and of the preeminent male role in the social hierarchy.

ROMAN LAW AND THE FEMALE CONDITION. Roman law, like Greek philosophy, underlay medieval thought and shaped medieval society. The ancient belief that adult property-owning men should administer households and make decisions affecting the community at large is the very fulcrum of Roman law.

About 450 B.C.E., during Rome's republican era, the community's customary law was recorded (legendarily) on twelve tablets erected in the city's central forum. It was later elaborated by professional jurists whose activity increased in the imperial era, when much new legislation was passed, especially on issues affecting family and inheritance. This growing, changing body of laws was eventually codified in the *Corpus of Civil Law* under the direction of the emperor Justinian, generations after the empire ceased to be ruled from Rome. That *Corpus*, read and commented on by medieval scholars from the eleventh century on, inspired the legal systems of most of the cities and kingdoms of Europe.

Laws regarding dowries, divorce, and inheritance pertain primarily to women. Since those laws aimed to maintain and preserve property, the women concerned were those from the property-owning minority. Their subordination to male family members points to the even greater subordination of lower-class and slave women, about whom the laws speak little.

In the early republic, the *paterfamilias*, or "father of the family," possessed *patria potestas*, "paternal power." The term *pater*, "father," in both these cases does not necessarily mean biological father but denotes the head of a household. The father was the person who owned the household's property and, indeed, its human members. The *paterfamilias* had absolute power—including the power, rarely exercised, of life or death—over his wife, his children, and his slaves, as much as his cattle.

Male children could be "emancipated," an act that granted legal autonomy and the right to own property. Those over fourteen could be emancipated by a special grant from the father or automatically by their father's death. But females could never be emancipated; instead, they passed from the authority of their father to that of a husband or, if widowed or orphaned while still unmarried, to a guardian or tutor.

Marriage in its traditional form placed the woman under her husband's authority, or *manus*. He could divorce her on grounds of adultery, drinking wine, or stealing from the household, but she could not divorce him. She could neither possess property in her own right nor bequeath any to her children upon her death. When her husband died, the household property passed not to her but to his male heirs. And when her father died, she had no claim to any family inheritance, which was directed to her brothers or more remote male relatives. The effect of these laws was to exclude women from civil society, itself based on property ownership.

In the later republican and imperial periods, these rules were significantly modified. Women rarely married according to the traditional form. The practice of "free" marriage allowed a woman to remain under her father's authority, to possess property given her by her father (most frequently the "dowry," recoverable from the husband's household on his death), and to inherit from her father. She could also bequeath property to her own children and divorce her husband, just as he could divorce her.

Despite this greater freedom, women still suffered enormous disability under Roman law. Heirs could belong only to the father's side, never the mother's. Moreover, although she could bequeath her property to her children, she could not establish a line of succession in doing so. A woman was "the beginning and end of her own family," said the jurist Ulpian. Moreover, women could play no public role. They could not hold public office, represent anyone in a legal case, or even witness a will. Women had only a private existence and no public personality.

The dowry system, the guardian, women's limited ability to transmit wealth, and total political disability are all features of Roman law adopted by the medieval communities of western Europe, although modified according to local customary laws.

CHRISTIAN DOCTRINE AND WOMEN'S PLACE. The Hebrew Bible and the Christian New Testament authorized later writers to limit women to the realm of the family and to burden them with the guilt of original sin. The passages most fruitful for this purpose were the creation narratives in Genesis and sentences from the Epistles defining women's role within the Christian family and community.

Each of the first two chapters of Genesis contains a creation narrative. In the first "God created man in his own image, in the image of God he created him; male and female he created them" (Gn 1:27). In the second, God created Eve from Adam's rib (2:21–23). Christian theologians relied principally on Genesis 2 for their understanding of the relation between man and woman, interpreting the creation of Eve from Adam as proof of her subordination to him.

The creation story in Genesis 2 leads to that of the temptations in

Genesis 3: of Eve by the wily serpent and of Adam by Eve. As read by Christian theologians from Tertullian to Thomas Aquinas, the narrative made Eve responsible for the Fall and its consequences. She instigated the act; she deceived her husband; she suffered the greater punishment. Her disobedience made it necessary for Jesus to be incarnated and to die on the cross. From the pulpit, moralists and preachers for centuries conveyed to women the guilt that they bore for original sin.

The Epistles offered advice to early Christians on building communities of the faithful. Among the matters to be regulated was the place of women. Paul offered views favorable to women in Galatians 3:28: "There is neither Jew nor Greek, there is neither slave nor free, there is neither male nor female; for you are all one in Christ Jesus." Paul also referred to women as his coworkers and placed them on a par with himself and his male coworkers (Phlm 4:2–3; Rom 16:1–3; 1 Cor 16:19). Elsewhere, Paul limited women's possibilities: "But I want you to understand that the head of every man is Christ, the head of a woman is her husband, and the head of Christ is God" (1 Cor 11:3).

Biblical passages by later writers (although attributed to Paul) enjoined women to forgo jewels, expensive clothes, and elaborate coiffures; and they forbade women to "teach or have authority over men," telling them to "learn in silence with all submissiveness" as is proper for one responsible for sin, consoling them, however, with the thought that they will be saved through childbearing (1 Tim 2:9–15). Other texts among the later Epistles defined women as the weaker sex and emphasized their subordination to their husbands (1 Pt 3:7; Col 3:18; Eph 5:22–23).

These passages from the New Testament became the arsenal employed by theologians of the early church to transmit negative attitudes toward women to medieval Christian culture—above all, Tertullian (*On the Apparel of Women*), Jerome (*Against Jovinian*), and Augustine (*The Literal Meaning of Genesis*).

THE IMAGE OF WOMEN IN MEDIEVAL LITERATURE. The philosophical, legal, and religious traditions born in antiquity formed the basis of the medieval intellectual synthesis wrought by trained thinkers, mostly clerics, writing in Latin and based largely in universities. The vernacular literary tradition that developed alongside the learned tradition also spoke about female nature and women's roles. Medieval stories, poems, and epics also portrayed women negatively—as lustful and deceitful—while praising good housekeepers and loyal wives as replicas of the Virgin Mary or the female saints and martyrs.

There is an exception in the movement of "courtly love" that evolved in southern France from the twelfth century. Courtly love was the erotic love between a nobleman and noblewoman, the latter usually superior in social rank. It was always adulterous. From the conventions of courtly love derive modern Western notions of romantic love. The tradition has had an impact disproportionate to its size, for it affected only a tiny elite, and very few women. The exaltation of the female lover probably does not reflect a higher evaluation of women or a step toward their sexual liberation. More likely it gives expression to the social and sexual tensions besetting the knightly class at a specific historical juncture.

The literary fashion of courtly love was on the wane by the thirteenth century, when the widely read *Romance of the Rose* was composed in French by the two authors of significantly different dispositions. Guillaume de Lorris composed the initial four thousand verses about 1235, and Jean de Meun added about seventeen thousand verses—more than four times the original—about 1265.

The fragment composed by Guillaume de Lorris stands squarely in the tradition of courtly love. Here the poet, in a dream, is admitted into a walled garden where he finds a magic fountain in which a rosebush is reflected. He longs to pick one rose, but the thorns prevent his doing so, even as he is wounded by arrows from the god of love, whose commands he agrees to obey. The rest of this part of the poem recounts the poet's unsuccessful efforts to pluck the rose.

The longer part of the *Romance* by Jean de Meun also describes a dream. But here allegorical characters give long didactic speeches, providing a social satire on a variety of themes, some pertaining to women. Love is an anxious and tormented state, the poem explains: women are greedy and manipulative, marriage is miserable, beautiful women are lustful, ugly ones cease to please, and a chaste woman is as rare as a black swan.

Shortly after Jean de Meun completed *The Romance of the Rose*, Mathéolus penned his *Lamentations*, a long Latin diatribe against marriage translated into French about a century later. The *Lamentations* sum up medieval attitudes toward women and provoked the important response by Christine de Pizan in her *Book of the City of Ladies*.

In 1355, Giovanni Boccaccio wrote *Il Corbaccio*, another antifeminist manifesto, although ironically by an author whose other works pioneered new directions in Renaissance thought. The former husband of his lover appears to Boccaccio, condemning his unmoderated lust and detailing the defects of women. Boccaccio concedes at the end "how much men naturally surpass women in nobility" and is cured of his desires.[3]

---

3. Giovanni Boccaccio, *The Corbaccio, or The Labyrinth of Love*, trans. and ed. Anthony K. Cassell, rev. ed. (Binghamton, N.Y., 1993), 71.

WOMEN'S ROLES: THE FAMILY. The negative perceptions of women expressed in the intellectual tradition are also implicit in the actual roles that women played in European society. Assigned to subordinate positions in the household and the church, they were barred from significant participation in public life.

Medieval European households, like those in antiquity and in non-Western civilizations, were headed by males. It was the male serf (or peasant), feudal lord, town merchant, or citizen who was polled or taxed or succeeded to an inheritance or had any acknowledged public role, although his wife or widow could stand as a temporary surrogate. From about 1100, the position of property-holding males was further enhanced: inheritance was confined to the male, or agnate, line—with depressing consequences for women.

A wife never fully belonged to her husband's family, nor was she a daughter to her father's family. She left her father's house young to marry whomever her parents chose. Her dowry was managed by her husband, and at her death it normally passed to her children by him.

A married woman's life was occupied nearly constantly with cycles of pregnancy, childbearing, and lactation. Women bore children through all the years of their fertility, and many died in childbirth. They were also responsible for raising young children up to six or seven. In the propertied classes that responsibility was shared, since it was common for a wet nurse to take over breast-feeding and for servants to perform other chores.

Women trained their daughters in the household duties appropriate to their status, nearly always tasks associated with textiles: spinning, weaving, sewing, embroidering. Their sons were sent out of the house as apprentices or students, or their training was assumed by fathers in later childhood and adolescence. On the death of her husband, a woman's children became the responsibility of his family. She generally did not take "his" children with her to a new marriage or back to her father's house, except sometimes in the artisan classes.

Women also worked. Rural peasants performed farm chores, merchant wives often practiced their husband's trades, the unmarried daughters of the urban poor worked as servants or prostitutes. All wives produced or embellished textiles and did the housekeeping, while wealthy ones managed servants. These labors were unpaid or poorly paid but often contributed substantially to family wealth.

WOMEN'S ROLES: THE CHURCH. Membership in a household, whether a father's or a husband's, meant for women a lifelong subordination to others.

In western Europe, the Roman Catholic Church offered an alternative to the career of wife and mother. A woman could enter a convent, parallel in function to the monasteries for men that evolved in the early Christian centuries.

In the convent, a woman pledged herself to a celibate life, lived according to strict community rules, and worshiped daily. Often the convent offered training in Latin, allowing some women to become considerable scholars and authors as well as scribes, artists, and musicians. For women who chose the conventual life, the benefits could be enormous, but for numerous others placed in convents by paternal choice, the life could be restrictive and burdensome.

The conventual life declined as an alternative for women as the modern age approached. Reformed monastic institutions resisted responsibility for related female orders. The church increasingly restricted female institutional life by insisting on closer male supervision.

Women often sought other options. Some joined the communities of laywomen that sprang up spontaneously in the thirteenth century in the urban zones of western Europe, especially in Flanders and Italy. Some joined the heretical movements that flourished in late medieval Christendom, whose anticlerical and often antifamily positions particularly appealed to women. In these communities, some women were acclaimed as "holy women" or "saints," whereas others often were condemned as frauds or heretics.

In all, although the options offered to women by the church were sometimes less than satisfactory, they were sometimes richly rewarding. After 1520, the convent remained an option only in Roman Catholic territories. Protestantism engendered an ideal of marriage as a heroic endeavor and appeared to place husband and wife on a more equal footing. Sermons and treatises, however, still called for female subordination and obedience.

THE OTHER VOICE, 1300–1700

When the modern era opened, European culture was so firmly structured by a framework of negative attitudes toward women that to dismantle it was a monumental labor. The process began as part of a larger cultural movement that entailed the critical reexamination of ideas inherited from the ancient and medieval past. The humanists launched that critical reexamination.

THE HUMANIST FOUNDATION. Originating in Italy in the fourteenth century, humanism quickly became the dominant intellectual movement in Europe. Spreading in the sixteenth century from Italy to the rest of Europe, it fueled the literary, scientific, and philosophical movements of the era and laid the basis for the eighteenth-century Enlightenment.

Humanists regarded the Scholastic philosophy of medieval universities as out of touch with the realities of urban life. They found in the rhetorical discourse of classical Rome a language adapted to civic life and public speech. They learned to read, speak, and write classical Latin and, eventually, classical Greek. They founded schools to teach others to do so, establishing the pattern for elementary and secondary education for the next three hundred years.

In the service of complex government bureaucracies, humanists employed their skills to write eloquent letters, deliver public orations, and formulate public policy. They developed new scripts for copying manuscripts and used the new printing press to disseminate texts, for which they created methods of critical editing.

Humanism was a movement led by males who accepted the evaluation of women in ancient texts and generally shared the misogynist perceptions of their culture. (Female humanists, as we will see, did not.) Yet humanism also opened the door to a reevaluation of the nature and capacity of women. By calling authors, texts, and ideas into question, it made possible the fundamental rereading of the whole intellectual tradition that was required in order to free women from cultural prejudice and social subordination.

A DIFFERENT CITY. The other voice first appeared when, after so many centuries, the accumulation of misogynist concepts evoked a response from a capable female defender: Christine de Pizan (1365–1431). Introducing her *Book of the City of Ladies* (1405), she described how she was affected by reading Mathéolus's *Lamentations:* "Just the sight of this book . . . made me wonder how it happened that so many different men . . . are so inclined to express both in speaking and in their treatises and writings so many wicked insults about women and their behavior."[4] These statements impelled her to detest herself "and the entire feminine sex, as though we were monstrosities in nature."[5]

The rest of *The Book of the City of Ladies* presents a justification of the female sex and a vision of an ideal community of women. A pioneer, she has received the message of female inferiority and rejected it. From the fourteenth to the seventeenth century, a huge body of literature accumulated that responded to the dominant tradition.

---

4. Christine de Pizan, *The Book of the City of Ladies*, trans. Earl Jeffrey Richards, foreword by Marina Warner (New York, 1982), 1.1.1, pp. 3–4.

5. Ibid., 1.1.1–2, p. 5.

The result was a literary explosion consisting of works by both men and women, in Latin and in the vernaculars: works enumerating the achievements of notable women; works rebutting the main accusations made against women; works arguing for the equal education of men and women; works defining and redefining women's proper role in the family, at court, in public; works describing women's lives and experiences. Recent monographs and articles have begun to hint at the great range of this movement, involving probably several thousand titles. The protofeminism of these "other voices" constitutes a significant fraction of the literary product of the early modern era.

THE CATALOGS. About 1365, the same Boccaccio whose *Corbaccio* rehearses the usual charges against female nature wrote another work, *Concerning Famous Women*. A humanist treatise drawing on classical texts, it praised 106 notable women: ninety-eight of them from pagan Greek and Roman antiquity, one (Eve) from the Bible, and seven from the medieval religious and cultural tradition; his book helped make all readers aware of a sex normally condemned or forgotten. Boccaccio's outlook nevertheless was unfriendly to women, for it singled out for praise those women who possessed the traditional virtues of chastity, silence, and obedience. Women who were active in the public realm—for example, rulers and warriors—were depicted as usually being lascivious and as suffering terrible punishments for entering the masculine sphere. Women were his subject, but Boccaccio's standard remained male.

Christine de Pizan's *Book of the City of Ladies* contains a second catalog, one responding specifically to Boccaccio's. Whereas Boccaccio portrays female virtue as exceptional, she depicts it as universal. Many women in history were leaders, or remained chaste despite the lascivious approaches of men, or were visionaries and brave martyrs.

The work of Boccaccio inspired a series of catalogs of illustrious women of the biblical, classical, Christian, and local pasts, among them Filippo da Bergamo's *Of Illustrious Women*, Pierre de Brantôme's *Lives of Illustrious Women*, Pierre Le Moyne's *Gallerie of Heroic Women*, and Pietro Paolo de Ribera's *Immortal Triumphs and Heroic Enterprises of 845 Women*. Whatever their embedded prejudices, these works drove home to the public the possibility of female excellence.

THE DEBATE. At the same time, many questions remained: Could a woman be virtuous? Could she perform noteworthy deeds? Was she even, strictly speaking, of the same human species as men? These questions were debated over four centuries, in French, German, Italian, Spanish, and English, by authors male and female, among Catholics, Protestants, and Jews, in ponderous volumes and breezy pamphlets. The whole literary genre has been called the *querelle des femmes,* the "woman question."

The opening volley of this battle occurred in the first years of the fifteenth century, in a literary debate sparked by Christine de Pizan. She exchanged letters critical of Jean de Meun's contribution to *The Romance of the Rose* with two French royal secretaries, Jean de Montreuil and Gontier Col. When the matter became public, Jean Gerson, one of Europe's leading theologians, supported de Pizan's arguments against de Meun, for the moment silencing the opposition.

The debate resurfaced repeatedly over the next two hundred years. *The Triumph of Women* (1438) by Juan Rodríguez de la Camara (or Juan Rodríguez del Padron) struck a new note by presenting arguments for the superiority of women to men. *The Champion of Women* (1440–42) by Martin Le Franc addresses once again the negative views of women presented in *The Romance of the Rose* and offers counterevidence of female virtue and achievement.

A cameo of the debate on women is included in *The Courtier,* one of the most widely read books of the era, published by the Italian Baldassare Castiglione in 1528 and immediately translated into other European vernaculars. *The Courtier* depicts a series of evenings at the court of the duke of Urbino in which many men and some women of the highest social stratum amuse themselves by discussing a range of literary and social issues. The "woman question" is a pervasive theme throughout, and the third of its four books is devoted entirely to that issue.

In a verbal duel, Gasparo Pallavicino and Giuliano de' Medici present the main claims of the two traditions. Gasparo argues the innate inferiority of women and their inclination to vice. Only in bearing children do they profit the world. Giuliano counters that women share the same spiritual and mental capacities as men and may excel in wisdom and action. Men and women are of the same essence: just as no stone can be more perfectly a stone than another, so no human being can be more perfectly human than others, whether male or female. It was an astonishing assertion, boldly made to an audience as large as all Europe.

THE TREATISES. Humanism provided the materials for a positive counterconcept to the misogyny embedded in Scholastic philosophy and law and inherited from the Greek, Roman, and Christian pasts. A series of humanist treatises on marriage and family, on education and deportment, and on the nature of women helped construct these new perspectives.

The works by Francesco Barbaro and Leon Battista Alberti—*On Marriage*

(1415) and *On the Family* (1434–37)—far from defending female equality, reasserted women's responsibility for rearing children and managing the housekeeping while being obedient, chaste, and silent. Nevertheless, they served the cause of reexamining the issue of women's nature by placing domestic issues at the center of scholarly concern and reopening the pertinent classical texts. In addition, Barbaro emphasized the companionate nature of marriage and the importance of a wife's spiritual and mental qualities for the well-being of the family.

These themes reappear in later humanist works on marriage and the education of women by Juan Luis Vives and Erasmus. Both were moderately sympathetic to the condition of women without reaching beyond the usual masculine prescriptions for female behavior.

An outlook more favorable to women characterizes the nearly unknown work *In Praise of Women* (ca. 1487) by the Italian humanist Bartolommeo Goggio. In addition to providing a catalog of illustrious women, Goggio argued that male and female are the same in essence, but that women (reworking the Adam and Eve narrative from quite a new angle) are actually superior. In the same vein, the Italian humanist Maria Equicola asserted the spiritual equality of men and women in *On Women* (1501). In 1525, Galeazzo Flavio Capra (or Capella) published his work *On the Excellence and Dignity of Women*. This humanist tradition of treatises defending the worthiness of women culminates in the work of Henricus Cornelius Agrippa *On the Nobility and Preeminence of the Female Sex*. No work by a male humanist more succinctly or explicitly presents the case for female dignity.

THE WITCH BOOKS. While humanists grappled with the issues pertaining to women and family, other learned men turned their attention to what they perceived as a very great problem: witches. Witch-hunting manuals, explorations of the witch phenomenon, and even defenses of witches are not at first glance pertinent to the tradition of the other voice. But they do relate in this way: most accused witches were women. The hostility aroused by supposed witch activity is comparable to the hostility aroused by women. The evil deeds the victims of the hunt were charged with were exaggerations of the vices to which, many believed, all women were prone.

The connection between the witch accusation and the hatred of women is explicit in the notorious witch-hunting manual *The Hammer of Witches* (1486) by two Dominican inquisitors, Heinrich Krämer and Jacob Sprenger. Here the inconstancy, deceitfulness, and lustfulness traditionally associated with women are depicted in exaggerated form as the core features of witch behavior. These traits inclined women to make a bargain with the devil—sealed by sexual intercourse—by which they acquired unholy powers. Such bizarre claims, far from being rejected by rational men, were broadcast by intellectuals. The German Ulrich Molitur, the Frenchman Nicolas Rémy, and the Italian Stefano Guazzo all coolly informed the public of sinister orgies and midnight pacts with the devil. The celebrated French jurist, historian, and political philosopher Jean Bodin argued that because women were especially prone to diabolism, regular legal procedures could properly be suspended in order to try those accused of this "exceptional crime."

A few experts such as the physician Johann Weyer, a student of Agrippa's, raised their voices in protest. In 1563, he explained the witch phenomenon thus, without discarding belief in diabolism: the devil deluded foolish old women afflicted by melancholia, causing them to believe they had magical powers. Weyer's rational skepticism, which had good credibility in the community of the learned, worked to revise the conventional views of women and witchcraft.

WOMEN'S WORKS. To the many categories of works produced on the question of women's worth must be added nearly all works written by women. A woman writing was in herself a statement of women's claim to dignity.

Only a few women wrote anything before the dawn of the modern era, for three reasons. First, they rarely received the education that would enable them to write. Second, they were not admitted to the public roles—as administrator, bureaucrat, lawyer or notary, or university professor—in which they might gain knowledge of the kinds of things the literate public thought worth writing about. Third, the culture imposed silence on women, considering speaking out a form of unchastity. Given these conditions, it is remarkable that any women wrote. Those who did before the fourteenth century were almost always nuns or religious women whose isolation made their pronouncements more acceptable.

From the fourteenth century on, the volume of women's writings rose. Women continued to write devotional literature, although not always as cloistered nuns. They also wrote diaries, often intended as keepsakes for their children; books of advice to their sons and daughters; letters to family members and friends; and family memoirs, in a few cases elaborate enough to be considered histories.

A few women wrote works directly concerning the "woman question," and some of these, such as the humanists Isotta Nogarola, Cassandra Fedele, Laura Cereta, and Olympia Morata, were highly trained. A few were professional writers, living by the income of their pens; the very first among them was Christine de Pizan, noteworthy in this context as in so many others. In addition to *The Book of the City of Ladies* and her critiques of *The Romance of the Rose*, she wrote *The Treasure of the City of Ladies* (a guide to social decorum for women), an advice book for her son, much courtly verse, and a full-scale history of the reign of King Charles V of France.

WOMEN PATRONS. Women who did not themselves write but encouraged others to do so boosted the development of an alternative tradition. Highly placed women patrons supported authors, artists, musicians, poets, and learned men. Such patrons, drawn mostly from the Italian elites and the courts of northern Europe, figure disproportionately as the dedicatees of the important works of early feminism.

For a start, it might be noted that the catalogs of Boccaccio and Alvaro de Luna were dedicated to the Florentine noblewoman Andrea Acciaiuoli and to Doña María, first wife of King Juan II of Castile, while the French translation of Boccaccio's work was commissioned by Anne of Brittany, wife of King Charles VIII of France. The humanist treatises of Goggio, Equicola, Vives, and Agrippa were dedicated, respectively, to Eleanora of Aragon, wife of Ercole I d'Este, duke of Ferrara; to Margherita Cantelma of Mantua; to Catherine of Aragon, wife of King Henry VIII of England; and to Margaret, duchess of Austria and regent of the Netherlands. As late as 1696, Mary Astell's *Serious Proposal to the Ladies, for the Advancement of Their True and Greatest Interest* was dedicated to Princess Anne of Denmark.

These authors presumed that their efforts would be welcome to female patrons, or they may have written at the bidding of those patrons. Silent themselves, perhaps even unresponsive, these loftily placed women helped shape the tradition of the other voice.

THE ISSUES. The literary forms and patterns in which the tradition of the other voice presented itself have now been sketched. It remains to highlight the major issues around which this tradition crystallizes. In brief, there are four problems to which our authors return again and again, in plays and catalogs, in verse and letters, in treatises and dialogues, in every language: the problem of chastity, the problem of power, the problem of speech, and the problem of knowledge. Of these the greatest, preconditioning the others, is the problem of chastity.

THE PROBLEM OF CHASTITY. In traditional European culture, as in those of antiquity and others around the globe, chastity was perceived as women's quintessential virtue—in contrast to courage, or generosity, or leadership, or rationality, seen as virtues characteristic of men. Opponents of women

charged them with insatiable lust. Women themselves and their defenders—
without disputing the validity of the standard—responded that women were
capable of chastity.

The requirement of chastity kept women at home, silenced them, isolated them, left them in ignorance. It was the source of all other impedi-
ments. Why was it so important to the society of men, of whom chastity
was not required, and who more often than not considered it their right to
violate the chastity of any woman they encountered?

Female chastity ensured the continuity of the male-headed household.
If a man's wife was not chaste, he could not be sure of the legitimacy of his
offspring. If they were not his and they acquired his property, it was not his
household, but some other man's, that had endured. If his daughter was not
chaste, she could not be transferred to another man's household as his wife,
and he was dishonored.

The whole system of the integrity of the household and the transmission
of property was bound up in female chastity. Such a requirement pertained
only to property-owning classes, of course. Poor women could not expect
to maintain their chastity, least of all if they were in contact with high-status
men to whom all women but those of their own household were prey.

In Catholic Europe, the requirement of chastity was further buttressed
by moral and religious imperatives. Original sin was inextricably linked with
the sexual act. Virginity was seen as heroic virtue, far more impressive than,
say, the avoidance of idleness or greed. Monasticism, the cultural institution
that dominated medieval Europe for centuries, was grounded in the renunciation of the flesh. The Catholic reform of the eleventh century imposed
a similar standard on all the clergy and a heightened awareness of sexual
requirements on all the laity. Although men were asked to be chaste, female
unchastity was much worse: it led to the devil, as Eve had led mankind to sin.

To such requirements, women and their defenders protested their innocence. Furthermore, following the example of holy women who had escaped
the requirements of family and sought the religious life, some women began to conceive of female communities as alternatives both to family and
to the cloister. Christine de Pizan's city of ladies with such a community.
Moderata Fonte and Mary Astell envisioned others. The luxurious salons of
the French *précieuses* of the seventeenth century, or the comfortable English
drawing rooms of the next, may have been born of the same impulse. Here
women not only might escape, if briefly, the subordinate position that life
in the family entailed but might also make claims to power, exercise their
capacity for speech, and display their knowledge.

THE PROBLEM OF POWER. Women were excluded from power: the whole cultural tradition insisted on it. Only men were citizens, only men bore arms, only men could be chiefs or lords or kings. There were exceptions that did not disprove the rule, when wives or widows or mothers took the place of men, awaiting their return or the maturation of a male heir. A woman who attempted to rule in her own right was perceived as an anomaly, a monster, at once a deformed woman and an insufficient male, sexually confused and consequently unsafe.

The association of such images with women who held or sought power explains some otherwise odd features of early modern culture. Queen Elizabeth I of England, one of the few women to hold full regal authority in European history, played with such male/female images—positive ones, of course—in representing herself to her subjects. She was a prince, and manly, even though she was female. She was also (she claimed) virginal, a condition absolutely essential if she was to avoid the attacks of her opponents. Catherine de' Medici, who ruled France as widow and regent for her sons, also adopted such imagery in defining her position. She chose as one symbol the figure of Artemisia, an androgynous ancient warrior-heroine who combined a female persona with masculine powers.

Power in a woman, without such sexual imagery, seems to have been indigestible by the culture. A rare note was struck by the Englishman Sir Thomas Elyot in his *Defence of Good Women* (1540), justifying both women's participation in civic life and their prowess in arms. The old tune was sung by the Scots reformer John Knox in his *First Blast of the Trumpet against the Monstrous Regiment of Women* (1558); for him rule by women, defects in nature, was a hideous contradiction in terms.

The confused sexuality of the imagery of female potency was not reserved for rulers. Any woman who excelled was likely to be called an Amazon, recalling the self-mutilated warrior women of antiquity who repudiated all men, gave up their sons, and raised only their daughters. She was often said to have "exceeded her sex" or to have possessed "masculine virtue"—as the very fact of conspicuous excellence conferred masculinity even on the female subject. The catalogs of notable women often showed those female heroes dressed in armor, armed to the teeth, like men. Amazonian heroines romp through the epics of the age—Ariosto's *Orlando Furioso* (1532) and Spenser's *Faerie Queene* (1590–1609). Excellence in a woman was perceived as a claim for power, and power was reserved for the masculine realm. A woman who possessed either one was masculinized and lost title to her own female identity.

THE PROBLEM OF SPEECH. Just as power had a sexual dimension when it was claimed by women, so did speech. A good woman spoke little. Excessive speech was an indication of unchastity. By speech, women seduced men. Eve had lured Adam into sin by her speech. Accused witches were commonly accused of having spoken abusively, or irrationally, or simply too much. As enlightened a figure as Francesco Barbaro insisted on silence in a woman, which he linked to her perfect unanimity with her husband's will and her unblemished virtue (her chastity). Another Italian humanist, Leonardo Bruni, in advising a noblewoman on her studies, barred her not from speech but from public speaking. That was reserved for men.

Related to the problem of speech was that of costume—another, if silent, form of self-expression. Assigned the task of pleasing men as their primary occupation, elite women often tended toward elaborate costume, hairdressing, and the use of cosmetics. Clergy and secular moralists alike condemned these practices. The appropriate function of costume and adornment was to announce the status of a woman's husband or father. Any further indulgence in adornment was akin to unchastity.

THE PROBLEM OF KNOWLEDGE. When the Italian noblewoman Isotta Nogarola had begun to attain a reputation as a humanist, she was accused of incest—a telling instance of the association of learning in women with unchastity. That chilling association inclined any woman who was educated to deny that she was or to make exaggerated claims of heroic chastity.

If educated women were pursued with suspicions of sexual misconduct, women seeking an education faced an even more daunting obstacle: the assumption that women were by nature incapable of learning, that reasoning was a particularly masculine ability. Just as they proclaimed their chastity, women and their defenders insisted on their capacity for learning. The major work by a male writer on female education—that by Juan Luis Vives, *On the Education of a Christian Woman* (1532)—granted female capacity for intellection but still argued that a woman's whole education was to be shaped around the requirement of chastity and a future within the household. Female writers of the following generations—Marie de Gournay in France, Anna Maria van Schurman in Holland, and Mary Astell in England—began to envision other possibilities.

The pioneers of female education were the Italian women humanists who managed to attain a literacy in Latin and a knowledge of classical and Christian literature equivalent to that of prominent men. Their works implicitly and explicitly raise questions about women's social roles, defining problems that beset women attempting to break out of the cultural limits that had bound them. Like Christine de Pizan, who achieved an advanced education through her father's tutoring and her own devices, their bold questioning makes clear the importance of training. Only when women were educated to the same standard as male leaders would they be able to raise that other voice and insist on their dignity as human beings morally, intellectually, and legally equal to men.

THE OTHER VOICE. The other voice, a voice of protest, was mostly female, but it was also male. It spoke in the vernaculars and in Latin, in treatises and dialogues, in plays and poetry, in letters and diaries, and in pamphlets. It battered at the wall of prejudice that encircled women and raised a banner announcing its claims. The female was equal (or even superior) to the male in essential nature—moral, spiritual, and intellectual. Women were capable of higher education, of holding positions of power and influence in the public realm, and of speaking and writing persuasively. The last bastion of masculine supremacy, centered on the notions of a woman's primary domestic responsibility and the requirement of female chastity, was not as yet assaulted—although visions of productive female communities as alternatives to the family indicated an awareness of the problem.

During the period 1300–1700, the other voice remained only a voice, and one only dimly heard. It did not result—yet—in an alteration of social patterns. Indeed, to this day they have not entirely been altered. Yet the call for justice issued as long as six centuries ago by those writing in the tradition of the other voice must be recognized as the source and origin of the mature feminist tradition and of the realignment of social institutions accomplished in the modern age.

We thank the volume editors in this series, who responded with many suggestions to an earlier draft of this introduction, making it a collaborative enterprise. Many of their suggestions and criticisms have resulted in revisions of this introduction, although we remain responsible for the final product.

PROJECTED TITLES IN THE SERIES

Margherita Sarrocchi, *La Scanderbeide*, edited and translated by Rinaldina Russell

Madeleine de Scudéry, *Selected Letters, Orations, and Rhetorical Dialogues*, edited and translated by Jane Donawerth with Julie Strongson

Justine Siegemund, *The Court Midwife of the Electorate of Brandenburg* (1690), edited and translated by Lynne Tatlock

Gabrielle Suchon, *"On Philosophy" and "On Mortality,"* edited and translated by Domna Stanton with Rebecca Wilkin

Sara Copio Sullam, *Sara Copio Sullam: Jewish Poet and Intellectual in Early Seventeenth-Century Venice*, edited and translated by Don Harrán

Arcangela Tarabotti, *Convent Life as Inferno: A Report*, introduction and notes by Francesca Medioli, translated by Letizia Panizza

Laura Terracina, *Works*, edited and translated by Michael Sherberg

Madame de Villedieu (Marie-Catherine Desjardins), *Memoirs of the Life of Henriette-Sylvie de Molière: A Novel*, edited and translated by Donna Kuizenga

Katharina Schütz Zell, *Selected Writings*, edited and translated by Elsie McKee

VOLUME EDITORS'
INTRODUCTION

A NEW AND DIFFERENT VOICE

Author of an important body of works that attest to her erudition, literary skill, and depth of thought, Isotta Nogarola (1418–1466) was a pioneering woman's voice—the voice of that gendered "other"—at the opening of the Renaissance and early modern era.[1] With her older contemporary, Christine de Pizan (1365–1431), an Italian-born French author raised at the royal court,[2] she launched the tradition of the learned woman in the early modern period, setting up the framework within which learned women expressed themselves over the next several centuries.

1. For Isotta Nogarola, see Margaret L. King, "Isotta Nogarola," in Rinaldina Russell, ed., *Italian Women Writers: A Bio-Bibliographical Sourcebook* (Westport, Conn.: Greenwood, 1994), 313–23, and sources there cited; also King, "The Religious Retreat of Isotta Nogarola (1418–1466)," *Signs* 3 (1978), 807–22; Lisa Jardine, "Isotta Nogarola: Women Humanists—Education for What?" *History of Education* 12 (1983): 231–44; for the Nogarola sisters in the Veronese context, Rino Avesani, *Verona e il suo territorio, 4: Verona nel Quattrocento,* part 2 (Verona: Istituto per gli studi storici veronesi, 1984), 60–76. The extensive introduction by editor Eugenius Abel to Nogarola's works, *Isotae Nogarolae Veronensis opera quae supersunt omnia; accedunt Angelae et Zeneverae Nogarolae epistolae et carmina,* collegit Alexander Comes Apponyi, ed. Eugenius Abel, 2 vols. (Vienna: apud Gerold et socios; Budapest apud Fridericum Kilian, 1886) [henceforth cited as Abel], i–clxxii, provides invaluable biographical and historical background for Nogarola's work and her family and correspondents. A recent synthesis has a substantial discussion of Nogarola, based largely on King's prior work. Prudence Allen, *The Concept of Woman: 2: The Early Humanist Reformation, 1250–1500* (Grand Rapids, Mich.: William B. Eerdmans Publishing Co., 2002), 944–69.

2. For Christine de Pizan, see esp. Charity Cannon Willard, *Christine de Pizan: Her Life and Works* (New York: Persea Books, 1984). Two major works are available in translation: *The Book of the City of Ladies,* trans. Earl Jeffrey Richards (New York: Persea Books, 1982); and *The Treasure of the City of Ladies,* trans. Sarah Lawson (New York: Viking Penguin, 1985; also trans. and introd. Charity Cannon Willard, ed. and introd. Madeleine P. Cosman (New York: Persea Books, 1989). Christine de Pizan et al., *Debate over the "Romance of the Rose,"* ed. and trans. Tom Conley and Virginie Greene with Elisabeth Hodges, is in press in this series, and two further works are planned: *Life of Charles V,* ed. and trans. Charity Cannon Willard; and *The Long Road of Learning,* ed. and trans. Andrea Tarnowski.

Nogarola entered into the world of humanist studies at a time when, in the highly urbanized context of northern Italy during the period called the Renaissance, humanism was the dominant intellectual phenomenon.[3] She did so, consciously, as a woman, often introducing her letters with professions of inadequacy on account of her sex and inserting into her works celebratory lists of famous women of classical and Christian antiquity (as did male correspondents in their works to her). At the same time, she emulated male thinkers, demonstrated a thorough knowledge of classical authors, ventured into the fields of philosophy and theology as well as the more standard humanistic pursuits, and produced important works in all the major humanist genres. In her dialogue on the relative sinfulness of Adam and Eve (see below, chap. 7), arguably her key work, and one of the most important works written by any woman in the early modern era, she confronts directly the paradoxes of the female condition in the age in which she lived, where blame and innocence, strength and weakness, were cultural categories that limited the possibilities of self-realization. Isotta Nogarola is presented here through translations of all her extant works known to the present editors (in addition to two by her correspondents), accompanied by extended discussions of their context that highlight the author's daring and originality.

THE CAREER OF ISOTTA NOGAROLA

Born probably in 1418, Isotta Nogarola received an excellent education when, still an adolescent, she entered into literary correspondence with important and learned men. In 1441, at about age twenty-three, she chose neither of the two careers normally open to a woman of her age and rank, marriage or the convent, but instead took up the life of a scholar in the household of her mother and brother. Over the next ten years, she won renown as a learned woman and a holy virgin. In 1451, her friendship with the governor of her city, Ludovico Foscarini, became the occasion for her most important work, a dialogue on the relative sinfulness of Adam and Eve. The dialogue was the opening volley in a series of major works published between 1453 and 1461, the year her mother died. Soon thereafter, she entered the household of her admirer Foscarini, who provided support and promoted her reputation as a holy woman, until her death in 1466.

---

3. See the articles on humanism in the *Encyclopedia of the Renaissance*, 6 vols. (New York: Charles Scribner's, 2000), and sources there cited; also Albert Rabil, Jr., ed., *Renaissance Humanism: Foundations, Forms, and Legacy*, 3 vols. (Philadelphia: University of Pennsylvania Press, 1988); and, most recently, Ronald G. Witt, *In the Footsteps of the Ancients: The Origins of Humanism from Lovato to Bruni* (Leiden and Boston: Brill, 2000).

These are the bare bones of a career that deserves a closer look. How did she acquire a humanist education and enter into the *res publica litterarum* ("republic of letters"), the society of humanism? Why did she choose to forego both marriage and convent in 1441, and to retire to live alone, with her mother as companion, in her brother's house? What were her personal and intellectual aims after 1441?

Humanist education and entry into humanist society. One of six daughters and four sons born to Leonardo Nogarola of Verona and Bianca Borromeo of Padua, both descendants of eminent northern Italian noble families, Nogarola was the only one of her family to choose to be a humanist scholar. With the death of Leonardo (between 1425 and 1433), Nogarola's mother undertook the management of a complex household and the education of her children. Under her care, the three brothers who survived childhood (Jacopo died young) went on to prominent careers fitting their social position. Leonardo, an intellectual considered learned in theology and philosophy, entered the church and attained the title of Apostolic Protonotary. Both Antonio, mentioned often in Isotta's correspondence, and Ludovico held important magistracies in the city of Verona and served on diplomatic missions, apparently mostly ceremonial.[4]

For her daughters, Bianca chose, remarkably, to hire as a tutor the Veronese scholar Martino Rizzoni. Rizzoni had been a student of the leading humanist scholar and teacher of northeastern Italy, Guarino Guarini, a native of Verona. Under Rizzoni's tutelage, two of the daughters—Isotta and Ginevra—excelled and began in their adolescent years to engage in the world of humanist discourse. They wrote letters in a classically informed Latin that at this time was the private language of an elite of young nobles and patricians aspiring to high positions in their city governments or the church and of the highly skilled scholars (some of whom had also mastered Greek) who taught them.

Those to whom they wrote responded, expressing admiration for the literary accomplishments of the two sisters, and further informed their friends and teachers. Guarino himself was impressed and engaged in an exchange with Nogarola. He commended the sisters to his young charge, Leonello d'Este, son and heir to the ruler of Ferrara, as well as to his own son, Battista

---

4. Abel, iv and n. 4 for Leonardo; xiii and nn. 24, 25 for Antonio and Ludovico. Leonardo and Antonio are often mentioned as young adults in the Nogarola correspondence of 1438–41. At this time, Ludovico was still young (as is revealed in Abel, letter xlii, 1:242–43, when Damiano dal Borgo rejoices that the child Ludovico has escaped the plague). It was Ludovico, who died in 1483, who would inherit the property left by his mother Bianca Borromeo and sister Isotta.

Guarini, who would succeed him as master pedagogue, and to several of his other distinguished students. At the same time, through Guarino's circle and through contacts with representatives of Venice posted to Verona where they became acquainted with the Nogarola family, Isotta Nogarola entered into correspondence with members of a unique generation of patrician humanists in Venice. By 1438, when she was twenty, she and Ginevra were famous within the northeastern Italian humanist coterie. Thereafter, Ginevra married and abandoned humanist commitments (so far as the record shows), although her learning and eloquence continue to be praised by contemporaries. Upon her return to Verona in 1441, after a two-year stay in Venice with her family from 1438 to 1440, Nogarola determined, alone, to continue these literary ventures in the full view of an educated public.

Nogarola's story, barely begun, is already remarkable. It is extraordinary that Bianca Borromeo—a woman who was by her own admission illiterate[5]—undertook the formal education of her daughters. Although at this time a significant fraction of women in highly urbanized Italy were literate, their literacy was in vernacular forms of Italian, which were useful in commercial dealings and for the consumption of popular devotional and fictional works. Latin, which gave access to the literature of the church and the learned traditions, was possessed by only a few. A few women committed to the religious life learned the Latin of prayer, of sermons, and of the Vulgate (the Latin version of the Bible used by the medieval church) from male priests or older nuns in their convents (and perhaps had only an oral command of the language). A very few women learned classical Latin from fond physician or lawyer fathers or as the companions of their student brothers. Before Nogarola, the European women known to have mastered classical Latin could be counted on the fingers of just one hand. By the end of the fifteenth century in which she lived, only a handful more could be added to the total. In the 1430s, only a woman of exceptional vision and receptivity to prevailing cultural trends would have thought to appoint a mature humanist scholar to teach her young daughters.[6]

---

5. Abel, xii and n. 23.

6. For women and learning, see esp. Pamela J. Benson, *The Invention of Renaissance Woman: The Challenge of Female Independence in the Literature and Thought of Italy and England* (University Park, Penn.: Pennsylvania State University Press, 1992); J. R. Brink, ed., *Female Scholars: A Tradition of Learned Women before 1800* (Montreal: Eden Press Women's Publications, 1980); Paul F. Grendler, *Schooling in Renaissance Italy: Literacy and Learning, 1300–1600* (Baltimore: Johns Hopkins University Press, 1989); Margaret L. King, *Women of the Renaissance* (Chicago: University of Chicago Press, 1991), chap. 3; Patricia H. Labalme, ed., *Beyond Their Sex* (New York: New York University Press, 1980); Letizia Panizza, ed., *Women in Italian Renaissance Culture and Society* (Oxford: Legenda, 2000); Bar-

The decision of 1441. Another extraordinary feature of this narrative is that Isotta, her humanist education completed, determined to pursue her avocation and to make of it a career.[7] Women of the elite classes did not have careers in the fifteenth century. In lower social strata, women labored in the peasant and urban economies or worked as midwives, servants, and shop assistants or as artisans within a family enterprise. In patrician and noble circles, however, young women normally had only two options: marriage or the convent. All of Nogarola's sisters who survived childhood married—this fact, and the fact that in every case they married men of prominent families, attests to the family's great social standing and wealth. Isotta alone, unique in this era, chose as her vocation the pursuit of humanist studies. From 1441 until a controversy in 1453 between her brothers and mother over the division of their father's property, she studied and wrote while living with her mother in the house of her brother Antonio; thereafter, until her mother's death in 1461, she lived in the house of her brother Ludovico.[8] It was not conceivable that a woman of Isotta's social standing could live alone as a never-married adult, so her decision to remain unmarried required the support of her family. It was her mother, who had seen to her education, who must have permitted

---

bara J. Whitehead, ed., *Women's Education in Early Modern Europe: A History, 1500–1800* (New York-London: Garland, 1999); and the volumes of the present Other Voice in Early Modern Europe series published by the University of Chicago Press.

7. Women of the elites (mostly likely to be educated) had virtually no career options in the Renaissance or early modern period beyond marriage or life in some form of religious community. For this problem, see especially Anthony Grafton and Lisa Jardine, *From Humanism to the Humanities: Education and the Liberal Arts in Fifteenth- and Sixteenth-Century Europe* (Cambridge, Mass.: Harvard University Press, 1986), chap. 2; Margaret L. King, "Book-Lined Cells: Women and Humanism in the Early Italian Renaissance," in Labalme, *Beyond Their Sex*, 66–90; King, *Women of the Renaissance*, chaps. 1 and 2; for cases most similar to Nogarola's, see Diana Robin's editions of the works of the humanists Laura Cereta and Cassandra Fedele in this series: *Collected Letters of a Renaissance Feminist* [Cereta] (1997) and Fedele's *Letters and Orations* (2000); also Albert Rabil, Jr., *Laura Cereta: Quattrocento Humanist* (Binghamton, N.Y.: MRTS, 1981). Women of the middling and lower strata, of course, did work (often as matrons), especially in northern Europe; see Monica Chojnacka, *Working Women of Early Modern Venice* (Baltimore: Johns Hopkins University Press, 2001); Barbara A. Hanawalt, ed., *Women and Work in Pre-Industrial Europe* (Bloomington, Ind.: Indiana University Press, 1986); and Merry Wiesner, *Working Women in Renaissance Germany* (New Brunswick, N.J.: Rutgers University Press, 1986).

8. The details of the property dispute are in Abel, 1:lix–lxi; see below, chap. 6. The date of her mother's death is fixed by her own words in her consolation for Jacopo Antonio Marcello on the death of his son in 1461: "Sed quo modo te consolabor, cum ipsa eadem consolatione egeam et omnis philosophiae ac religionis oblita terga dare visa sim, meque dolor et moeror, quem ex morte sanctissimae ac dulcissimae matris meae cepi, captivam ducant, ex qua incredibilem ac graviorem quam unquam existimassem concepi dolorem?" Abel, 2:164; and below, chap. 10, no. 32. Foscarini's letters indicate that she joined his household in 1461; she was probably still there, and certainly in close contact with him, in 1464 and 1466; see below, chap. 6.

and fostered this secular vocation of one of her daughters—as she assured by her will, with great prudence, Nogarola's welfare and maintenance after her death.[9]

What motivated Nogarola to make that remarkable decision in 1441? A confluence of events during the years 1438–1440, when she lived in Venice with her family, must have stimulated her to consider what were her future choices and to make the choice she did.[10] During these years, when she achieved the peak of her renown, her communications with learned and important men might have inclined her to pursue her scholarly goals. In 1438, Isotta's sister Ginevra, the companion of her studies, married. Isotta was presented with the reality that she too might marry and that marriage would likely present an impediment to the pursuit of her studies; or that, if she did not marry, she would pursue her career without the companionship of her talented sister. In 1439, furthermore, she was targeted by a nasty anonymous invective, which accused her of adultery, promiscuity, and incest. Although the charges were dismissed as spurious in a response by the Venetian patrician humanist Niccolò Barbo, the notoriety might have triggered thoughts of retreat from the public eye.[11] Nogarola's correspondence, finally, with Damiano dal Borgo from 1438 to 1441, might also have been unsettling, particularly Damiano's suggestion that she might have been spurned in love.[12]

Nogarola's later career: 1441–1466. Whatever causes triggered her decision, it was firmly made by 1441. Nogarola returned to Verona and took up residence, along with her mother, in her brother Antonio's house. After 1453, with her mother, she resided with her other brother Ludovico. After 1461, she joined the household of Foscarini. Throughout these years, then, she was under the protection of a male householder, which social norms would have absolutely required. It was unusual that a woman of Nogarola's age and rank would not have married or joined a religious community. It was unthinkable that she could live alone.

Nogarola could and did leave the household in which she was resident and venture out into the world. She journeyed to Rome at least once (in

---

9. Bianca's will, with extraordinary ample provisions for Isotta, who inherited almost equally with her brother Ludovico, is printed in full in Abel, 1:cxlv–clii. See discussion below, chap. 6, at n. 30.

10. For the events described in this discussion, see chapters 3 and 4 below; also Abel's discussion, introduction, 1:xli, of possible reasons for Nogarola's near decade-long silence after 1441.

11. For this imbroglio, see Arnaldo Segarizzi, "Niccolo Barbo patrizio veneziano del secolo XV e le accuse contro Isotta Nogarola," *Giornale storico della letteratura italiana* 43 (1904): 39–54.

12. Abel notes Damiano dal Borgo's accusations voiced in his letter of April 19, 1440 (Abel 1: 259–60; no. 48) that she had stopped writing him because of her love for a certain young man.

1450), together with family members, and perhaps twice (in 1450 and 1459). She was free to circulate in her city; on at least two occasions she delivered orations there to a public audience and may have engaged with Foscarini in a public debate on the matter of the relative sin of Adam and Eve.

Nevertheless, she was isolated. She (her mother's presence is sometimes recorded) received visitors—the churchmen Matteo Bosso, Paolo Maffei, and Ermolao Barbaro the Elder; her physician; and Foscarini. She received them in her *libraria cella*, or *cellula*—her "little room" or "library", or as one of the present editors first termed it, her "book-lined cell" because it was adorned with holy objects and prayer, hymn singing, and pious conversation are named as activities that transpired there, a space of combined study and contemplative seclusion. It was a setting suitable to the mission that Nogarola apparently set for herself after 1441: the pursuit of "sacred studies"— the Latin tradition viewed from a Christian perspective, represented by the late-ancient fathers of the church who wrote masterfully in that language (including Lactantius, Jerome, Augustine, Ambrose, and Gregory).

We do not hear of this decision from Nogarola herself. Rather, it is reported by male correspondents, at least two of whom had visited her in her book-lined cell, who reported and enthusiastically applauded her commitment to the sacred tradition.[13] Other correspondents from the 1440s, in contrast—the humanists Costanza Varano and Andrea Contrario and the Venetian philosopher Lauro Quirini—commend her serious commitment to advanced learning, philosophical as well as humanist in Quirini's case, without specifying a focus on the sacred tradition.

Nevertheless, Nogarola's later works, all written between 1451 and 1461 after a ten-year silence, do show that she added to her already masterful knowledge of classical literature extensive study in the sacred tradition. These works are more infused by Christian literary references than her early works and are devoted to subjects that are theological, devotional, moral, or ecclesiastical. In no way, however, does she indicate in these works any renunciation of classical literature or inattention to the stylistic and technical features of that tradition.

Not only did Nogarola engage in sacred studies; she was perceived, by at least some observers, as having committed herself not merely to sacred studies, but also to a sacral vocation. In their letters of admiration and letters of advice, these male admirers depict Nogarola as a type of the "holy woman" much revered in Italy in the period 1300–1600: a living saint who combined mystical experience with personal asceticism and sacrificial service to the

---

13. See chapter 5 for a discussion of Nogarola's relations with Bosso, Maffei, Barbaro, Varano, Contrario; and chapter 6 for those with Foscarini.

poor or ill.[14] Nogarola did none of these things. She reports no mystical visions, literary models of which were amply available; and she seems to have engaged in no personal asceticism or frequent service beyond the self-discipline she imposed upon herself by renouncing marriage and retiring to the household of her male kin. To some male observers, however, for whom the "holy woman" model was available and sanctioned (as for Bosso and Foscarini) and who had never before experienced the phenomenon that Isotta personified—an unmarried female aristocrat, devoted to scholarship, and living respectably in her household—the choice was clear. Viewing Nogarola through the veil of their particular cultural norms, they saw her as a *beata*, a holy woman. They then deposited with her, amid their admiring words, a cargo of advice about her commitment to virginity and to sacred pursuits.

How did Nogarola respond to these messages? By not expressly responding at all, at least in any surviving work, she appears to resist them. Yet, by remaining in contact with two of these male observers (Barbaro and Foscarini), who are lavish both in their praise and their admonitions, she seems not to resist forcefully. Her oration on Saint Jerome, the author (among many other achievements) of the archetypal provirginity text, appears to signal obedience to that message with which he was principally associated; yet in her celebration of Jerome's heroic and unconventional qualities, Nogarola appears to resist the pale ideal of chastity. In pioneering the role of woman scholar, she was no doubt uneasy about her role in a world closely hemmed in by social, gender, and religious hierarchies.

After her mother died in 1461, Nogarola composed her last surviving work. From then until her death, we have nothing more from her hand. The letters of Foscarini, in whose household she probably lived from 1461 to 1466, indicate that she continued her literary work while she suffered from a chronic and painful illness.[15] When she died in 1466, she was not yet fifty. It was twenty-five years after she had made the unique decision, unprecedented in her social world, to devote her life to humanist studies.

---

14. For the phenomenon of the holy woman, see especially Rudolph Bell and Donald Weinstein, *Saints and Society: The Two Worlds of Western Christendom 1000–1700* (Chicago: University of Chicago Press, 1982); Caroline Walker Bynum, *Holy Feast and Holy Fast: The Religious Significance of Food to Medieval Women* (Berkeley: University of California Press, 1987); Richard Kieckhefer, *Unquiet Souls: Fourteenth-Century Saints and Their Religious Milieu* (Chicago: University of Chicago Press, 1984); King, *Women of the Renaissance*, chap. 2; André Vauchez, *La sainteté en Occident aux derniers siècles du moyen age après les procès de canonisation et les documents hagiographiques* (Rome: Ecole française de Rome, 1981). For a case study of a woman who aspired to be such a holy woman, see Cecilia Ferrazzi, *Autobiography of an Aspiring Saint*, ed. and trans. Anne Jacobson Schutte (Chicago: University of Chicago Press, 1996).

15. For a discussion of the correspondence of 1461–66, see chap. 6.

Nogarola did not intend to create a revolution. She was respectful of existing hierarchies—the political hierarchies of the cities of Verona and Venice, the intellectual hierarchies of humanist society, and ecclesiastical hierarchies. Yet her mission was unique and important, and she has left behind her works, which record, amid their silences, her struggle to be heard in a world that did not want to listen.

NOGAROLA'S HUMANISM AND INTELLECTUAL DEVELOPMENT

Nogarola's intellectual development falls into three discrete periods: 1434–40, the youthful writings that comprise her humanist letterbook; 1441–49, the fallow middle years that represent a period of intellectual awakening in which she attempts to syncretize classical, biblical, and patristic texts previously unknown to her; and 1450–61, the rich late period, during which she experiments in her writings with new genres and her new syncretism of pagan and Christian thought.

The collection of one's Latin correspondence and its presentation and circulation in a bound volume, a letterbook, was expected of any writer who aspired to a place in the *res publica litterarum*. Although Nogarola was the first major woman humanist in Italy, one hundred years of humanist epistolography—by such writers who "published"[16] their collected Latin letters as Petrarch, Salutati, Bruni, Barbaro, Poggio, and Filelfo—had already preceded her.[17] For professional writers in the Renaissance, the letterbook was the *de rigueur* vehicle for self-promotion. In such letter collections, the humanists displayed their friendships, education, philosophical and literary leanings, and adventures; their expertise in foreign languages and classical rhetoric, its tropes and genres; and their accomplishments and honors. Although public speech was considered an impropriety for the female sex in fifteenth-century Italy, the women humanists freely circulated and published their correspondence.[18]

16. In manuscript culture before the age of the printed book, to "publish" (*prodere, promere, edere, in lucem producere*) meant to circulate a finished manuscript copy of one's compositions among friends and acquaintances. The work would then be copied and recopied and thus disseminated as widely as possible.

17. On the humanist letterbook as a important Renaissance genre see Diana Robin, *Filelfo in Milan: Writings, 1451–1427* (Princeton: Princeton University Press, 1991), esp. 5–6 and 11–55.

18. See Benjamin G. Kohl and Ronald G. Witt, eds., *The Earthly Republic: Italian Humanists on Government and Society* (Philadelphia: University of Pennsylvania Press, 1978): 177–228; Margaret L. King and Albert Rabil, Jr., eds., *Her Immaculate Hand: Selected Works by and about the Women Humanists*

Nogarola's early letterbook offers one of the first European defenses of the female sex, a theme that will take center stage in Italian literature after 1480 and will remain a key literary trope on the continent and in England until the end of the eighteenth century.[19] Nogarola's defense of women in no way stands out as anomalous in a letter collection that otherwise reflects all the typically male humanist themes—the mandate to seek virtue through knowledge, the key role of learning and eloquence in civic life, the spirituality of true friendship, the ethic of *pietas* (loyalty to family, friends, and city), and the twin imperatives of moderation and humility. Drawing her images of famous women in antiquity from Valerius Maximus rather than from Boccaccio or Christine de Pizan,[20] Nogarola centers her *defensio mulierum*, which addresses to Damiano dal Borgo, on the figure of the female orator and poet: Cornelia, Amesia, Affrania, Hortensia, and Sappho are her heroes.[21] Similarly, in an earlier letter to Guarino Veronese, citing the story from Diogenes Laertius's *Lives of the Philosophers* of Lasthenia of Mantinea and Axiothea of Phlius, who disguised themselves in men's clothing in order to gain access to Plato's seminars, she argues that women had always studied philosophy and instructed great men.[22] As we shall see, this figure—of the woman orator

---

of *Quattrocento Italy*, 2d rev. ed. (Binghamton, N.Y.: Medieval and Renaissance Texts and Studies, 1991), 11–30.

19. Virginia Cox, in her edition and translation of Moderata Fonte, *The Worth of Women: Wherein Is Clearly Revealed Their Nobility and Their Superiority to Men* (Chicago: University of Chicago Press, 1997), 13, notes that between 1524 and 1632, fifty defenses of women were published.

20. See now Giovanni Boccaccio, *Famous Women* [composed ca. 1361 under the title *De claris mulieribus*], ed. and trans. Virginia Brown (Cambridge, Mass.: Harvard University Press, 2001); and Christine de Pizan's revision of Boccaccio's history of women, *The Book of the City of Ladies* [composed ca. 1405 under the title *Cité des dames*], 1982.

21. See Nogarola's letter to dal Borgo (April 18, 1439 or 1440), chap. 4, no. 24; see also Nogarola's letter to Guarino Veronese (October 11, 1436), chap. 2, no. 6, not a defense of women per se but in which Nogarola cites Faunia, Nicaula, Cornificia, and Portia, who were all women famed for their learned speech. For various views on Sappho's role as a public figure in seventh-century B.C.E. Greece and her early European transmission see Eva Stehle, *Performance and Gender in Ancient Greece* (Princeton: Princeton University Press, 1997); on the same theme see also Holt N. Parker, "Sappho Schoolmistress," in Ellen Greene, ed., *Re-Reading Sappho: Reception and Transmission* (Berkeley: University of California Press, 1996), 146–83; and Andre Lardinois, "Who Sang Sappho's Songs?" in E. Greene, ed., *Reading Sappho: Contemporary Approaches* (Berkeley: University of California Press, 1996), 150–74. While Lardinois emphasizes the tradition of Sappho as public performer, Parker, who debunks the "myth" of Sappho as an educator, nonetheless cites the ancient testimony that Sappho indeed taught publicly in the widely disseminated Byzantine historical encyclopedia known as the *Suda* (tenth century C.E.) and in Philostratus's *Life of Apollonius of Tyana* (ca. 200 C.E.), a work Nogarola cites extensively in her letterbook.

22. See Nogarola's letter to Antonio Borromeo (ca. 1436–37), chap. 1, no. 4; citing Diogenes Laertius 3.46 and 4.2. The story from Diogenes Laertius's *Lives* is so obscure that no other

and public performer—will dominate Nogarola's presentations of herself in her late works.

In her letters of 1434–40, Nogarola does not cite biblical or patristic texts—except once, in a consolatory letter.[23] In her early epistles, she quotes abundantly from numerous classical works including, among others, Cicero's *Brutus, De amicitia, De officiis,* and *Pro Roscio;* Juvenal 6; Petronius' *Satyricon;* Aulus Gellius's *Attic Nights;* Philostratus's *Life of Apollonius of Tyana;* Plutarch's *Lives of Artaxerxes, Alexander, Aristides,* and *Demetrius;* Diogenes Laertius's *Lives of the Philosophers;* Valerius Maximus's *Memorabilia;* and Virgil's *Eclogues.* Her interests throughout the 1430s remain classical and secular.

Nogarola's second period, the years 1441–49, represents a time of intense study, expansion of her knowledge base, and developing syncretism. Although this is a period in which no writings of her own survive, we know from the enormous number of extended quotations and references in her writings after 1451 to classical, biblical, and patristic texts she had never previously cited that she must have spent the eight or nine years after her return from Venice reeducating herself. Certainly she was urged to do precisely that by the young Venetian patrician and University of Padua–trained Aristotelian Lauro Quirini, from whom she received a long list of suggested readings sometime around 1448.[24] Quirini's letter recommended that she undertake a serious course in ancient philosophy, Paduan style—whereas Florence as early as the 1450s was the center in Italy for studies in Plato, Padua remained the hub for quattrocento Aristotelians and their students. His list included Aristotle's *Moralia, Physics, Metaphysics,* the *De interpretatione,* and the *Categories.* He also directed her to familiarize herself with the medieval Christian and Islamic commentaries on Aristotle (Boethius, Aquinas, Averroes, and Avicenna); Cicero's philosophical works; and Livy's histories, which she had never cited and had probably not read prior to the 1450s.

---

fifteenth-century woman writer cites it or mentions Lasthenia or Axiothea; and in the sixteenth century, as far as we know, only Lucrezia Marinella alludes to the story of the disguised women philosophers. Marinella mistakenly attributes the story to Plutarch (Lucrezia Marinella, *The Nobility and Excellence of Women and the Defects and Vices of Men,* ed. and trans. Anne Dunhill; intro. Letizia Panizza (Chicago: University of Chicago Press, 1999), 89.

23. To Damiano dal Borgo (1438); see chap. 4, no. 16.

24. For Quirini's letter to Nogarola, see chap. 5, no. 25. On Quirini, see Margaret L. King, *Venetian Humanism in an Age of Patrician Dominance* (Princeton: Princeton University Press, 1986), 419–21. Quirini, a relative of Leonardo Giustiniani, was an exact contemporary of Nogarola's; he was born in 1420 and died ca. 1475. Relevant to Quirini's advice to Nogarola is that in 1449 (around the time of his letter to Nogarola, dated variously by Abel, 2: 9–22 as ca. 1448–52) he was teaching Aristotle's *Ethics* in the public school in Venice and in 1452 he was offered a teaching position at the university of Padua. He received a doctorate in liberal arts in 1440 and a second doctorate in canon law in 1448, both at the university of Padua.

The nine years Nogarola spent in concentrated study paid off in the third period of her career, 1450–61. These years represent the time of her greatest productivity and the coming to fruition of all her reading, writing, and study, as well as of her friendships with other intellectuals, in a series of major works. In the decade that began in 1450, Nogarola wrote six works for public performance: an oration presented in the jubilee year of 1450 at the papal court of Nicholas V in Rome (the only one of these late six major works that is no longer extant); a dialogue in 1451 on sex, gender, and original sin; an encomium for Ermolao Barbaro on the occasion of his accession to the bishopric of Verona in 1453; a public lecture on the life of Saint Jerome in 1453; a sermon against the Turks, written for the congress Pope Pius called at Mantua in 1459; and, lastly, a *Consolation* written for the prestigious volume of eulogies that the Venetian statesman Jacopo Antonio Marcello published to commemorate the death of his son in 1461. Two themes mark Nogarola's major late works: her conflation of classical, biblical, and patristic learning and thought in a syncretism that characterizes early Italian humanism, as Paul Oskar Kristeller and Eugene Rice have shown;[25] and her performance of the role of public orator—of public intellectual—in her community.

According to her correspondent Matteo Bosso, in 1451 Nogarola engaged in a public debate with Foscarini, which she later recorded as a *Dialogue on the Equal or Unequal Sin of Eve and Adam: A Debate over Saint Augustine's Dictum, Namely That Adam and Eve Sinned Unequally by Sex, but Equally in Pride*. With the exception of her 1438 consolatory letter to dal Borgo, which contains references to the book of Job, John, Romans, and Peter along with quotations from Cicero's letters and Virgil's *Eclogues*,[26] none of Nogarola's earlier works contain biblical or Christian references. Thus the *Dialogue* marks a turning point in Nogarola's career because for the first time she introduces references from patristic texts and both the Old and New Testaments, mingling passages from Genesis, Ecclesiastes, the Psalms, Matthew, Mark, John, and Romans with citations from Aristotle's *Nicomachean Ethics* and *Posterior Analytics*.

Nogarola's *Dialogue* is both more and less than her own work. Although she unquestionably wrote it, it was based on a *viva voce* debate with Foscarini, or perhaps a series of letters exchanged between them. Presumably, some of the arguments it contains are not hers, therefore, but her opponent's.

---

25. See Eugene Rice, *Saint Jerome in the Renaissance* (Baltimore: Johns Hopkins University Press, 1985); and Rice, "The Renaissance Idea of Christian Antiquity: Humanist Patristic Scholarship," in Albert Rabil, Jr., ed., *Renaissance Humanism, Foundations, Forms, and Legacy*, 3 vols. (Philadelphia: University of Pennsylvania Press, 1988), 1:17–28; and Paul Oskar Kristeller, *Eight Philosophers of the Renaissance* (Stanford: Stanford University Press, 1964).

26. See chap. 4, no. 16.

Nonetheless, the issue is clearly hers, and her arguments are the ones that lend originality and drama to the debate.

In composing the *Dialogue,* Nogarola spans two genres and two worlds. The dialogue is a literary form second only in popularity to the letterbook among quattrocento humanists.[27] It permits authors to present views for consideration that are not necessarily their own and to portray the complexity of ideas without arguing for a particular position. Very different is the university disputation, an academic exercise in which two opposing viewpoints are presented, followed by a regular sequence of contrary positions and rebuttals, culminating in a victory for one or the other claims. Nogarola's *Dialogue* is structured like the university disputation—and well it might be, because her opponent Foscarini, like all the learned men of her milieu, was a university product. Yet it resembles the humanist dialogue in its playful presentation of alternative viewpoints.

Nogarola's *Dialogue* splits Augustine's teaching that the first man and woman were equally responsible for the Fall into two opposing sides represented by the interlocutors "Isotta" and "Ludovico" (Nogarola's friend Foscarini). While the character Isotta, who supposedly represents the real Isotta's views and the female point of view, argues that Eve was less guilty than Adam because she was weaker and intellectually inferior, Ludovico plays the role of Adam's advocate. He argues that it was Eve whose sin was greater because she seduced Adam into disobeying God. Nogarola's arguments are largely indebted to Augustine's *City of God* and his *On the Literal Meaning of Genesis,* but the originality of her work lies in her reframing the questions his writings raise about the Fall as a debate between two interlocutors who argue nothing less than the nature of gender. What is woman? What is man? And do the two sexes have different natures, or are gender behaviors determined by situation and context rather than by inborn characteristics? As the first work of its kind in European literature, Nogarola's *On the Equal or Unequal Sin of Adam and Eve* stands among the founding works of the controversy on gender and the nature of woman (the *querelle des femmes*) that persisted on the continent and in England until the end of the eighteenth century. Nogarola's brilliant characterizations of the two allegorical figures in this dialogue, a man and a woman, mocked assumptions deeply imbricated in the ideology of humanism regarding woman's supposed inferiority.

27. On the genre, see David Marsh, *The Quattrocento Dialogue. Classical Tradition and Humanist Innovation* (Cambridge, Mass.: Harvard University Press, 1980); and Virginia Cox, *The Renaissance Dialogue: Literary Dialogue in Its Social and Political Contexts, Castiglione to Galileo* (Cambridge: Cambridge University Press, 1992).

In the two public orations that Nogarola delivered to the people of Verona in 1453, the first welcoming the new presiding bishop, the Venetian Ermolao Barbaro, to the city and the second an encomium of Saint Jerome, she seized the opportunity to display both the classical and biblical learning she had acquired during the previous decade. In these two orations, she quotes or paraphrases passages from an impressive new repertoire of both classical and religious works she seems not to have known prior to 1451; nowhere are they cited in her letterbook of 1434–40. Her new references include Cicero's *Pro Cluentio*, Plutarch's *Lives of Cicero* and *Demosthenes*, Seneca's *Excerpta controversiarum*, a fragment from Ennius' largely lost hexameter epic, the *Annales* (ca. 180 B.C.), and Statius' *Silvae*, while from the Bible she cites texts from Exodus, Jeremiah, and the Song of Solomon as well as Jerome's *Letter to Eustochium*. The virtues she celebrates as Jerome's reflect in a sense her own values, namely, his contempt for wealth; his critical stance toward the established church, its pomp, and complacency; his embrace of alien lands in his search for truth; his mastery of ancient and forgotten languages as gateways to new knowledge; and, above all, the profound syncretism of his learning in the classical, Christian, and eastern traditions.

Nogarola's next major public oration was written for presentation at the congress Pope Pius II held at Mantua in August 1459. He had summoned prelates, heads of state, and their orators from England and the continent to mount a crusade to free Constantinople, which had fallen to the Turks in 1453 after a brutal siege—the city that for the Italian humanists represented the last bastion of Christendom in the East and of ancient Greek civilization for the West. The most evangelical and characteristic of her late works in its conflation of classical and biblical allusions, her speech is a call to arms against the Ottoman Turks, whom she excoriates as "an evil race of men," "a savage nation," "infidels," and "blasphemers of the Lord" in the dour slogans of the humanists after Constantinople's fall. As in her public orations of 1453, she mingles classical reminiscences and anecdotes from Aulus Gellius, Cicero, Plutarch's *Life of Artaxerxes*, and Virgil with texts from Numbers, Isaiah, Daniel, Corinthians, Revelations, and the Psalms. A tour de force, her speech is a call for unity among Christians and, ultimately, for blood sacrifice. In it, humble apologies are followed by hymns of jubilation, and bursts of righteous anger lead to pulpit-pounding calls for vengeance. The oration is also an encomium for Pius. She praises the pope's gentle nature, his mercy, clemency, and concern for the most humble of his subjects. Yet in this, the most violent of her works, she urges this "man of peace" to raise his sword against the Antichrist. Paraphrasing Jeremiah, she tells the pope he is the angel the Lord, "set over all nations and kingdoms to root out and

destroy, to build and to plant."[28] Quoting Virgil's *Aeneid*, she exhorts the pope
to "crush the proud and show mercy to the humble."[29] Addressing "the Very
Reverend Cardinals of the Church," she ends the oration with the promise
of her support and that of the whole Nogarola family.

Nogarola's last major work, her *Consolatory Letter for Jacopo Antonio Marcello
on the Death of His Son Valerio* (1461), consolidated her place as a public intellectual among the members of the dominant class in Venice and its client cities
in the 1450s and '60s. Surely acting on the recommendations of Foscarini,
Barbaro, and other prominent Venetians, Jacopo Antonio Marcello, soldier,
statesman, and patron of writers, invited Nogarola to join his roster of famous men as a contributor to the volume he was producing as a memorial to
his son who had died that year. The publication of the *Consolatio*, her most
elegant and polished work to date, in Marcello's monument to his son sealed
Nogarola's fame among men of letters. She had now composed in all four of
the major early humanist genres—the letterbook, the dialogue, the sermon,
and the consolation—and each of these works had met with critical acclaim.
More syncretic still than any of her previous works, the *Consolatio* combines
classical and biblical consolatory texts in such a way that her familiarity with
the treatments of the genre by such modern writers as Petrarch and Salutati,
Filelfo and Marsuppini is clear.[30] Again, in this late work we see her quoting
from classical texts she had not cited before in her works. Among the new
works from which she now drew were Pseudo-Plutarch's *Consolatio ad Apollonium*; Plutarch's *Lives of Pericles, Aemilius Paullus, Cato the Younger,* and *Gaius and
Tiberius Gracchi*; Cicero's *De oratore*; and Seneca's *De providentia*. From the Scriptures, she paraphrased and translated passages from John, Luke, Philippians,
Romans, Corinthians, James, Peter, Isaiah, Ecclesiastes, and Job.

In defining Nogarola's humanism, we should consider the story she
retells in several of her letters about Euclides, the man from Megara who
walked twenty miles from his home to Athens to converse with Socrates, in
defiance of a law that condemned any Megaran found in the city to be put to
death.[31] Euclides succeeded in crossing the border into Athens elaborately
disguised, with trailing hemline and multicolored head scarf, as a woman.

28. Jer 1:10.

29. *Aen.* 6.852–53.

30. On the genre in the early Renaissance, see George W. McClure, *Sorrow and Consolation in
Italian Humanism* (Princeton: Princeton University Press, 1991).

31. The anecdote about Euclides the Socratic (not the mathematician, fl. ca. 300 B.C.E.) is
in Aulus Gellius *Attic Nights* 7.10 [*The Attic Nights of Aulus Gellius*, trans. John Rolfe (London:
Heinemann Ltd., and Cambridge, Mass.: Harvard University Press, 1968): 2.119–20].

But what was the attraction of this anecdote for Nogarola? The themes it foregrounds—those of disguise, gender itself as a role or mask, travel across forbidden borders, and the primacy, even at the risk of one's life, of the quest for wisdom, here represented in the figures of Socrates and Athens—are dominant in her writings. Among the philosophers she admires most are Apollonius of Tyana and Saint Jerome,[32] ascetics who relinquished the manly clothing of their cultures, grew their hair long, and became unrecognizable to their countrymen. These men traveled to India, Egypt, and the Holy Land in search of truth and knowledge. They learned ancient and little-known languages on their journeys to the East, chose lives of privation, renounced the pleasures of the world, and yet returned to the world through their writings and their speech.

It is also no surprise that the source of this favorite anecdote of Nogarola's was not an early church father or a Golden Age writer from Augustan Rome, but an Italian educated in Athens: Aulus Gellius (fl. 180 C.E.), a learned synthesizer and collector of Greek and Roman antiquities. Nogarola's writing and thought is, above all, profoundly syncretic, like all the varied forms that humanism took in Renaissance Italy. Nogarola was a Ciceronian in her belief in the cultivation of *scientia, disciplina,* and *eloquentia* as the foundation for the well-ordered and just republic. She shared not at all the distrust of writing and speech so deep-seated in Florentine Platonism. For her, the performance of letters, whether in books or oratory, was necessary to the culture and cultivation of the good state. And yet her writings show her pulling away from the materiality of Roman culture. She was drawn to the asceticism and syncreticism of East-leaning writers Augustine, Apollonius of Tyana, and Jerome, on the one hand, and to the West-leaning classicist syncretists Plutarch, Gellius, Philostratus, Valerius, and Diogenes Laertius of the second and third centuries C.E., on the other. At the same time, her writing is thoroughly imbued with the authors of the Old Testament and the apostles.

In her writings, Nogarola self-consciously crosses the barriers imposed by and for her sex, her rank, and her era. A favorite descriptor for herself is the Latin word *aliena*: she feels uncomfortably alien as a woman, as an aristocrat, and as an actor in her own historical age. Most of her letters broach the problem of the strangeness of a woman as writer and orator. She is always in

---

32. The Apollonius whom Nogarola admires is the first-century C.E. mystic portrayed in Flavius Philostratus's (b. ca. 170 C.E.) *Life of Apollonius,* a work commissioned by Julia Domna, the wife of the Roman emperor Septimius Severus. On the widespread fascination among the Italian humanists with the life and work of Saint Jerome, see Rice, *Saint Jerome;* and Rice, "The Renaissance Idea of Christian Antiquity."

disguise, always defying borders, yet with hardly—unlike Gellius's Euclides of Megara—a sure home to which to return.

NOGAROLA'S LEGACY

Nogarola was renowned in her own day and remained after her death one of the most famous—and of those most famous, the first—of the learned women of the Italian Renaissance. Immediately after her death, she was celebrated in a lengthy poem by the humanist Giovanni Mario Filelfo (son of the more famous Francesco): the *Isottaeus liber*, a funeral eulogy for Isotta dedicated to her brother Ludovico Nogarola.[33] Filelfo portrays her as a poet and prophetess who nobly rejected marriage for a life of study—indeed, of immortality: "This woman . . . always followed immortality and gave herself to the pursuit of fame and glory in all her efforts."[34] In subsequent years, she was often included in biographical compilations of famous women's lives (a favorite genre in the late-fifteenth and sixteenth centuries), such as the *De claris mulieribus* ("On Famous Women") of Jacopo Filippo da Bergamo.[35] Her presence in these standard works shows the extent to which Nogarola became a model for aspiring women and artists.

Far more important—especially for the readers of this edition—than the recognition accorded Nogarola by the male learned community is the impact she had on later women authors and thinkers. Nogarola's writings provide a matrix for several generations of subsequent learned women writers in Italy. Her writings experiment with the genres and themes that women writers took up. Her letterbook anticipates the substantial letter collections of Cassandra Fedele, Laura Cereta, and Veronica Franco[36]: women who were among the first professional writers of their sex in early modern Italy. Her dialogue, in which she portrays herself as an intellectual duelist engaged in combat with a male humanist, looks forward to the sixteenth-century poet Tullia d'Aragona's erotic dialogue, *The Infinity of Love*, in which she and the

---

33. Published by Abel, 2:365–87. See also Avesani, 75–76.

34. Abel, 2:365, ll. 13–16: "Haec mulier teneris nondum satis apta sub annis / Virtuti praebere manus, aeterna secuta / Semper erat studiis laudum famaeque per omneis / Dedita conatus . . ."

35. Jacobus Philippus Bergomensis, *De memorabilibus et claris mulieribus, aliquot diversorum scriprorum opera* (Paris: Ex aedibus Simonis Colinaei, 1521; orig. 1497), and other editions. Other important catalogues of this sort are by Battista Campofregosa (Venice 1483); Jean Tixier Ravisius (Paris 1521); Giovanni Battista Egnazio (Venice 1554); Giacomo Alberici (Bologna 1605); and Jacopo Filippo Tomasini (Padua 1644).

36. See Cereta, *Collected Letters*; Fedele, *Letters and Orations*; Veronica Franco, *Poems and Selected Letters*, ed. and trans. Ann Rosalind Jones and Margaret F. Rosenthal (Chicago: University of Chicago Press, 1998).

Florentine scholar Benedetto Varchi are the principal interlocutors.[37] Nogarola's rejection of the culture of misogyny foreshadows the writings of the later Italian Renaissance feminists Moderata Fonte and Lucrezia Marinella and the polemicist Arcangela Tarabotti.[38] Her daring in having chosen writing and speaking as a way of life and a very public one—though she did so with neither the assurance of tradition nor the institutionalized patronage of women authors that becomes a by-product of print culture—nonetheless provide a model for several successive generations of Italian women who enter the republic of letters in the era of the printed book.

NOTE ON THE TEXT

The works to and from Nogarola, published in 1886, were gathered by the Hungarian count Alexander count Apponyi for publication in honor of his grandmother, a much later descendant of the Nogarola family. These were edited by Eugenius Abel, with full biobibliographical introduction: *Isotae Nogarolae veronensis opera quae supersunt omnia, accedunt Angelae et Zenevrae Nogarolae epistolae et carmina* (Vienna: apud Gerold et socios; Budapest: apud Fridericum Kilian, 1886).[39] This collection includes eighty works, of which thirty are by Nogarola herself. It contains also additional sections with works by her aunt Angela Nogarola, an author of Latin moral verse[40]; by her sister Ginevra (four early letters)[41]; and by authors commenting on her achievement in the

---

37. See Tullia d'Aragona, *Dialogue on the Infinity of Love*, ed. and trans. Rinaldina Russell (Chicago: University of Chicago Press, 1997).

38. See Fonte, *The Worth of Women*; Marinella, *The Nobility and Excellence of Women*; and Arcangela Tarabotti, *Paternal Tyranny*, ed. and trans. Letizia Panizza (Chicago: University of Chicago Press, forthcoming).

39. Abel, introduction, ii; and clvi–clxxii for the manuscript works Abel consulted. Corrections to Abel's edition of Nogarola's works are found in Remigio Sabbadini, "Notizie sulla vita e sugli scritti di alcuni dotti umanisti del secolo XV . . . V.: Isotta Nogarola," *Giornale storico della letteratura italiana* 6 (1885): 163–64; and Remigio Sabbadini, "Isotta Nogarola," *Archivio storico italiano*, 4th ser., vol. 18 (1886): 435–43. Two modern translations of Nogarola's dialogue, *De pari aut impari Evae atque Adae peccato*, are now available in print in King and Rabil, *Her Immaculate Hand*; and Maria Ludovico Lenzi, ed., *Donne e madonne: l'educazione femminile nel primo Rinascimento italiano* (Turin: Loescher, 1982), 214–16.

40. Angela was the sister of Isotta's father Leonardo and of the unfortunate Giovanni Nogarola (see below, chap. 1), all children of Antonio, and the wife of the Vicentine nobleman Antonio de Arco (1396): see Abel, genealogies, 1: *Tabula* and 1:7; also Avesanti, 23–26. Angela's works are published by Abel at 2:293–326.

41. Abel publishes four letters written by Ginevra: to Jacopo Foscari (2:329–34); to Johannes Papiensis, a teacher of sacred theology (2:335, a mere six lines); and to Damiano dal Borgo (2:336–39 and 339–42). The letters of Ognibene Leoniceno and Giorgio Bevilacqua in chap.

years and generations after her death (including the extensive *Isottaeus liber* of Giovanni Mario Filelfo[42]). We publish here all thirty of Nogarola's works published by Abel, plus two of the most important of those written to her.

Abel's critical edition rests on three principal manuscript witnesses from Verona, Vienna, and the Vatican, all of which also contain her *Dialogue*.[43] All of these must be derived from Nogarola's own letterbook. We know from her own testimony that she copied out and collected her letters to assemble them for publication in a bound manuscript volume.[44] Many more codices listed by Abel, or subsequently identified by later scholars, contain two or more of her letters or other works. The impressively wide diffusion of Nogarola's works, which are often embedded in humanist miscellanies including works by the leading humanists of the Renaissance, testify as much as the praise of contemporaries to her great reputation and influence.

Nogarola wrote works that are not extant. Known to be missing are her letters to Foscarini in the year 1453, a year in which he wrote her twenty letters evidently responding to matters she had raised, all now extant. It is also highly likely that Nogarola responded to the letters of the other figures named in the pages that follow who wrote her, especially during the silent period 1440–49. These works may be lost. Alternatively, and more probably, they were suppressed (especially the correspondence with Foscarini)— possibly by Nogarola herself, who left them out of her letterbook or consigned them to the flames, or by members of her family who would have had the disposition of her papers after her death.

---

1 are addressed to both sisters, as are the letters of Girolamo Guarino (1:93–102), Ludovico Cendrata (1:109–15), Tobia dal Borgo (1:121–28), and Niccolò Venier (1:164–69); thereafter, correspondence is directed to Nogarola alone.

42. Abel, 2:365–87. See also Avesani, 75–76.

43. Abel, 1:clvii–clxi lists his manuscript sources, including the three principal manuscripts in Vienna, Rome, and Verona (Vindobonensis 3481, Vaticanus 5127, and Veronensis 256), and some twenty more containing one, two, or several letters from major European collections in Rome, Florence, Venice, Milan, Mantua, Munich, Paris, London, Vienna, and Basel—a truly impressive diffusion. Further details of these and other manuscript versions of Nogarola's works are listed in Paul Oskar Kristeller, *Iter Italicum, accedunt alia itinera: A Finding List of Uncatalogued or Incompletely Catalogued Humanistic Manuscripts of the Renaissance in Italian and Other Libraries*, 6 vols. plus index (London: Warburg Institute-Leiden: E.J. Brill, 1967–97); see the cumulative index in vol. 7. In most cases, these entries refer to humanist miscellanies of the fifteenth through seventeenth centuries, containing one or a few of her letters.

44. See Abel on this, 1: clvi: "Isottae igitur et Zenevrae epistolas mature iam in volumen redactas esse et ipsam Isotam diligentem in epistolis suis describendis et colligendis operam posuisse ex nunnullis eius litterarum locis intellegitur."

VOLUME EDITORS'
BIBLIOGRAPHY

For a broader introduction to the literature on women and learning in the early modern era, see the series editors' bibliography at the end of this volume. Books listed here are not repeated there.

PRIMARY SOURCES

Ambrose, Saint. *Hexameron, Paradise, and Cain and Abel*. Translated by John J. Savage. *Fathers of the Church*, 42. Washington, D.C.: Catholic University Press, 1977. Originally published in 1961.

Augustine, Saint. *Augustine: Earlier Writings*. Translated by J.H.S. Burleigh. Library of Christian Classics, 6. Philadelphia: Westminster Press, 1953.

————. *The Literal Meaning of Genesis*. Translated by John Hammond Taylor. In *Ancient Christian Writers* (New York: Newman Press, 1982).

Bergomensis, Jacobus Philippus. *De memorabilibus et claris mulieribus, aliquot diversorum scriptorum opera*. Paris: Ex aedibus Simonis Colinaei, 1521. Originally published in 1497.

Bernard, Saint. *On Grace and Free Choice*. Vol. 7 of *The Works of Bernard of Clairvaux*. Translated by D. O'Donovan. Introduction by B. McGinn. Kalamazoo, Mich.: Cistercian Publications, 1971.

Boccaccio, Giovanni. *Famous Women*. Edited and translated by Virginia Brown. Cambridge, Mass.: Harvard University Press, 2001.

Boethius, Anicius Manlius Severinus. *The Consolation of Philosophy*. Translated by Richard Green. New York: Macmillan, 1962.

Cereta, Laura. *Collected Letters of a Renaissance Feminist*. Edited and translated by Diana Robin. Chicago: University of Chicago Press, 1997.

D'Aragona, Tullia. *Dialogue on the Infinity of Love*. Edited and translated by Rinaldina Russell. Chicago: University of Chicago Press, 1997.

De Pizan, Christine. *The Book of the City of Ladies*. Translated by Earl Jeffrey Richards. New York: Persea Books, 1982.

————. *The Treasure of the City of Ladies*. Translated by Sarah Lawson. New York: Viking Penguin, 1985. Also translated and introduction by Charity Cannon

Willard, edited and introduction by Madeleine P. Cosman (New York: Persea Books, 1989).

Diogenes Laertius. *Lives of Eminent Philosophers.* Translated by R.D. Hicks. Loeb Library. Cambridge Mass.: Harvard University Press, 1980.

Fedele, Cassandra. *Letters and Orations.* Edited and translated by Diana Robin. Chicago: University of Chicago Press, 2000.

Ferrazzi, Cecilia. *Autobiography of an Aspiring Saint.* Edited and translated by Anne Jacobson Schutte. Chicago: University of Chicago Press, 1996.

Fonte, Moderata. *The Worth of Women: Wherein Is Clearly Revealed Their Nobility and Their Superiority to Men.* Edited and translated by Virginia Cox. Chicago: University of Chicago Press, 1997.

Franco, Veronica. *Poems and Selected Letters.* Edited and translated by Ann Rosalind Jones and Margaret F. Rosenthal. Chicago: University of Chicago Press, 1998.

Gellius, Aulus. *The Attic Nights of Aulus Gellius.* Translated by John Rolfe. London: Heinemann; Cambridge, Mass.: Harvard University Press, 1968.

Gregory, Saint. *Morals on the Book of Job.* Translated by J. Bliss. 3 vols. Oxford: J.H. Parker, 1844–50.

Gregory, Saint. "St. Gregory's Pastoral Rule." In *Nicene and Post-Nicene Fathers,* ser. 2. 12, edited by Philip Schaff and Henry Waceser. Peabody, Mass.: Hendrickson Publishers, 1994. Originally published in 1890.

Guarino Veronese. *L'epistolario di Guarino Veronese.* Edited by Remigio Sabbadini. 3 vols. R. deputazione veneta di storia patria. Ser. III: Miscellanea di storia veneta. Vols. 8, 11, 114. Venice: la Società, 1915–19. Anastatic reproduction Turin: Bottega d'Erasmo, 1967.

Jerome, Saint. *Selected Letters of St. Jerome.* Translated by F.A. Wright. London: Heinemann, and New York: G.P. Putnam, 1933.

King, Margaret L., and Albert Rabil, Jr., eds. *Her Immaculate Hand: Selected Works by and about the Women Humanists of Quattrocento Italy.* 2d rev. ed. Binghamton, N.Y.: Medieval and Renaissance Texts and Studies, 1991.

Kohl, Benjamin G., and Ronald G. Witt, eds. *The Earthly Republic: Italian Humanists on Government and Society.* Philadelphia: University of Pennsylvania Press, 1978.

Marinella, Lucrezia. *The Nobility and Excellence of Women and the Defects and Vices of Men.* Edited and translated by Anne Dunhill, introduction by Letizia Panizza. Chicago: University of Chicago Press, 1999.

Nogarola, Isotta. *Isotae Nogarolae veronensis opera quae supersunt omnia, accedunt Angelae et Zenevrae Nogarolae epistolae et carmina.* Edited by Eugenius Abel. Vienna: apud Gerold et socios, and Budapest: apud Fridericum Kilian, 1886.

Tarabotti, Arcangela. *Paternal Tyranny.* Edited and translated by Letizia Panizza. Chicago: University of Chicago Press, forthcoming.

Vergerio, Pier Paolo. *The Character and Studies Befitting a Free-Born Youth* [*De ingenuis moribus*]. In *Humanist Educational Treatises,* edited and translated by Craig W. Kallendorf, 2–91. Cambridge, Mass.: Harvard University Press, 2002, 2–91.

———. *De ingenuis moribus.* In *Vittorino da Feltre and Other Humanist Educators,* edited by William H. Woodward, 93–118. Cambridge: Cambridge University Press, 1897. Reprint with introduction by Eugene F. Rice, Jr. New York: Bureau of Publications, Teachers College, Columbia University, 1963.

SECONDARY SOURCES

Allen, Prudence. *The Concept of Woman: 2: The Early Humanist Reformation, 1250–1500.* Grand Rapids, Mich.: William B. Eerdmans Publishing Co., 2002.

Avesani, Rino. *Verona e il suo territorioa.* Vol. 4 of *Verona nel Quattrocento.* Tomo 2 of *La civiltà delle lettere.* Parte terza of *La letteratura.* Verona: Istituto per gli Studi Storici Veronesi, 1984. 51–76.

Bell, Rudolph, and Donald Weinstein. *Saints and Society: The Two Worlds of Western Christendom, 1000–1700.* Chicago: University of Chicago Press, 1982.

Benson, Pamela J. *The Invention of Renaissance Woman: The Challenge of Female Independence in the Literature and Thought of Italy and England.* University Park, Penn.: Pennsylvania State University Press, 1992.

Black, Robert. *Benedetto Accolti and the Florentine Renaissance.* Cambridge: Cambridge University Press, 1985.

Brink, Jeanie R., ed. *Female Scholars: A Tradition of Learned Women before 1800.* Montreal: Eden Press Women's Publications, 1980.

Bynum, Caroline Walker. *Holy Feast and Holy Fast: The Religious Significance of Food to Medieval Women.* Berkeley: University of California Press, 1987.

Chojnacka, Monica. *Working Women of Early Modern Venice.* Baltimore: Johns Hopkins University Press, 2001.

Chojnacki, Stanley. *Women and Men in Renaissance Venice: Twelve Essays on Patrician Society.* Baltimore: Johns Hopkins University Press, 2000.

Cox, Virginia. *The Renaissance Dialogue: Literary Dialogue in Its Social and Political Contexts, Castiglione to Galileo.* Cambridge: Cambridge University Press, 1992.

Dizionario biografico degli Italiani. 55 vols. Rome: Istituto della Enciclopedia Italiana, 1960–.

Encyclopedia of the Renaissance. 6 vols. New York: Charles Scribner's Sons, 2000.

Frank, Maria Esposito. *Le insidie dell'allegoria: Ermolao Barbaro il Vecchio e la lezione degli antichi.* Venice: Istituto Veneto di Scienze, Lettere ed Arti, 1999.

Grafton, Anthony, and Lisa Jardine. *From Humanism to the Humanities: Education and the Liberal Arts in Fifteenth- and Sixteenth-Century Europe.* Cambridge, Mass.: Harvard University Press, 1986.

Grendler, Paul F. *Schooling in Renaissance Italy: Literacy and Learning, 1300–1600.* Baltimore: Johns Hopkins University Press, 1989.

Grubb, James S. *Provincial Families of the Renaissance: Private and Public Life in the Veneto.* Baltimore: Johns Hopkins University Press, 1996.

Hale, John R., ed. *Renaissance Venice.* London: Faber & Faber, and Totowa, N.J.: Rowman and Littlefield, 1973.

Hanawalt, Barbara A., ed. *Women and Work in Pre-Industrial Europe.* Bloomington, Ind.: Indiana University Press, 1986.

Hull, Suzanne W. *Chaste, Silent and Obedient: English Books for Women, 1475–1640.* San Marino, Calif.: The Huntington Library, 1982.

Jardine, Lisa. "Isotta Nogarola: Women Humanists—Education for What?" *History of Education,* 12 (1983): 231–44.

Kieckhefer, Richard. *Unquiet Souls: Fourteenth-Century Saints and Their Religious Milieu.* Chicago: University of Chicago Press, 1984.

King, Margaret L. "Book-Lined Cells." In *Beyond Their Sex: Learned Women of the European Past*, edited by Patricia H. Labalme, 66–90. New York: New York University Press, 1980.

————. *The Death of the Child Valerio Marcello*. Chicago: University of Chicago Press, 1994.

————. "Goddess and Captive: Antonio Loschi's Epistolary Tribute to Maddalena Scrovegni (1389)." *Medievalia et humanistica*, NS 1 (1980): 103–27.

————. "Isotta Nogarola." In *Italian Women Writers: A Bio-Bibliographical Sourcebook*. Edited by Rinaldina Russell, 313–23. Westport, Conn.: Greenwood, 1994.

————. "The Religious Retreat of Isotta Nogarola (1418–1466)." *Signs* 3 (1978): 807–22.

————. "Thwarted Ambitions: Six Learned Women of the Renaissance." *Soundings*, 59 (1976): 280–304.

————. *Venetian Humanism in an Age of Patrician Dominance*. Princeton: Princeton University Press, 1986.

————. *Women of the Renaissance*. Chicago: University of Chicago Press, 1991.

Kristeller, Paul Oskar. *Eight Philosophers of the Renaissance*. Stanford: Stanford University Press, 1964.

————. *Iter italicum, accedunt alia itinera: A Finding List of Uncatalogued or Incompletely Catalogued Humanistic Manuscripts of the Renaissance in Italian and Other Libraries*. 7 vols. London: Warburg Institute, and Leiden: E.J. Brill, 1963–1997.

Labalme, Patricia H., ed. *Beyond Their Sex: Learned Women of the European Past*. New York: New York University Press, 1980.

Lane, Frederic C. *Venice: A Maritime Republic*. Baltimore: Johns Hopkins University Press, 1973.

Lardinois, Andre. "Who Sang Sappho's Songs?" In *Reading Sappho: Contemporary Approaches*, edited by E. Greene, 150–74. Berkeley: University of California Press, 1996.

Lenzi, Maria Ludovico, ed. *Donne e madonne: l'educazione femminile nel primo Rinascimento italiano*. Turin: Loescher, 1982.

Marsh, David. *The Quattrocento Dialogue. Classical Tradition and Humanist Innovation*. Cambridge, Mass.: Harvard University Press, 1980.

Martin, John, and Dennis Romano, eds. *Venice Reconsidered: The History and Civilization of an Italian City-State, 1297–1797*. Baltimore: Johns Hopkins University Press, 2000.

McClure, George W. *Sorrow and Consolation in Italian Humanism*. Princeton: Princeton University Press, 1991.

Panizza, Letizia, ed. *Women in Italian Renaissance Culture and Society*. Oxford: Legenda, 2000.

Parker, Holt N. "Sappho Schoolmistress." In *Re-Reading Sappho: Reception and Transmission*, edited by Ellen Greene, 146–83. Berkeley: University of California Press, 1996.

Rabil, Albert. *Laura Cereta: Quattrocento Humanist*. Binghamton, N.Y.: Medieval and Renaissance Texts and Studies, 1981.

————., ed. *Renaissance Humanism: Foundations, Forms and Legacy*. 3 vols. Philadelphia: University of Pennsylvania Press, 1988. Paperback reprint 1991.

Rice, Eugene F. *Saint Jerome in the Renaissance*. Baltimore: Johns Hopkins University Press, 1985.

————. "The Renaissance Idea of Christian Antiquity: Humanist Patristic Scholarship." In Vol. 1 of *Renaissance Humanism, Foundations, Forms, and Legacy* 3 vols. Edited by Albert Rabil, Jr., 17–28. Philadelphia: University of Pennsylvania Press, 1988.

Robin, Diana. *Filelfo in Milan: Writings, 1451–1477.* Princeton: Princeton University Press, 1991.

Sabbadini, Remigio. *Guariniana* [photostatic reproduction of Sabbadini's *Vita di Guarino Veronese* and *La scuola e gli studi di Guarino Guarini Veronese*]. Edited by Mario Sancipriano. Turin: Bottega d'Erasmo, 1964.

————. "Isotta Nogarola." *Archivio storico italian.* 18, ser. 4 (1886): 435–43.

————. "Notizie sulla vita e sugli scritti di alcuni dotti umanisti del secolo XV . . . V.: Isotta Nogarola." *Giornale storico della letteratura italiana* 6 (1885): 163–64.

Segarizzi, Arnaldo. "Niccolò Barbo patrizio veneziano del secolo XV e le accuse contro Isotta Nogarola." *Giornale storico della letteratura italiana* 43 (1904): 39–54.

Stehle, Eva. *Performance and Gender in Ancient Greece.* Princeton: Princeton University Press, 1997.

Vauchez, André. *La sainteté en Occident aux derniers siècles du Moyen Age après les procès de canonisation et les documents hagiographiques.* Rome: Ecole Française de Rome, 1981.

Warner, Marina. *Alone of All Her Sex: The Myth and the Cult of the Virgin Mary.* New York: Knopf, 1976.

Whitehead, Barbara J., ed. *Women's Education in Early Modern Europe: A History, 1500–1800.* New York-London: Garland, 1999.

Wiesner, Merry. *Working Women in Renaissance Germany.* New Brunswick, N.J.: Rutgers University Press, 1986.

Willard, Charity Cannon. *Christine de Pizan: Her Life and Works.* New York: Persea Books, 1984.

Witt, Ronald G. *In the Footsteps of the Ancients: The Origins of Humanism from Lovato to Bruni.* Leiden-Boston: Brill, 2000.

ABBREVIATIONS

DBI   *Dizionario biografico degli italiani.* Rome: Istituto della Enciclopedia italiana, 1960–.

NPNF   *Select Library of the Nicene and Post-Nicene Fathers of the Christian Church. First Series.* 14 vols. Edited by Philip Schaff. Peabody, Mass.: Hendrickson Publishers, 1994. Originally published 1886–90. *Second Series.* 14 vols. Edited by Philip Schaff and Henry Wace. Peabody, Mass.: Hendrickson Publishers, 1994. Originally published 1890–1900.

PL   *Patrologia latina* = Migne, Jacques-Paul (1800–75), *Patrologiae cursus completus. Series Latina. Patrologiae cursus completus, sive biblioteca universalis, integra, uniformis, commoda, oeconomica, omnium SS. Patrum, doctorum scriptorumque eccelesiasticorum qui ab aevo apostolico ad usque Innocentii III tempora floruerunt . . . Series Latina, in qua prodeunt Patres, doctores scriptoresque Ecclesiae Latinae, a Tertulliano ad Innocentium III.* 221 vols. Paris: 1844–64.

I

KIN, FRIENDS, AND BOOKS

(1 4 3 4 – 3 7)

The early letters by and to Isotta Nogarola, sometimes jointly with her elder sister Ginevra, circulated among a close circle of humanistically trained aristocrats closely related to the Nogarola family, one of the leading noble clans of Verona. The quality of those relationships was conditioned to some extent by the longer history of the author's city and family.

Today a flourishing city of northeastern Italy, Verona was then a considerable town that had only recently lost its independence to its grander neighbor, the republic of Venice, perched on the Adriatic Sea.[1] From its origins until the last years of the fourteenth century, Venice had looked seaward and had expanded down the Balkan coast and eastward toward the Levant. After its last mighty struggle with archrival Genoa, however, in the Chioggian war of 1378–80, Venice turned away from maritime preoccupations and launched a project of territorial expansion in northern Italy that, at its high tide, reached as far west as, and even a little beyond, the other most populous northern city, Milan. In the early years of the fifteenth century, Venice acquired the nearby strongholds of Padua (home to the major university of the region), Vicenza, and Verona (in 1405), among others. With those acquisitions, Venice became an imperial ruler of the *terra ferma*, or "solid land," as it had been and continued to be of its maritime colonies and protectorates.

The warrior nobility of the mainland cities, the social stratum to which the Nogarola clan belonged, underwent a significant transformation with the

1. For Venice, see the entry in the *Encyclopedia of the Renaissance* and bibliography there cited; esp. Frederic C. Lane, *Venice: A Maritime Republic* (Baltimore: Johns Hopkins University Press, 1973); John R. Hale, ed., *Renaissance Venice* (London: Faber & Faber; Totowa, N.J.: Rowman and Littlefield, 1973); John Martin and Dennis Romano, eds., *Venice Reconsidered: The History and Civilization of an Italian City-State, 1297–1797* (Baltimore: Johns Hopkins University Press, 2000).

Venetian conquest. Previously, the supporters of the *signori*, or local despots, who themselves had emerged from the noble clans, they now became the loyal clients of the Venetian state, from which they could expect economic opportunities, political offices, and the possibility of advantageous marriages. The Nogarola marriages attest to the shift. From the fourteenth and into the fifteenth century, Nogarolas married into some of the major families of northern Italy: della Scala (Scaligeri), Lamberto, Malespina, della Porcia, Castronovo; and Isotta's sister Laura married into the Venetian nobility, becoming the wife of Niccolò Tron.[2] At the same time, the Nogarola men continued to achieve important career advancement in the Veronese state (under Venetian overlordship) and the church.[3] In addition, the Nogarolas established relationships with the Venetian military and civilian governors and diplomats who rotated into office in Venice and with a Venetian cleric who won the important position of Bishop of Verona. The letters and orations of Isotta Nogarola often commented upon these relationships and reaffirmed her family's loyalty to the dominant state that had, in fact, just a generation earlier overrun her town and that, in 1414, had caused the execution for treason of her paternal uncle, whose avocation was the writing of verse.[4]

If the Nogarola family was deeply involved in past and present politics, another aspect of its tradition was its important participation in cultural life. In the century before Isotta's emergence as a humanist author, both male and female Nogarolas had been noted for their scholarship and literary pursuits. Early in the fifteenth century, Isotta's aunt Angela, the sister of the unfortunate Giovanni, was a productive author, largely of moralizing verse—and, having married into a Vicentine family, became mother and grandmother of learned men.[5]

The intellectual careers of Nogarola's forebears, male and female, unfolded in an age before humanism had become the dominant intellectual tradition that it would become in the fifteenth century. The evidence of naming suggests an interest among some Nogarola ancestors in late-medieval romance literature. The name of Isotta's grandfather's grandfather, Gufredus,

2. Abel, genealogies, *Tabula I.*

3. For Isotta's brothers Ludovico, Leonardo, and Antonio, see volume editors' introduction, n. 4.

4. For Isotta's uncle Giovanni, condemned to death on December 2, 1412, see Abel, iii and n. 3; Avesani, 22. His perceived guilt must have caused other members of the Nogarola family some discomfiture as they tried to establish themselves as loyal supporters of the new Venetian regime.

5. See volume editors' introduction, n. 40.

is the Italianized form of "Siegfried," a central figure of Germanic romance.[6] Some family members of an older generation must have suggested the names given Isotta and her sister Ginevra, Italian forms, respectively, of the romance heroines Isolde and Guinevere. These were not names commonly chosen in the Veronese or Venetian cultural milieu, where the names of saints and exemplary ancestors were favored. They are tantalizing suggestions of the literary world of Isotta's Nogarola forebears, whose taste for ultramontane romance matter accords well with their participation in the social stratum of the warrior nobility in a northern Italian milieu more generally characterized by an urbanized and commercial culture.

Although Leonardo, the father of Isotta and Ginevra, died young (between 1425 and 1433), their mother Bianca, from the Paduan Borromeo clan (similar in many ways to the Veronese Nogarolas) actively supervised the rearing of her many children—and, conspicuously, although she herself was illiterate,[7] the education of her daughters in the latest humanist mode. The Nogarola brothers—Ludovico, Antonio, and Leonardo (Jacopo had died young) all proceeded to important careers as statesmen, intellectuals, or clergy, attainments indicating that they had received, under a tutor or at a school perhaps chosen at Bianca's direction, a solid education through the secondary level. For her daughters, Bianca chose as tutor the Veronese teacher Martino Rizzoni (1404–88), who lived with the household for several years afer 1431.[8] Rizzoni was himself the student of the even more famous Veronese intellectual, the greatest of the generation, Guarino Guarini, known as Guarino "Veronese" or "Guarino from Verona." Guarino, a master of Greek as well as Roman literature, was one of the major pedagogues of the first generation of mature Italian humanism (who include also Pier Paolo Vergerio, Vittorino da Feltre, Gasparino Barzizza, and the like).[9] Isotta's sisters Bartolommea, Laura, Samaritana, and Isabella[10] may also have studied

---

6. Abel, 1, genealogies, *Tabula I*.

7. Abel, xii and n. 23.

8. For Rizzoni, see Abel, xvi and n. 30; Rino Avesani, *Verona e il suo territorio*, 4: *Verona nel Quattrocento*, part 2 (Verona: Istituto per gli studi storici veronesi, 1984), 51–59.

9. For Guarino Veronese, see especially the *Epistolario di Guarino Veronese*; Sabbadini, *Guariniana*; for his pedagogical role, William H. Woodward, *Vittorino da Feltre*; Anthony Grafton and Lisa Jardine, *Humanism and the Humanities*, chap. 2; for his activity in Verona, Avesani, 31–50; for his activity in Venice, Margaret King, *Venetian Humanism*, passim.

10. We know of the other sisters only that Samaritana died young, Bartolommea married Jacopo Lavagnola, Isabella married, first, Francesco Fracastoro and then Giovanni da Mosto, and Laura married, first, Cristoforo Peregrino, and then the nobleman Niccolò Tron. See Abel, genealogies, *Tabula I*.

with Rizzoni, along with Isotta and Ginevra. But it was these latter two who excelled and who in their adolescence attracted the attention of local notables and intellectuals because of their extraordinary progress in the difficult humanist curriculum—one to which at this time only a handful of privileged men had access.

Two such local figures appeared among the earliest correspondents of the two sisters. The first, Ognibene da Lonigo—or Leoniceno, an Italianized form of the Latin *Leonicenus*—was a humanist teacher of the Guarinian type, who would attain a wide reputation in Venice and the Veneto.[11] A young man in the 1430s, he had received the patronage of Bianca Borromeo, the mother of the Nogarola sisters (as appears from his letter) and would later be supported in his career by Leonardo Nogarola; and at an unspecified date he would recite in Vicenza the funeral oration for Elisabetta Nogarola, the sister of Isotta's father, who had resided there, the wife of the nobleman Jacopo da Thiene. Ognibene subsequently became the teacher of Benedetto Brognoli (1427–1502), who would in 1466 become the master of Venice's publicly funded humanist school for future state secretaries; and of the eminent Venetian nobleman, humanist, and statesman Francesco Diedo (1433–84), a correspondent, in turn, of the nobleman Ludovico Foscarini, who will appear often in these pages. In 1454, he delivered an oration celebrating the award of a degree in canon law to Pietro Foscari, papal notary, *primicerius* (head chaplain) of the doge's vast chapel of San Marco in Venice and nephew of doge Francesco Foscari (whose son Jacopo would soon join the roster of Nogarola correspondents). To have been selected to give an oration for a person of such eminence is a clear indicator of the high reputation Ognibene had achieved a generation after his letter to the Nogarola sisters, with which their correspondence opens.

Ognibene wrote the two sisters at some point during the period 1433–36, when Isotta turned eighteen.[12] His letter alludes to Bianca Borromeo's support for him and commends the sisters for their great accomplishments in the study of the liberal arts.[13] As a gift to them and to their mother, he had translated from the Greek a work by the early church father John Chrysos-

---

11. For Ognibene Leoniceno, a student of Vittorino da Feltre's who taught in Venice in the 1440s and '50s, see *Venetian Humanism*, 343, 362, 374; also Abel, xv and nn. 28, 29.

12. Abel, 1:3–5, probably from Vicenza, 1433–36?

13. A testimony of Ognibene's continued relation to the Nogarola family is the oration he gave for the death (date unknown) of Elisabetta Nogarola (Isotta's aunt, the sister of Isotta's father Leonardo), who had married the Vicentine nobleman Jacopo da Thiene (Abel, 2:407–18 for the oration; see also 1:cv–cvi, n. 29).

tom, *On Virginity*, and now sends them a copy of his Latin version.[14] A slight thing, this first letter is nevertheless striking for two reasons: first, because of the seriousness with which the young women's studies are viewed; and, second, because of the introduction of the theme of virginity, virtually a constant in the history of the intellectual lives of women in the premodern West. Virginity was conceived of, not only by Ognibene but by centuries of male thinkers and experts, as the ideal state, especially for women, and even more so for women who had acquired literacy and aspired to higher learning.[15]

No letter survives in which either Nogarola sister responds to Ognibene. This lacuna does not mean that such a letter was not written. The letter collections of this period are both artful constructions and the product of accident. In some cases, letters were written which their authors or others decided not to preserve. In others, letters were written, but have been lost over the course of nearly six hundred years, all the more likely to have happened in the age before print because of the rarity and fragility of manuscript versions. These comments pertain to all those situations where letters appear to be "missing" from the Nogarola correspondence.

A second local figure in communication with the Nogarola sisters was Giorgio Bevilacqua (1406 to after 1463), a Veronese nobleman of considerable humanist reputation.[16] A student of Guarino's who studied law at Padua and Bologna, Bevilacqua later threw his lot in with the dominant Venetian Republic. He dedicated works to the Venetian noblemen Marco Donato, Zaccaria Barbaro, and Ludovico Foscarini, and became the secretary and literary counselor of another one: Jacopo Antonio Marcello, to whom Isotta also would dedicate a work many years later (see chapter 10). Like Isotta Nogarola and Ognibene Leoniceno, as a citizen of a mainland north Italian city that had come under Venetian sway, Bevilacqua's career was intricately involved with figures from Venetian political and cultural life.

In these early years of his career, however, he was a university student, the friend of Isotta's brother Antonio and of Jacopo Lavagnola, also

---

14. John Chrysostom, one of the Greek fathers of the church (ca. 347–407). The work "On Virginity" may describe one of his many sermons.

15. For the theme of virginity, see esp. Suzanne W. Hull, *Chaste, Silent and Obedient: English Books for Women, 1475–1640* (San Marino, Calif.: Huntington Library, 1982); King, *Women of the Renaissance*; and Marina Warner, *Alone of All Her Sex: The Myth and Cult of the Virgin Mary* (New York: Knopf, 1976).

16. For Bevilacqua, see Margaret King, *The Death of the Child Valerio Marcello* (Chicago: University of Chicago Press, 1994), esp. 45–47; King, *Venetian Humanism* 273, 326, 370, 396, 446; Abel, 1: xviii–xxi; and Avesani, chap. 4.

Veronese, a fellow university student who had studied with Guarino and who, by 1438, would marry Isotta's sister Bartolommea.[17] In the extant correspondence, he writes the Nogarola sisters three times: in February and April 1436 and in June 1437 (but possibly 1436)[18]; Isotta responds to him twice, in July 1437 (see below). In his first letter, from the university town of Padua, which trained most of the lawyers and physicians of the Veneto, and its native aristocracy, Bevilacqua recalls having seen the sisters in Verona—"and found you amid your studies and the rich books of Cicero like the handmaidens of Calliope"—and sends them a copy of a work by Lactantius and requests the return of his copy of Livy.[19] In the second, also from Padua, he especially commends their mother, whom he likens to Cornelia, the daughter of Roman general Scipio Africanus and famed as the mother of Tiberius and Gaius Gracchus, two heroic and principled Roman statesmen who were killed for their political stands; like her, Bianca Borromeo has chosen the finest tutors for her children.[20] In this letter, too, he praises the letter (not extant, to our knowledge) that he received from them, which testified, he believed, to their humanist achievements. In the third, from Bologna, he notes that the sisters' fame is public knowledge in that city and that Verona had won renown not only for its learned men but, because of them, for its learned women. In addition, he sends them another gift, a book, like the first, and like the Chrysostom sent by Ognibene, Christian in theme: a devotional work on the death of Saint Jerome.[21]

It is noteworthy that these promoters of learning in the two Nogarola women, by the nature of the books they chose as gifts, fostered their pursuit of sacred literature. This pattern could indicate some underlying distrust of women's pursuit of learning, with the intent to channel those aspirations in the safe direction of sacred studies. Or it could point to standards of social decorum that would encourage young men to send books to young women

17. For Lavagnola, see Abel, 1:xviii and no. 34. Jacopo, the son of Thomas Lavagnola of Verona, from a family of ancient noble heritage, from which derived several physicians and learned men in the fifteenth century, would hold important magistracies in his native Verona, and perform diplomatic missions. He died in Rome in 1453 and was buried in a chapel in the church of Saint Anastasia, Verona. His four sons also went on to significant civic careers.

18. Abel, 1:12–17; 1:18–24; 1:25–35.

19. Calliope is the Greek muse of epic poetry; Lactantius (240–ca. 320 C.E.) is one of the most read Latin fathers of the Christian church, author of the *Divine Institutes*. Bevilacqua does not state which work of Lactantius's she sent.

20. See Val. Max. 4.4; and Plutarch *Lives of Tiberius* and *Gaius Gracchus*.

21. Unidentifiable; there were many works in circulation that could be described with the title *The Death of Saint Jerome*, a saint whose cult flourished in this period. See Rice, *Saint Jerome*, which mentions a hagiographical work on Jerome by Giovanni d'Andrea, but gives no date.

that were properly devotional in nature. Whatever the intent on the part of the givers, the message to the recipients must have been clear: in response to their publicized entry into the *res publica litterarum,* the "republic of letters," they received mainly Christian works.

Two other correspondents of Nogarola's in these earliest years were the Venetian nobleman Ermolao Barbaro (1410–71),[22] known to the family through Lavagnola, and the Paduan nobleman Antonio Borromeo, her maternal uncle. Borromeo, to whom Isotta writes in 1436 or 1437 and at whose Venetian home the family stays during the years 1438–40, is known only to be a substantial figure of the Paduan elite.[23] Ermolao Barbaro, however, was a conspicuous figure. The nephew of Francesco Barbaro, perhaps the most famous Venetian nobleman of this generation when large reputations were won in the Milanese wars, Ermolao was a student at the University of Padua at least intermittently betwen 1431 and 1436. It was during this period that Nogarola wrote him, probably in 1434, at his request and that of Lavagnola. Already holding the prestigious title of apostolic protonotary (precociously, since he was only 24 years old at the time of Isotta's letter), Barbaro went on to have a notable clerical and humanist career. He was made bishop of Treviso in 1443 and Bishop of Verona in 1453; in Verona, at that much later date, he would renew his acquaintance with Isotta Nogarola (see below, chapter 8). Barbaro was also an author of several works, most notably of the *Orationes contra poetas* (*Orations against the Poets*), a humanist attack on the study of secular classical authors.[24]

These, then, were the figures surrounding Nogarola as she and her sister first attempted to make themselves known to the male intellectuals of their era. They included teachers and students and noblemen from both the interior mainland towns and the preeminent republic of Venice. They were related to the young women as figures known to the Nogarola family, especially to mother Bianca, or vouched for by close friends or kin.

22. *Venetian Humanism,* 320–22, and sources there noted; Abel, 1:xvii, no. 31; for Barbaro's episcopacy in Verona, see Avesani, chap. 5. This Ermolao Barbaro is known as "the Elder" to distinguish him from his younger second cousin, a contemporary of the humanists Angelo Poliziano and Giovanni Pico della Mirandola.

23. Abel, 1:xix and no. 35. Borromeo was a very wealthy man, with property in Bologna, Verona, and Padua, where he retired, and apparently also in Venice. He died between 1443 and 1454. That the family stayed in the Borromeo home in Venice is known from Damiano dal Borgo's letter to Nogarola of August 20, 1438. Abel, 1:206–9; see chap. 4); at the end (1:209), the letter is addressed to Nogarola: Venetiis in domo spectabilis militis domini Antonii Borromei.

24. See *Venetian Humanism,* 157–61; Maria Esposito Frank, *Le insidie dell'allegoria: Ermolao Barbaro il Vecchio e la lezione degli antichi* (Venice: Istituto Veneto di Scienze, Lettere ed Arti, 1999).

The correspondence with these figures is uncertainly dated, but its outside limits are 1434 to 1437, a period during which Isotta matured from
sixteen to nineteen years of age. Although a political career was barred to
the two sisters because of their gender, literary ventures were not; and there
were women writers among their Nogarola forebears who could guide them
on that path. It is a path they undertook together in the mid-1430s.

I

Isotta Nogarola to Ermolao Barbaro: Verona, probably 1434

*Since he had invited her to do so, through a family friend (and future brother-in-law), Jacopo
Lavagnola, Nogarola introduces herself to Barbaro as an author of letters in classical Latin
style and thus a member of the coterie of youthful humanist professionals and amateurs. She
praises Barbaro and his prominent Venetian noble family.*

*P*etronius Arbiter,[25] a most learned man, seems truly to have made the
greatest fun of certain men who criticized others but were inarticu-
late and speechless themselves, who thought that they themselves were the
sons of Minerva when they listened to an oration of Cicero or some verses of
Virgil. For after one of these men, he said, wove together verse in meters and
delicate sentiment in balanced periods, he thought that he had arrived at the
Helicon. I am afraid that the same could be said of me, most reverend father,
who, although I have barely sampled a taste of the study of the humanities,
would not hesitate to expose my own writings—or really my foolishness—
to be examined by critics and even to write to an accomplished man such
as you who are endowed with such a degree of dignity, modesty, humanity, gravity, as well as the finest eloquence and knowledge of pontifical law.
But my sex itself will provide the greatest excuse for me among some men,
since it may be very difficult to find a silent woman, as our comic playwright
says.[26] Among other men, your excellence will be the witnesss that I took up

---

25. Nogarola's "aliquis versum pedibus instructum sensumque tenuiorem verborum ambut in-
texuit, putavit se continuo in Heliconem venisse" (Abel, 1:6) is an almost verbatim quote from
Petronius *Satyricon* 118. Petronius Arbiter, first-century author of the bawdy Latin novel the
Satyricon (of which *Trimalchio's Feast* is the most famous episode). According to Tacitus, Petronius
was characterized as the *arbiter elegantiae* at Nero's court. For Nogarola's knowledge of Petronius
and a manuscript of his work from her collection (Biblioteca Apostolica Vaticana, cod. Bar-
beriniano Lat., 4 [VIII 4]) that bears the family coat of arms as well as a medallion of a young
woman, se Avesani, 61, 63; Kristeller, *Iter* 6:387b.

26. Plautus *Aulularia* 124: "Nec mutam profecto repertam ullam esse."

this role of writing to you at your urging and the suggestion of our brother Antonio and our Lavagnola.[27] I would gladly have refused this burden, but I preferred to be judged impudent rather than disobey your orders and those men's wishes.

But, most excellent father, I would not want you to wait for an oration worthy neither of your character nor your acclaim since the rhetorical elegance and eloquence of a very learned man might be sullied by my praises. But such a thing would also seem superfluous, and I would be wasting my labor, as they say.[28] For your virtue places you at such a level that whatever things you do and say can never fail to attract fame. For you have never neglected anything that might possibly increase and embellish your erudition. Nature has endowed you with innumerable gifts; foremost of these is sweetness of speech and wonderful eloquence that you have augmented with your incredible talent and spirit. And rightly so. For what is more lasting than eloquence, which among every free people and in every republic is held in the highest esteem when it is strengthened by good customs? For eloquence is the companion of peace and tranquility and the daughter of the well-governed city, one might say.[29] From this emanate the loves of princes, their honors, and the prestige of republics—I need not mention the knowledge of divine and human law, to which you have devoted as much time as other men devote to dealing with their own affairs, celebrating the feast days and games, to various other pleasures, and to the relaxation of the mind and body. All this proceeds from the greatness and nobility of a divine mind.

For who does not know the distinguished family of the Barbaro, which the foremost citizens of the city of Venice celebrate and honor? From this clan you have received as much honor and praise as you return to it with your own character, gravity, magnanimity, prudence, fairness, and the rest of your virtues the proof of which you exhibit both at home and abroad, accompanied by the highest acclaim and praise of all men. And so it is that because of these gifts you are loved by God and admired by men. For the pope himself wanted you, despite your extreme youth, to be made a member of the sacred college of protonotaries as a reward for your virtues. O distinguished glory of our age! O superb jewel of the Venetian republic! O rare

27. Jacopo Lavagnola; see above, n. 18.

28. *Agere acta*: to do things that have already been done, i.e., to waste one's labor.

29. "Pacis est enim otiique socia et bene constitutae civitatis quasi alumna quaedam eloquentia": a standard humanist formulation connecting the public good (*bene constituta civitas*) with private intellectual and literary pursuits (*otium*). In fact, Nogarola here is quoting Cicero almost verbatim. Cf. Cicero *Brutus* 45: "Pacis est comes otioque socia et iam bene constitutae civitatis quasi alumna quaedam eloquentia."

bird on earth, like a black swan![30] But lest my writings should seem to you to be too verbose, even if an encomium of you demands a longer oration, I shall bring my letter to a close lest I be rightly accused of what Aristotle said to a certain overly garrulous man whom men shunned whenever he entered a room so that they would not have to suffer the tedium of his speeches. For when this man visited Aristotle and complained about this, he answered, "I am only surprised that anyone who has feet stays to hear you."[31] For here you have a long-winded letter, which as long as it does not displease you as a witness of my esteem, will allow me to be happy that I have not taken the trouble to write in vain. Vale.

II

Isotta Nogarola to Giorgio Bevilacqua: Verona, July 1436 or 1437

She has received his letter and is grateful to him for interrupting his intense studies at the university in Padua, for his expressions of admiration and affection, and for his gift of the book on the death of Saint Jerome (to which she responds with a quote from Cicero). She looks forward to seeing him again and will comfort herself in the meantime with his letters.

If you are well, I am glad. I too am well. I was very pleased with your letter when I read your explanation of why so much time has passed since you have sent your elegant letters to me. This was gratifying because I now understand that you neglected to write to us not from lack of regard but because of your constant and unceasing study. And so, you have freed us from the greatest sorrow and anxiety, since your letter has left me no doubt of how much you esteem me. Really, you could not possibly have written the praises you lavished on my writing without love. And though I shall not be able to respond to you in words, I shall respond unfailingly with a wordless love; for your excellence, which appears greater to us each day, affects me daily with such a great desire for you that I seek only one consolation for that longing—that our desire for each other may be assuaged by long and frequent letters.

All that is left is to assure you that the book you sent us on the death of Saint Jerome, another clear token of your love, pleased us wonderfully; I have read it with delight and continue to read it and most diligently will cherish

---

30. Juvenal 6.165: "rara avis in terris nigroque simillima cygno."

31. Nogarola's source for the anecdote on Aristotle and the nonstop talker is Plutarch *Moralia* 502B–503B. The topic heading is "De Garrulitate" (*Peri adoleschias*).

it. And so, I shall lovingly adorn this parting[32] from you with Cicero's words: I shall impatiently await your return, remember you while you are gone, and by sending letters, I shall allay my desire to receive them.[33] Farewell.

III

Isotta Nogarola to Giorgio Bevilacqua: Verona, July 1436 or 1437

She expresses her appreciation of his affection for her and the joy she feels when she reads the book he sent.

*E*ven though I have known for a long time now that I am extraordinarily well loved by you,[34] still I am more keenly aware of it every day. For I see such a great store of goodwill in the letter I have here from you that I wonder how there can be room for more. As a matter of fact, when I thought that you who are endowed with such great wisdom had stopped writing to me, I became so distressed that I nearly succumbed to despair. For I was unhappy that I had lost the great patron[35] I saw in you because I thought that I had found a herald who would make me immortal in everyone's eyes. And it is very helpful to me, I think, that those letters of yours have so much weight and authority that one would think it was not you but Cicero himself speaking. Indeed, all our citizens boast about you and boldly call you the most eminent man in the city. Therefore, it is impossible to say how glad I am that I have won your friendship, and as long as I have it I shall rejoice. That you extol me to the skies, however, I attribute to your incredible love for me,[36] and I give you the greatest thanks and trust that your opinion of

---

32. This translation prefers the alternate reading "profectionem" in ms. V to the reading "perfectionem" chosen by Abel because it accords with the sense of the Cicero quotation that follows.

33. Cicero *Ad. Fam.* 15.21.5: " . . . tuam profectionem amore prosequar, reditum spe expectem, absentem memoria colam, omne desiderium litteris mittendis accipiendisque leniam."

34. "Etsi iam diu, Giorgi amantissime, me a te vehementer amari intellexeram." So the letter begins. It is impossible to get the exact sense of "vehementer amari," which we take to be formulaic in humanist letters and very much in the idiom of the *amicitia* or patronage relationship. On the language and idioms of patronage see Diana Robin, *Filelfo in Milan*, esp. chap. 1 and in particular Filelfo's letter to Traversari (42).

35. Nogarola uses here the explicit term *patronus*, a somewhat rare usage in patronage correspondence where euphemisms prevail and expressions suggesting that a friendship (*amicitia*) might lead to material advantages tend to be suppressed.

36. " . . . tuo incredibili tribuo *amori*" (our italics): here again her use of the word *amor* is attributed to her need to display her command of the hyperbolic language of humanist affiliation.

me will be a tremendous help. I cannot tell you how useful all your kindness has been. For what could please me more at this time than your giving me the little book on the death of Jerome?[37] For this is an undying memento of your love for me, and whenever I take it in my hands (and I shall take it up often) I myself become better and wiser. Therefore, again and again I give you everlasting thanks and I shall continue to do so as long as I have life and breath in these limbs. Vale.

IV

Isotta Nogarola to Antonio Borromeo:
Verona, 1436 or 1437

Recalling the many learned women of the past, she dares to write him, her maternal uncle, although she characterized her own writing, modestly, as "crude." She asks him for money to buy a book by the Roman historian Livy.

I had often planned to send you my unpolished and unworthy writings, but when I thought of how many men there are—if they deserve to be called men—who consider learning in women a plague and public nuisance, this deterred me from the task. But it seems to me that these men—who approve of nothing except what they themselves do and think—are themselves a different kind of plague, that of men envious of others' glory, which comes from ignorance and baseness of spirit. I know for a certainty that they have not read with how much fame and renown those illustrious and remarkable women are celebrated, who each in her own era spent all her energy, care, and effort in study. The Muses themselves were women, who instructed and inspired great men and godlike poets. Clearly Virgil was not ashamed to invoke their aid when he wrote, "Come Sicilian Muses, let us sing of loftier themes."[38] Certainly in Plato's circle women were not unoccupied with divine philosophy: for example, Lasthenia of Mantinea and Axiothea of Phlius, and she, they say, wore men's clothing in order to study with him.[39] In how many poems has Cornelia the mother of the Gracchi[40] been honored! Our ancestors have rightly preserved for later ages the memory of that

---

37. See above, n. 21.

38. P. Vergilius Maro *Eclogues* 4.1: "Sicelides Musae, paulo maiora canamus!"

39. Diogenes Laertius, *Lives of Eminent Philosophers* 3.46 and 4.2, trans. R.D. Hicks (Cambridge, Mass.: Harvard University Press, 1980).

40. See Val. Max. 4.4; and Plutarch *Lives of Tiberius* and *Gaius Gracchus.*

remarkable woman Proba, the wife of Adelphus, a Christian by religion, who was so learned that they say she knew Virgil by heart and composed a clear and beautiful version of the New Testament.[41] And so, does not learning exist among women—although woman is considered the origin and source of evil?[42] Does not their learning letters warrant respect for women? Has it not made them more worthy of admiration that these women have surpassed not only other women in learning, but men as well?

Given all of this, I have decided to throw off my embarrassed timidity and send you these trifling works, since I am aware that you, for the sake of honor, will punish and destroy the envy and slander of those cowardly and malevolent men, and if there were anyone who wished to injure me, I do not doubt that you, in accord with your usual kindness and generosity toward me, will stand firm and defend me when I am not with you.

It remains to be said that by these crude works I hope to impress upon you that I am in need of your help, for at the moment I lack only money to be able, even if I am not worthy to be numbered in the circle of those women whom I have named above, at least to run in their footsteps. The lovely, the most beautiful *Decades*[43] of Livy of Padua are in my hands and offered to me for purchase. To buy it I would need to raid fifty gold florins from my money chest, which I cannot do; and so I fly to you and humbly beg for your assistance. For I know that your benevolence and love for me is so great that you will choose to humor me in this matter—you are my father, my patron, and I have put all my hope in you. And so I beg you, if it is possible, to take care to send it, since there is an amazing shortage of such books here and those that are here are much sought after, they say. If you do this, I shall be most grateful to you, both because the book is useful to me and because it will give me extraordinary delight. But since I know that you know this, I do not wish to pile on more words; rather I shall put an end to my writing and implore you to help me in this, since I believe that you will find it no burden to do so. Farewell; I commend myself to you.

41. See Boccaccio *Famous Women*, chap. 97.

42. The notion of woman as the font of all evil is a prevailing theme of Western culture. It is explicit in the Greek myth of Pandora, who opened the locked box with which she was entrusted and released all the evils that plague human kind; and it is implied in the Genesis account of the actions of Adam and Eve in Eden and consequent fall of Man (Gen 2:15–3:24); see chap. 7 below for Nogarola's understanding of this passage.

43. A section of Livy's *Ab urbe condita* (*History of Rome from the Founding of the City*).

II

GUARINO'S CIRCLE (1 4 3 6 – 3 8)

A set of thirteen letters written between 1436 and 1438 by Isotta Noga-rola, her sister, and their correspondents center on the figure of Guarino Veronese. Guarino Veronese has been encountered in chapter 1 as a compa-triot of the Nogarola family and the teacher of Martino Rizzoni, the tutor appointed by Bianca Borromeo to train her daughters in the latest humanistic studies. Guarino was in Ferrara, where he had taken up residence in 1429, having been invited to set up a school at court for the d'Este heir, Leonello, and other young aristocrats from the region.[1] In these years, Isotta's works include six letters (and Ginevra's total collection of four includes one) written to friends, relatives, and students of Guarino, as well as to the master him-self. By engaging in this correspondence with a preeminent humanist and his circle, Isotta became known to the leading humanists of northeastern Italy and also to groups beyond.

In a letter that has not survived, the Nogarola sisters apparently ap-proached the nobleman Francesco Barbaro, the uncle of the young protono-tary Ermolao Barbaro encountered in chapter 1 and one of the most impor-tant of the inner circle of Venetian rulers at this critical period of the city's expansion on the Italian mainland.[2] The elder Barbaro must have redirected the sisters to his own younger compatriot, Jacopo Foscari. At this time Fos-cari, in his early twenties, was also Barbaro's protegé in humanistic studies.[3]

---

1. For Guarino and his school, see chap. 1, n. 10. Leonello subsequently ruled Ferrara (1441–50).

2. For Francesco Barbaro (1390–1454), see King, *Venetian Humanism*, 323–25 and *ad indices* for many further references. See also DBI 6:101–3; and Barbaro letters, republished by Claudio Griggio, 2 vols. Florence: L.S. Olschki, 1991– .

3. For Jacopo Foscari, see King, *Venetian Humanism*, 372–73. Jacopo Foscari (b. 1415–d. 1457),

As son of the doge of Venice, Francesco Foscari (r. 1423–57), Jacopo Foscari had enormous potential as a patron of humanist endeavors. He included among his correspondents the noted Florentine humanists Poggio Bracciolini and Leonardo Bruni, as well as Guarino Veronese. Nogarola directed a letter (no. 5, below) to Jacopo in September 1436, praising the liberal arts and inviting Jacopo's friendship. Her sister Ginevra did so as well.[4]

Any letter Jacopo may have written to the sisters in response has not survived. He did, however, send the two Nogarola letters on to Guarino Veronese. Guarino (who had for the moment taken refuge in Valpolicella from the risk of plague in Ferrara) was impressed. Guarino's letter to Jacopo of October 7, 1436,[5] first extols Jacopo and his family; then lavishes praise on both the letters for their erudition and style—comments that would have been read as an endorsement of the young women's efforts and an encouragement of their further attempts to reach out to the literati of the day.

> What shall I say of the gift itself, concerning which when I have said a great deal, much more remains to be said. What, when you read through these pages, could be better constructed or more harmonious than their phrases, or more elegant than their purity and clarity, or more true to Latin norms than the propriety and choice of words? Richness of thought, variety of substance, knowledge of antiquity . . . [6]

Verona should be proud to have produced such daughters, Guarino continued, equal in their greatness to heroic women of antiquity such as the dutiful wife Penelope, who cleverly wove and unwove her tapestry as she waited the return of Odysseus; or the skillful spinner Arachne; or the warrior maidens Camilla and Penthesilea.

Guarino then further advertised the sisters' arrival on the threshold of

---

son of Francesco Foscari (doge, 1423–57) was convicted twice of bribery and exiled twice (1445, 1451, and possibly also in 1456). He corresponded with the most famous humanists of the period: Leonardo Bruni, Francesco Filelfo, Poggio Bracciolini, Lauro Quirini, Guarino Veronese and Ciriaco d'Ancona; he studied with Francesco Barbaro. While no works of his are known, his fame as an intellectual rests on his knowledge of Greek literature, his library of classical manuscripts, his friendships with leading humanists, and perhaps his martyrdom as an exile.

4. Abel, *Zeneverae Nogarolae Epistolae*, 2:329–34.

5. Abel, 1:55–60.

6. Abel, 1:58: "Quid de dono ipso praedicem, de quo cum plura dixero, plura dicenda restabunt? Quid, cum scripta ipsa perlegas, aut apta verborum constructiore concinnius aut ipsa puritate et lucidate elegantius aut sermonis proprietate consuetudineque Latinius? Crebrae sententiae, rerum varietas, antiquitatis notitia . . . "

fame by writing his young charge Leonello d'Este on October 11, 1436, enclosing the letters of the two Nogarolas.[7] While Ferrara was his new "nurse," he wrote, Verona and its region was his homeland; and he was proud to find that Verona had yielded these two "fruits," the two women of the Nogarola clan: "For these are the fruits of genius and of study, born of two maidens of my city, which, ripened, I have picked, and I have sent the harvest to your magnificence."[8] He prods Leonello, as he had also prodded Jacopo, with Cicero's words to the young men of Rome: "Are you young men behaving like women, and that woman like a man?"[9] The Nogarola sisters, once on stage, were an implicit threat to the young men of their social milieu.

Word came to Nogarola of Guarino's promotion of her work, and her sister's. She was encouraged to introduce herself directly to Guarino, so as to become more centrally involved in his prestigious circle. And here she met her first setback. It is described in a series of three letters (two of Isotta's and one of Guarino's) that mark a point of intensity in Isotta's work and a crisis in her development as an independent thinker. For the first time, she confronts what it may mean to be a woman attempting to join the intellectual world inhabited, with rare exceptions, only by men.

Soon after Guarino had written Leonello, Isotta wrote Guarino a very long letter (no. 6, below), praising his wisdom and eloquence and acclaiming him as the "prince of orators," while confessing that she was herself a mere novice of humanistic letters. Yet she dared to write because he had praised her and invited him, in effect, to hoist her reputation still higher by taking note of her work.

After six months, he had not responded. Early in April 1437, she wrote again (no. 7, below), a curt and reproachful letter this time, reporting the mockery to which she was subjected especially by the women of Verona because she had publicly approached so great a man for his approval, and he had publicly, or so it seemed, spurned her.

To this emotional appeal, Guarino responded immediately, on April 10, 1437.[10] He reproved her for her lack of confidence—she must have a "manly

7. Abel, 1:61–64. Leonello subsequently responded to Guarino, mentioning the sisters; and then Guarino to him. This correspondence of November 3 and December 3, 1436 is excerpted in Abel, 1:cxiii–cxiv, no. 37, and is taken from Remigio Sabbadini, *Guarino Veronese e il sul epistolario edito e inedito* (Salerno 1885) no. 135, 18; no. 403, 39.

8. Abel, 1:63: "Sunt namque ingenii fructus et studiorum, quos e duabus nostrae civitatis virginibus pullulantes collegi, collectos ad tuam magnificentiam misi."

9. Abel, 1:64: "Vos etenim iuvenes animum geritis muliebrem illaque virgo viri?" Cicero *De officiis* 1.18.61. Girolamo Guarini also quotes this phrase; see Abel, 1:96.

10. Abel, 1:83–92.

soul," he chided, and not be abject and "so like a woman." "Your own conscience and your memory of all you have done well should make you happy,
joyful, brilliant, generous, steady. You must create a man within the woman,"
he told her, so that equipped thus with a manly soul, she could withstand
whatever might happen.[11] He had been busy, that was all—domestic, professional, personal obligations had prevented him from writing earlier. He
urged her to aspire to the highest achievements in her studies and recommended to her the examples of Virgil's heroine Dido, the ruler of Carthage;
Cornelia, the Roman matron who raised the Gracchi brothers, Tiberius and
Gaius, Roman heroes and martyrs; and the Muses, who inspire the creators
of all arts, and the holy women who do so much for the Christian religion.
Such a letter, lengthy and weighty, would have affirmed Isotta's humanist
ambitions in the eyes of the citizens of the *res publica litterarum*.

Certainly it did among Guarino's associates, with whom Isotta now
freely corresponded. Guarino's own son Girolamo Guarini, who would one
day succeed him as northen Italy's master pedagogue, wrote both the sisters
on December 31, 1437.[12] He expressed his admiration for them, of whom he
had heard the report of Jacopo Foscari and his father Guarino. He compared
them to several ancient heroines and pronounced them worthy to be numbered among the most learned men.[13] Isotta responded to Girolamo Guarini
in early 1438 no. 8, below), praising him and his father, and exalting the
study of the liberal arts and the pursuit of virtue.

Around the same time, another young student of Guarino's, Ludovico
Cendrata, wrote a letter of praise to the two Nogarola sisters. He refers to the
young women's tutor Martino Rizzoni—I am aware, he wrote, "how much
learning you have both abundantly adorned yourselves under that learned
man, your teacher Martino"—and, at the end, salutes Isotta's brother Antonio and her mother, whom he must have known personally.[14] Isotta responded, once again at approximately the same point in early 1438 (no. 9

---

11. Abel, 1:85: "Ipsa te conscientia et recte factorum recordatio laetam, hilarem, renidentem,
magnanimam, constantem et in muliere virum faciat opus est, quidquid obveniat . . ."

12. Abel, 1:93–102. For Girolamo Guarini, see Anthony Grafton and Lisa Jardine, *From Humanism to the Humanities: Education and the Liberal Arts in Fifteenth- and Sixteenth-Century Europe* (Cambridge,
Mass.: Harvard University Press, 1986), 1–28 and passim.

13. Abel, 1:101: " . . . quis dignis ad sidera vos laudibus sublimes efferat aut digno quisquam
veneretur honore, cum inter tam doctos peritissimosque viros doctae numerandae videa-
mini? . . . Ita et cum singulari propter virtutes vestras ac litterarum studium palma sapientes
inter viros digne versari liceret . . . "

14. Abel, 1:109–15; at 1:110: "Quippe me minime latet, quanta doctrina praeceptore Martino
viro peritissimo vos ambas cumulatissime decoraveritis . . . " For Cendrata, see Abel, 1:xxvii
and n. 39.

below), commending his studies with Guarino and reporting that Rizzoni spoke well of the young man's talents.

Cendrata was, like Lavagnola and Bevilacqua, a member of the patriciate of the northeastern Italian towns. His father, Battista, was a public notary who held civic offices and was in correspondence with Guarino Veronese; Guarino was in turn married to a different Cendrata, Thaddea, the daughter of Niccolò. Ludovico's mother was the sister of Isotta's Veronese friend and frequent correspondent, Damiano dal Borgo (see chapter 4). These complex relationships reveal a network of kinship, as well as of literary friendship, uniting the Veronese families in whose circle Isotta worked. A student of Guarino's in Ferrara from the late 1430s, a notary like his father, Cendrata graduated to a significant public career in Verona, holding magistracies and performing diplomatic missions.

A final exchange in this flurry of letters to and from the young pupils around Guarino dates from the same early months of 1438. Tobia dal Borgo, another young scion of the Veronese patriciate—related to Damiano dal Borgo, Cendrata's uncle and Nogarola's later correspondent—wrote to the two sisters. Isotta alone replied, as she alone had replied to Girolamo Guarini and Ludovico Cendrata, during the same period.[15] Tobia writes to the two sisters very deferentially—he is apparently very young—contrasting his modest works with "your very weighty writings, which now travel the whole globe."[16] He alludes at the outset to his great reverence for the Nogarola family, as would be proper for a dal Borgo, whose family would have been more modestly ranked in the Veronese social hierarchy. In the litany of praise that constitutes the bulk of his letter, he returns to the Veronese theme, calling the sisters "the special ornament of our city" and predicting that their achievements will bring honor to Verona. In closing, he congratulates the family on the wedding then in progress, which he also will mention in the poem he encloses with his letter. The wedding to which he alludes must have been that between Ginevra and Brunorio Gambara of Brescia.

In this sequence of letters written between 1436 and 1438, Nogarola enters a humanist circle that is broader than her family and her city, although its members remain linked to those anchors. The chief achievement was to win the attention of Guarino Veronese, whose own fame and connections to a broader Italian public would boost her image among the learned. In

---

15. Tobia dal Borgo's letters in Abel, 1:121–28. For dal Borgo, see Abel, 1:xxvii and nn. 40 and 41.

16. Abel, 1:22: "Cum enim in tantas manus meas perventuras litterulas animadverterem, acutissimum vestrum de me iudicium maxime, fateor, non formidare non poteram, cum gravissima scripta vestra, quae toto iam orbe vagantur, ingenioli mei vires metirer exiguas."

approaching Guarino, she risked the shame of being rejected and for several months felt herself mocked by the Veronese community and especially the women, for whom her pretensions to status in the intellectual world might have seemed both perplexing and threatening. In the end, Guarino affirmed her bid for recognition. His encouragement was delayed long enough, however, to require Nogarola to confront explicitly the contradictions that enmeshed her as a woman who sought entry to the *res publica litterarum*.

V

Isotta Nogarola to Jacopo Foscari: Verona, September 1436

After a modest apology for having presumed to write, Nogarola praises Jacopo's commitment to books and to study, praises his father, the doge of Venice, and his mentor, the noble statesman and humanist Francesco Barbaro.

I beseech you, although hesitantly, most distinguished man, not to accuse me of arrogance if I have dared to send you such uncultivated and boorish letters since, relying on your kindness, I believe you have allowed me to do this. For this kindness of yours is so great that I do not doubt you gladly receive gifts, imitating Artaxerxes, the king of the Persians. When a very poor and humble man happened to meet the king who was enjoying a stroll on horseback, the man offered him water he had taken from the river with both his hands, for it was the custom of the Persians to greet the king with a gift.[17] The king received the gift with pleasure and smiled because he valued the spontaneity of the giver more than the price of the gift. A certain poor man brought him an apple that had grown to a very beautiful size, and on receiving it graciously he said: "By god, it seems to me that this man could make even a small city great—if it were his—by his work and his diligence."[18]

Likewise, I have been spurred on by such enthusiasm that I could not fail to congratulate you when I was told that effort, care, and every sort of diligence has brought you to this eloquence as a speaker and this fame as a man of letters, a sphere in which all your ancestors excelled. Therefore,

17. Plutarch *Artaxerxes* 5.1 contains the anecdote about the man who gave the king river water.

18. Plutarch *Artaxerxes* 4.3–4 contains the anecdote about the peasant's gift of an enormous piece of fruit—a pomegranate there—and is also the source for Nogarola's almost verbatim translation from the Greek of the king's remark about the man's ability to make a city great. Nogarola's aphorism about the king valuing the act of giving more than the gift is suggested in both the water and pomegranate stories in Plutarch.

you who were born to a lofty rank have recognized rightly that nothing is better than complementing beautiful furnishings with a harmonious and useful collection of books, which, as Cicero has put it,[19] will always be available at your command and also so that we who live now may speak to posterity. For when Cato went out to the country with his entourage to enjoy himself, he always carried books with him as if they were beloved friends, and likewise when the senate was convened he used to read books in the meeting hall.[20] And we have heard the same thing about Caesar, Alexander, and Augustus, whose custom it was to both read and write when they were encamped with their troops. Why then should we who are free from all care be able to pursue a different interest of our own? For we read that Apollonius, whether "the great," as he is commonly called, or "the philosopher," as the Pythagoreans[21] refer to him, went to Persia, crossed over into the Caucasus, Albania, Scythia, and the land of the Massegetes; he penetrated the kingdoms of richest India and after crossing an extremely wide river, the Hyphasis,[22] he arrived at the land of the Brahmans so that he could see

---

19. " . . . nil melius agere posse quam supellectilem praeclaram et iocundam familiam librorum frugi et bene morigeram, ut Cicero appellat, convenire . . . " This is an unusual formulation in humanist letters with unusual vocabulary and odd pairings of vocabulary (*supellectilem praeclaram*, "distinguished furnishings"; *familia librorum*, "family of books"). One manuscript, G, reads "liberorum," but that does not fit the context that follows. The nearest resemblance we can find to it is Cicero's strange personification of friends as the best and most beautiful *furnishings* one can "get" (*parare*) in life: "Quid autem stultius quam parare quae parantur pecunia, amicos non parare— optimam et pulcherrimam vitae, ut ita dicam, *supellectilem?*" "What could be more foolish than to pursue whatever can be pursued with cash, and yet not pursue friends (and friendships), the best and most beautiful furnishings in life" (*De amicitia* 15.55). Note also the unusual use by Nogarola of *convenire* ("to agree with", "to fit", "to come together agreeably", "to be in harmony"), which in Cicero is often used in philosophical contexts.

20. The details of Cato's obsession with reading, how he even took books with him to read during the senate's sessions in the curia, is in Val. Max. 8.7.2.

21. She refers to the fascinating figure, Apollonius of Tyana (b. ca. 30 B.C.E.), a Neo-Pythagorean philosopher, prophet, and magician who toured the Mediterranean and Middle East during the reigns of the emperors Nero, Titus and Vespasian, Domitian, and Nerva. Nogarola's source on Apollonius is the philosopher and rhetorician Philostratus's massive biography of the Pythagorean. Philostratus (b. 172 C.E. in Lemnos) is identified with the Second Sophistic and the literary salon of the empress Julia Domna and the Roman emperor Septimius Severus. Apollonius was an ascetic who gave up his inheritance, refused to wear shoes, and let his hair grow long. He traveled to Persia, Jerusalem, and Egypt, where he sought out the Gymnosophists (the naked philosophers), and to India, where he studied with the Brahmans. He was promoted by some pagans of the period as a rival of Jesus Christ.

22. Philostratus, *Life of Apollonius of Tyana*, trans. F. C. Conybeare (Cambridge, Mass.: Harvard University Press, and London: Heinemann, 1919), 2.33: "Hyphasis" is Conybeare's transliteration of the Greek name for the river near the Ganges that Apollonius crossed on his way to India. Nogarola transliterates it as "Physon."

Iarchas[23] sitting on his golden throne, drinking from the fountain of Tantalus, and hear him discoursing among a few of his disciples on nature, ethics, and the revolutions of the stars. Next he went to the lands of the Elamites, the Babylonians, the Chaldeans, the Medes, the Assyrians, the Parthians, the Phoenicians, the Arabians, the Palestinians, and turning back toward Alexandria he reached Ethiopia in his journey to see the Gymnosophists and the famous table of the Sun in the sand.[24] Apollonius discovered that he learned something everywhere and that in his perpetual travels he was always becoming a better man. For we are all drawn, as Cicero reminds us, to desire knowledge,[25] and we think it a beautiful thing to excel in this pursuit. But to slip, to err, to be ignorant and misled, we see as a shameful evil. Socrates scanned the last frontiers in his quest for wisdom. Anaxagoras too embarked on a long journey for the purpose of study, and when he discovered after many years that he had lost all his own possessions, he said, "I would not have found myself had I not lost everything."[26]

However, it has been given to you, so it appears, to surpass your own lineage in every kind of virtue and in every species of excellence. Indeed, what should I say about the illustrious doge, your father, whose fame is known in the heavens? Under his leadership, the reputation of this fortunate city and the name of your glorious family increases every day. I shall say nothing about the justice, extraordinary life, and the integrity of character of this man whom everyone refers to as a virtual Cato, so that a poem about his life could deservedly be called "A Third Cato Has Come Down to Us from Heaven." O most fortunate Venetian Senate! Since your leader happens to be so celebrated and excellent a Doge, whom all think worthy to be loved and worshiped like a god on earth. His famous name, his celebrated kindness, and his shining piety toward everyone are hymned all over the world.

But you also have other examples of illustrious men in Venice who should serve to spur you on in your pursuit of virtue and honor. But let me

---

23. Iarchas was a famous Indian philosopher whose celebrated springs supposedly had the power to restore old men to youth. Apollonius's visit to Iarchas is described in Philostratus *Life of Apollonius* 3.16.

24. Philostratus *Apollonius* 2.24 and 2.43 describes the altars of Sol (the Sun) in the sand.

25. "Omnes enim trahimur ad cognitionis et scientiae cupiditatem." Nogarola quotes almost verbatim from Cicero *De officiis* 1.6.18: "Omnes enim trahimur et ducimur ad cognitionis et scientiae cupiditatem."

26. Philostratus *Apollonius* 1.2 compares Socrates and Anaxagoras to Apollonius in this passage. Nogarola's reference is to Anaxagoras's journey to Egypt in search of knowledge and Socrates' metaphysical travels (she writes, "Socrates ultimas regiones acquirendae sapientiae causa perlustravit"), since he, unlike most philosophers, writes Diogenes Laertius in his *Life of Socrates*, had no need to travel.

pass over the rest of them. Suffice it to mention the most eloquent Francesco Barbaro, the elegance of whose speech is so great that everyone in Venice boldly declares this one man the most outstanding. For I have been told that you became a devotee of literary studies under the aegis and guidance of Francesco Barbaro and that the thing that was truly the most pleasing to you was that you had such a brilliant mentor for your studies. You will achieve the highest praise if you choose to imitate the virtue of the most just and good men, since as Cicero says, "There is nothing, believe me, more beautiful than virtue and nothing more worthy of our esteem."[27] Therefore, embrace this virtue with your whole heart—although it is certainly not necessary for me to urge you on. If you do follow my advice, however, as the beginnings of your noble youth seem to promise,

> As long as rivers flow through the narrows, as long as shadows traverse the mountains, as long as the earth's pole nourishes the vault of the heavens, your honor, your name, and your praises will always remain.[28]

Vale. From Verona.

VI

Isotta Nogarola to Guarino Veronese: Verona, shortly after October 11, 1436

Verona is fortunate to have had Guarino as its son, and yet its citizens have insufficiently honored him, Nogarola writes. He will now bring fame to Ferrara. She rejoices that he has amplified her own position by his greatness, likening her (and her sister) to the great women of antiquity, and invites him to dignify her work by correcting it.[29]

I have been reluctant, illustrious Guarino, to write you, since I did not think it fitting that I, a beginner in the world of letters, should send my work to you, the prince of orators. Now the occasion has arisen

---

27. Cicero *Epistulae ad familiares* 9.14.4: "Nihil est enim, mihi crede, virtute formosius, nihil pulchrius, nihil amabilius." Again Nogarola quotes nearly verbatim: "Nihil est enim, mihi crede, virtute formosius nihil amabilius."

28. Virgil *Aen.* 1.607–609:
   In freta dum fluvii current, dum montibus umbrae
   lustrabant convexa, polus dum sidera pascet,
   semper honos nomenque tuum laudesque manebunt.

29. This letter reads as though it might have originally been a public encomium for Guarino commemorating his departure from his native city to Ferrara. Perhaps Nogarola wrote or even delivered such an encomium but subsequently revised it and sent it to Guarino as a letter.

where your authority may prevail over my timidity since, moved by your praise of me, which I understand to be the reward of my virtue (if I have any), I could not fail to thank you enormously—although however grateful I may be, my gratitude still will not equal the abundance of your benevolence toward me. For you have judged me worthy of such honor and, with your singular humanity, you have heaped upon me such praise, that I do not know how I might calculate the value of a repayment to you for the honor you have given me. Many thanks are owed also to the lord Jesus, since I see clearly that it was his Eternal Light that brought you to the study of letters—and me to the pursuit of virtue—in whom we shall rejoice, and this city, as long as it endures, shall delight.

This situation also prompts me to lament your absence from this place—if such a thing does not seem improper on my part. Father, O eternal power of men and gods! For truly is there anyone or anything we can call on now? What kind of god, O citizens, what madness bestirs you that you do not revere this man, seemingly sent to us as a divine gift from the high heavens, and that you do not, as you should, show him the utmost respect? For we have read, to quote you, that many men traveled to Olympus from distant places by land and sea in order to feast their eyes, ears, and souls on Plato, forgetful of every pleasureable indulgence to attend Plato, to admire Plato, and so to linger with Plato in a most pleasant resting place.[30]

What could be more absurd do you think, citizens of Verona, than not seeking out so great and distinguished a man, who was born here in our republic and who is overflowing with virtue? O immortal gods! Do you not understand how much virtue should be esteemed, which, to use Cicero's words, can neither be taken away nor stolen, which neither shipwreck nor fire destroy, which the disruptions of neither storms nor circumstances alter.[31] Only those endowed with virtue are truly rich, for they alone possess fruitful and eternal goods, and they alone are content with what they have, which is the true meaning of wealth. They are satisfied with what they have, they desire nothing, they need nothing, they yearn for nothing, they require nothing. And it has been said by the wisest men, gold and silver have no power greater than that of virtue. All things are good when accompanied by virtue.[32]

30. Diogenes Laertius *Lives of the Philosophers* 3.46; perhaps taken by Nogarola from Guarino's *Life of Plato*: see Sabbadini, ed., *Epistolario di Guarino Veronese*, 3:340.

31. Cicero *Paradoxa* 6.51: " . . . quanti virtus aestimanda est, quae nec eripi nec surripi potest umquam, nec naufragio nec incendio amittitur, nec vi tempestatum nec temporum perturbatione mutatur. Qua qui praediti sunt soli sunt divites; soli enim possident res fructuosas et sempiternas solique, quod proprium est divitiarum, rebus suis contenti sunt. Satis esse putant quod est, nihil appetunt, nulla re egent, nihil sibi deesse sentiunt, nihil requirunt."

32. Plautus *Amphitruo* 2, 2, 21.

Shall we not exalt the illustrious Prince Leonello[33] to the stars who, in advance of his years, bears the soul and character of a man who has so clearly understood this; for he felt it not beneath his dignity to have a Nestor to counsel him, just as it had been honorable to Agamemnon himself, the king of kings, to have such a counselor. For he prudently accomplished many things, and they say none were done more magnificently or more excellently or more salutarily for his republic, since he put in practice Plato's sound maxim: most blessed are those republics if their rulers are either wise or seekers of wisdom.[34] And so, Leonello should be praised by all, since he has embraced Guarino most amiably with such zeal and fervor, and since he has behaved toward Guarino as Pompey treated Cato. For ignorant of who he was, those men who neglected Cato on the road soon afterward admired him, for they were converted to admiration by Pompey himself. For when Cato arrived in Ephesus he went to salute Pompey, since he was the greater in age and authority, yet Pompey, when he saw Cato, would not suffer that nor wait for Cato to find him seated, but rising quickly as if to honor someone greater than he, he strode forward and seized his right hand amid the circle of onlookers, and long after Cato's departure so spoke in praise of Cato's virtues that all those who heard learned to regard Cato highly.[35] And Leonello has also followed Caesar's example, who won glory for his knowledge and shone in Greek and Latin eloquence:[36] and he has also concurred with the maxim of Posidonius, that one day among the learned was to be valued more than an eon with the ignorant;[37] and the renowned prince Leonello has recognized what Sallust taught, that greatness of mind is worth more than strength of body.[38] And since our enjoyment of life is brief, it is right that we extend our memory as long as we can.

Permit me, glorious Guarino, to speak further in praise of you; and do not persuade yourself that I am a flatterer, although you do rightly believe that those who do not sing your praises should be judged envious rather

33. Leonello d'Este, son of Niccolò III d'Este, duke of Ferrara, Guarino's patron; see n. 1.

34. Cicero Epistulae ad Quintum Fratrem 1.1.29: "atque ille quidem princeps ingenii et doctrinae Plato tum denique fore beatas res publicas putavit, si aut docti et sapientes homines eas regere coepissent aut ii qui regerent omne suum studium in doctrina et sapientia conlocassent hanc coniunctionem videlicet potestatis et sapientiae saluti censuit civitatibus esse posse."

35. Plutarch Cato the Younger.

36. Gaius Julius Caesar, Roman general, consul (59 B.C.E., and dictator (49–44 B.C.E.), perhaps known to Nogarola in the Life of Caesar by Plutarch.

37. See Cicero Tusculan Disputations 2.61, for the story of Pompey's pilgrimage to see the Stoic philosopher Posidonius (135–50 B.C.E.).

38. Paraphrasing Sallust De coniuratione Catilinae 1.2, 1.5.

than that those who do should be thought flatterers. For who in Italy is more famous than you? Who more eloquent? Your life, fortune, and glory are such that nothing could surpass them. How much utility and honor, Guarino my father, shall I accrue from you, the wellspring of virtue and probity, when I see myself and my name approved by you, so honored a man! "I am happy" (as Cicero reported that Hector said, as he believed he had read in Naevius), "that I am praised by you, father, who has received praise."[39] It is indeed pleasing praise that is offered by those who themselves have lived in honor. I indeed by your testimony, or rather that of your letter, have now achieved immortality and need no longer be anxious about the public's opinion and estimation of me. So Cicero, since he had been praised by Cato, easily bore the criticism of others.[40] So Socrates, defended by Plato, was able to disdain the opinion of others.[41]

For nothing could be more laudable than your eulogy of me (would that I were worthy of your praise). You have so raised me up by your abundant dignity and authority that I seem to shine splendidly in your shade. For you are one who never ceases in your clemency and humanity to adorn those whom you embrace. How much you should be treasured! Is not Italy flourishing as though the foster child of your teaching? Have you not brought to us the art of speaking of Greece and its literature? For with regard to the Greeks, that excellent and memorable judgment of Apollonius concerning Cicero also applies to you.[42] For when Cicero came to Rhodes, he declaimed in Greek at Apollonius's request since he knew no Latin. And when Cicero's speech was over, while the others who there stood about stupefied by such eloquence were praising him, Apollonius himself neither gave a sign of his approval nor praised the declamation in any way, but stood a long time silently apart. When after a time, as was right, all looked at Apollonius and awaited his judgment, at last he broke the silence and spoke: "I praise and admire you, Cicero. It was a certain sadness and wretchedness that caused me to stand silent so long when I heard your declamation. For I reviewed in my mind how in former times the Greeks exceeded all other nations in arms and in the governance of republics and domestic institutions. In these spheres, the Romans clearly now surpass us, and all agree that with a true

---

39. Cicero *Epistulae ad familiares*, 15.6.1: "'laetus sum laudari me,' inquit Hector, opinor, apud Naevium 'abs te, pater, a laudato viro"; also *Tusculan Disputations* 4.67.

40. Plutarch *Cicero* 23.

41. Cicero *De oratore* 3.129.

42. Plutarch *Cicero* 4:4–5. The anecdote here refers to Apollonius the Rhodian orator, not Apollonius the Pythagorean.

and incredible virtue they have taken the palm of victory. One last and sole glory—that of learning and eloquence—remains, which I now see also has been taken from us by you and is transferred to the Romans, so that nothing of excellent worth is left to us."

So much benefit have you, Guarino, brought us that we are not only not ignorant of Greek letters, but we are even judged learned and expert. Do not all excellent and leading citizens show themselves obedient to your counsels and precepts? Do not all men call Ferrara most fortunate, and extol her with praises to heaven for her merit, since she did not hesitate to take Guarino Veronese into her bosom? If we consider Ferrara, will we not judge it to be like Plato's Academy? All men cherish you, all venerate you, on you alone they fix their eyes. Why do I delay? You alone are he on whose virtue Italy depends, and you the hero who towers above all learned men; nor will Italy vaunt itself so great in eloquence because of any other of its children.

The weakness of my mind and my sex limit my ability to express what I have to say; and I do not myself seek, most learned man, nor do I wish to be believed to be one of those most famous women whom antiquity so extols, such as were Cornificia, Nicaula from Ethiopia, Faunia the sister of Faunus, Cornelia, Portia, and others.[43] I shall collect myself and impose a limit to my words, once I have begged you to view these trifling works of mine not with a critical eye, but by your humanity to emend and correct them, and to not condemn me if I have overstepped the bounds of silence especially imposed on women and appear ignorant of Vergerio's precept that the young should say little, since in much speech there is always something to blame.[44] And Sophocles also called silence women's special adornment.[45] But impelled by your praise of me, which I have set to myself as a spur to virtue, I could neither stay silent nor fail to send you this letter. Receive it in a

---

43. Boccaccio *Famous Women* chap. 86 for Cornificia; 43 for Nicaula; 82 for Portia. For Cornelia, see Plutarch *Tiberius Gracchus* 1; *Gaius Gracchus* 4. Faunia, or Fauna, also known as *Bona Dea*, was the prophesying sister of the god Faunus; see Macrobius *Saturnalia* 1, 12; Lactantius 1, 22, 9.

44. Pier Paolo Vergerio, *De ingenuis moribus*: "Nothing so injures a young man in the eyes of serious people as exaggeration and untruthfulness. Indeed, a master will be well advised to inculcate generally a habit of speaking little, and seldom, and of answering questions rather than asking them. For a youth who is silent commits at most but one fault, that he is silent; one who is talkative probably commits fifty." There is a more recent translation: *Humanist Educational Treatises*, ed. and trans. Craig W. Kallendorf, The I Tatti Renaissance Library (Cambridge, Mass.: Harvard University Press, 2002), 17. We have cited, however, the freer and more elegant rendering of the nineteenth-century translation: *Vittorino da Feltre and Other Humanist Educators*, trans. William Harrison Woodward, with a foreword by Eugene F. Rice (New York: Teachers College, 1963), 99.

45. Sophocles *Ajax* 293: "Silence is an ornament for women."

kindly spirit, therefore (as you are accustomed to do always), and if it seems
to you not to thank you sufficiently, and if there is anything further that
should be said or told, ascribe the failure not to my will but to the slightness
of my intellect. For I give and commit myself to your most ample worthiness,
wisdom, and authority, and so much reverence have I devoted to you, father,
that I esteem you in the place of my own father, and now, venerable father, I
receive you with a whole heart, and whatever there is in me that is honorable
or praiseworthy, I declare it has come from you. Farewell.

VII

Isotta Nogarola to Guarino Veronese: Verona, April 10, 1437

*Deflated and anxious because she had not received a response to her glowing letter to Guarino
of October 1436, Nogarola writes Guarino reproachfully, bewailing her condition as a
woman, which has left her vulnerable to criticism, especially that of the other women of
Verona, because she had dared to approach so great a man.*

Since I often ponder what the worth of women is, it occurs to me to
bemoan my fate since I was born female and women are ridiculed by
men in both word and deed. I raise this issue privately so I will not have to
ask in public how it happens that you consider me a joke. For I am distressed
as never before that you have been unfair to me in what you have written.
Really, I had forebodings that I was writing you to no avail when I did write.
But your kindness enticed me to do so, since I thought of Cicero's words
when he warned that however superior to others we are, that is the extent
to which we are obligated to behave more humbly toward them.[46] But by
Hercules, I see that you are unmoved and disagree with his teaching. I was
glad when I sent you that letter. Indeed, I thought it followed directly from
your praise of me, since there was nothing in your report that I felt misun-
derstood me. Now, however, sorrow eclipses all my joy, since I know that
things have turned out differently. I made use of your friendship, although it
was useless and you had no more regard for me than if I had never been born.

46. Cicero *De officiis* 1.90: "qui monent, ut quanto superiores simus, tanto nos geramus summis-
sius." Cicero offers this precept commenting on Philip of Macedonia's humility and gentility in
comparison with his son Alexander's arrogance. Nogarola quotes here: "qui monet, ut quanto
nos superiores sumus, tanto nos geramus submissius," with only verb changes and the repetition
of the subject pronoun.

For I am ridiculed throughout the city; the women mock me.[47] There is no safe shelter[48] for me in this city. The asses tear me apart with their teeth, the bulls charge me with their horns. Even if I have deserved your contempt, it was shameful of you to do this. Why do you dismiss me in this way, father Guarino? Ah, how unhappy I am! While once my thoughts wavered between hope and fear, now I have lost all hope, and my fear has turned to despair. And so, if you judge me worthy of your kindness, I beg you to help me in this distress of mine and also—if I can speak more frankly—in the matter of my reputation; and I ask you not to allow yourself to dishonor me by your actions. But you would help me, since I am lacking in literary skill, if you lend your great dignity to my style and if you put a stop to those cruel tongues

47. Nogarola says: "meus me ordo deridet" ("my *order* mocks me"). We have translated this to read, "the women mock me." There is sound evidence for doing so. Throughout the Renaissance, a woman's *ordo*, or rank, reflected her position with regard to men: she was a virgin, a matron, a widow (or old woman)—or a whore, if she were mature and presumed sexually active and without a male householder to protect her. Women did not consciously refer to the social rank they held, for they held none; their rank was determined by the male figure (father, husband, brother, sometimes but rarely uncle or brother-in-law) in whose household they lived. The suggestion could be made that Nogarola conceives her "order" as being that of the "republic of the learned," the *res publica litterarum*, or *litteratorum*, in which she so much desired to participate. Renaissance society did not provide language as yet for such a concept, however. Given these points, the following also tip the balance toward our interpretation of *ordo* here as the "community of women": (1) Nogarola opens this letter with a statement about the condition of being female; this is her theme. (2) Nogarola also complains of the *scelestas linguas* ("wicked tongues") that mock her. Those tongues are in the feminine gender, and gossip, the work of "wicked tongues," was conventionally in this era seen as characteristic of matrons (and, when the wickedness gets too much to bear, of witches, the most negative version of a mature woman in the public mind). Guarino in his response to Nogarola (*Epistolario di Guarino Veronese*, ed. Sabbadini, B.307) similarly refers to the scyllaeos latratus ("Scyllan barks"), an echo of the *scelestas linguas*. This phrase again suggests that the nasty gossipers are women, since the "barks" must be those of the hounds belonging to Scylla, a woman whom the jealous Circe, also female, had turned into a sea monster. (3) Sabbadini, one of the leading nineteenth-century scholars of humanism as well as Guarino's biographer and editor of his letters, identifies Nogarola's accusers as the women of Verona; *Vita di Guarino Veronese* (in *Guariniana*), no. 282. (4) In 1436, Giorgio Bevilacqua had warned Nogarola that she might be the target of the mockery of other women, spiteful of her attainments; Abel, 1:15.1–9. (5) Later in the century, another woman humanist, Laura Cereta, also had difficulties with envious and spiteful females ("the gabbing and babbling women who . . . harm with their petulant talk not only their sex but themselves") in the not dissimilar social world of Brescia; Cereta, *Collected Letters*, no. 19 (81–82). It is "a counterattack on women who abuse other women, explaining that they are envious of women who are achievers because they are frustrated, because their lives are empty, and because they lack the self-confidence they would need to work at becoming educated themselves" (81).

48. In our translation of *stabile stabulum* (stable or shelter) to suggest barnyard images, we are reading this passage as a clear reference to Plautus's *Aulularia* 232–35, which Nogarola almost exactly quotes: "meus me ordo deridet, neutrobi habeo stabile stabulum, asini me mordicus scindunt, boves me incursant cornibus."

that call me a tower of audacity and say that I should be sent to the ends of the earth for my boldness.[49] Nor do I know what I have done to be the cause of such words, but I do confess that I have done wrong and deserve blame for it. I come to you to ask this: that you attend to what troubles my spirit and accomplish what I ask, and that I may undo the wrong that you have done.[50] Vale.

VIII

Isotta Nogarola to Girolamo Guarini: Verona, beginning of 1438

After her despair of April 1437, Nogarola was boosted by Guarino's encouraging response, and even more when Guarino forwarded the letters of the Nogarola girls to his circle of students in Ferrara, which included the d'Este heir Leonello and many other young aristocrats, as well as Guarino's own son and successor Girolamo. Here Nogarola responds to the latter's letter praising the two sisters, thanking him for the honor that he bestowed.

*Y*ou said many things in your letter both wise and excellent, which can easily lead the soul of any reader to love and cherish your virtue, and with elegance and dignity you affirm your points with many examples of our ancestors. And you do rightly; for what is more pleasant than virtue itself? Seneca used to say that leisure without letters was death and a living man's tomb.[51] Cato never willingly put down his book.[52] What could our ancestors have found more excellent than letters? For we have read of the great honor in which learning itself was enshrined. And do we

---

49. "quando . . . addideris atque *istas* scelestas linguas comprimes": a pair of future tense verbs (the first future), which should both be translated as presents in this conditional clause. "Istas" (those; those belonging to you), which is the strongest and most venomous demonstrative there is in Latin, conjures up an angry finger being pointed at the addressee or addressees, in this case not only the bulls and asses she mentions above but also Guarino himself who on some level (from what she says in this letter) has been a participant in the slander circulating about her.

50. Notice the bumpy cadence here: a triplet of subordinate present subjunctives. But the first two are second person verbs "ut facias et efficias," which each depend on the supine in -*um* "oratum" (to ask): "Id advenio ad te oratum ut facias et efficias; literally, "I come to you *to ask* this: to do . . . and to accomplish"), each having its own relative clause. This doublet is followed by an abrupt switch into the first person "auferam" and a purpose construction that depends on "advenio": "and I come so that I may undo . . . ." A bumpy end to an angry and disturbing letter.

51. Seneca *Epist.* 82.3.

52. For the love of reading of Marcus Porcius Cato the Younger, see Val. Max. 8.7.2; and Plutarch *Cato the Younger* 19, 20, 68.

not see that those men in whom there was a capacity for learning prospered as though divine? When Plato returned from Sicily as though to a feast of the Olympian gods, there came to greet him a huge assembly from all over the globe, the rejoicing crowds honoring him as though he were a god sent to earth from heaven.[53] Socrates died of the poison given to him in the public prison. Not many days after that monstrous deed the unstable mob changed its mind and, too late repenting of its prior judgment, lamenting the killing of Socrates who had been worthy of reverence for his sanctity and every kind of virtue. All mourned openly, the workshops closed, the gymnasia were deserted, the theaters emptied. Justice at last was done in the city. Plans to punish Socrates' accusers were made, and while the others fled into exile and seized safety in flight, Meletus was sentenced to death and Anitus, upon arriving in Heraclea, was ignominiously ejected by the citizens and his goods confiscated for the public treasury. A bronze statue, the work of Lysippus, was erected to Socrates.[54]

Good gods, how happy I am when I hear of the many things you have done, with what toil, anxiety, and zeal you strive for virtue, since virtue itself reaches not for the enticements or lascivious pleasures of the body; but it is rather by the sweat of exertion, as Hesiod says, that the gods recognize human virtue: "the road to evil is smooth . . . but on the road to virtue the gods placed sweat."[55] And Aristotle, the prince of philosophy, reasoned that virtue involved the performance of difficult and arduous things.[56] In this matter truly your father is an excellent witness, who rightly has traced the footsteps of our ancestors and who, along those long roads, across such diverse regions, through various circumstances, through so many dangers, has pursued eloquence. Here is someone, studious youth, whom you may imitate. For if Publius Scipio and Quintus Fabius said that they were greatly inspired by considering the images of illustrious men,[57] what should happen to you, whenever you look upon that living face and example? I do not doubt, therefore, that you will undertake excellent studies. Great God, what a great poverty we have of such adolescents! For there is in you a truly mature ability, by which now you begin to undertake some excellent and unusual pursuit; for I anticipate that you will soon win glory for yourself, honor for

---

53. Diogenes Laertius *Lives of the Philosophers* 3.46.

54. For the Athenians' remorse after the death of Socrates, see Diogenes Laertius *Lives of the Philosophers*, *Socrates* 43.

55. Based on Hesiod *Works and Days* 287f.

56. Aristotle *Nicomachean Ethics* 2.3.

57. We have not identified the source of this statement.

your father, and benefit for your city; for you have shown yourself to be a son worthy of such a parent. So the fathers and sons Thelamon and Ajax, Peleus and Achilles, Aeneas and Ascanius, Caesar and Octavian[58] undertook a rivalry among themselves for excellence.

And so, having received your gift may I not glory a little? For your words were gifts to me so pleasing that I cannot express myself in words. For there is in them the fruit of your genius and studies, the love of letters, a sweetness of expression, a clarity of speech, and what I especially value, a variety of matter, a knowledge of antiquity, an abundance of examples. Hence it can be said of you what Homer said of Nestor: that from his mouth flowed speech sweeter than honey.[59] My ignorance will not permit me to say more, for in me there is no divine genius, no great prudence won by experience; and lest I bore you with my trifles I shall now make an end to my writing. Farewell, for my soul gives and owes you as much gratitude as it is capable of doing. Again, farewell. From Verona.

IX

Isotta Nogarola to Ludovico Cendrata: Verona, beginning of 1438

Guarino Veronese's student Ludovico Cendrata, a scion of the Veronese patriciate, has followed Guarino's son Girolamo's lead in writing a letter praising the achievements of the Nogarola sisters. Isotta responds, encouraging Cendrata in his studies and sending regards from her own tutor Martino Rizzoni and greetings to Guarino and Girolamo.

I received your letter sparkling with the light of virtue and greatly appreciated it, since I saw in it a fraternal spirit full of love and humanity, and saw also how you are flourishing in the studies of the best arts and disciplines. Certainly, the learned men who have read it have so assessed and judged it, since nothing in it could have been said more elegantly or richly, so adorned, distinguished, refined it is; wherefore you may claim for yourself no slight reputation. For I hear that you have by now sent abroad many letters, which you send both to your excellent parent and to others,

---

58. Ajax, the son of Telamon, is one of the Greek heroes in the Trojan War as described by Homer in the *Iliad*; the principal hero in the same epic work is Achilles, son of Peleus. Ascanius, the son of Aeneas, legendarily established the city of Alba Longa, where Romulus and Remus were born; Ascanius's birth is noted in Livy 1.1; his founding of Alba Longa, in 1.3. Octavian, who became the emperor Augustus, was the great-nephew and adoptive son of Julius Caesar.

59. Homer *Iliad* 1.249.

who see that they were excellent prophets concerning you, since you are revealing yourself to be that man whom your great potential always promised you would become. Proceed, therefore, and may you so increase your virtue that what was hoped and expected of you may be admired, although the admiration you have already won seems great to me. For our most learned tutor Martin[60] speaks approvingly and admiringly about you, and many other most learned men greatly admire your sharpness of mind that now offers so many splendid flowers of virtue and knowledge. If there is any greater or better sign of your excellence, I do not know what it would be.

Accordingly, you should give the greatest thanks to your father who, just as king Philip of Macedon wished Alexander to learn his first letters under Aristotle,[61] assigned you to be instructed under that most excellent man Guarino. For so much do the wisest men commend Guarino that I am not sure whether Aristides was that highly commended by Plato, who spoke of Aristides as the only man among all the sages who flourished at Athens who was worthy of esteem, praise, and admiration.[62] In Guarino there is a certain high understanding of Greek and Latin letters, so that he is in fact a kind of lamp or star of Italy. You are truly fortunate, therefore, to be given the opportunity to pursue good and sound studies with him. How can my meager talent attempt to speak about his achievements, when it could achieve not even the least part of them? But you are he who is worthy of that task of honoring Guarino.

Your praise of me I consider to be a spur to the study of virtue and honor; for this I thank you greatly, and my love for you grows hourly, "just as the green alder shoots up in early spring."[63] Farewell, and if I have responded tardily, do not wonder, since we cannot ourselves do all things.[64] I pray that you will commend me to the most learned Guarino Veronese; and salute with special warmth that delightful and outstanding youth Girolamo Guarino, and thank him amply for me for his great and beautiful gift to us, since he clearly now can play the pipes that the Muses gave to the old bard of Ascra: "wherewith as he sang, he would draw the unyielding ash trees down the

---

60. Martino Rizzoni, Guarino's student, tutor to the Nogarola sisters; see Avesani, *Verona nel Quattrocento*, part 2: 51–59.

61. Plutarch *Alexander* 7.1–5; 8.1–4.

62. Plutarch *Aristides* 6. Aristides, son of Lysimachus, was a revered Athenian leader of the generation after the defeat of the Persians at the battle of Marathon.

63. Virgil *Eclogues* 10:73–74: "Gallo, cuius amor tantum mihi crescit in horas, / quantum vere novo viridis se subicit alnus."

64. Cicero *Pro Sex. Roscio* 111: "non enim possumus omnia per nos agere."

mountainsides."[65] And such then, Ludovico, is his gift to us: "like sleep on the grass to the weary, as in summer heat the slaking of thirst in a dancing rill of sweet water. Not with the pipe alone, but in voice do you match your master."[66] Farewell.

X

Isotta Nogarola to Tobia dal Borgo: Verona, January or February 1438

Yet another Veronese aristocrat under Guarino's tutelage, Tobia del Borgo, had written the two sisters, enclosing poems with his letters that Nogarola here commends, extending her comment at some length to include the praise not only of poetry but of eloquence—describing a number of famous orators in a virtuoso show of her knowledge.

I am afraid you may think I am not responding as a friend should because of my slowness to write. If by any chance you had any such suspicion, please erase it from your mind, since I did this neither because I forgot you (since I especially keep you in my thoughts) nor because I deeply distrusted myself. Moved by the expression of your affection for me, I have decided, to the best of my womanly ability,[67] to accept my duty to respond. I know this work will not pose a heavy burden for me, however things turn out, although I do know that the Pythagorean philosopher instituted a rule applicable to me when he commanded his disciples at the beginning of their studies to remain silent for no less than two years[68] lest, shamefully, they should seem to commit errors, make mistakes, pursue fallacies, or stubbornly defend

65. Virgil *Eclogues* 6.69–71 (English trans. H. Rushton Fairclough [Loeb Library: Harvard University Press, 1999]): Gallo, cuius amor tantum mihi crescit in horas, / quantum vere novo viridis se subicit alnus."

66. Virgil *Eclogues* 5:46–48: "Tale tuum carmen nobis, divine poeta, / quale sopor fessis in gramine, quale per aestum / dulcis aquae saliente sitim restinguere rivo: / nec calamis solum aequiparas, sed voce magistrum . . ."

67. "Pro muliebri mea": a play on *pro virili mea parte*, "to the best of my ability."

68. Pythagoras's rule that his students had to keep silence for their first five years of study with him is in Diogenes Laertius *Lives of the Philosophers* 8.10, and Philosotratus *Life of Apollonius* 1.14 tells of Apollonius's own rule of silence for a period of five years at the beginning of his studies. Here Nogarola wavers when it comes to the question of her sex, between assertions of her difference and denial of that difference. In the previous sentence she slipped in a dig (*pro muliebri mea*), noting that after all this is only a woman talking. Now she suggests that it is not because she is a girl that she is expected to be silent, but rather because she is a novice at the study of rhetoric just like any one of Pythagoras's boys. So, she wavers constantly between identification with males and feelings of utter alienation from them and their world.

precepts they understood too little. Isocrates too put his students under oath before he would teach them, extracting from them an oath of silence.[69]

I, however, lured by the sweetness and loveliness of your poems, am unable to be silent, although this goes against feminine decorum. And so it is that I am never more struck with admiration than when I consider that poems themselves were often capable of rousing Alexander the Great to such a pitch of anger that he took up arms and went to war and that, likewise, poetry could lull him into a state of tranquility and calm.[70] For I think what Cicero wrote is completely true: he says he heard it said by the greatest and most erudite men that pursuits in all other spheres depend on training, rules, and skill, but that the poet is able to be inspired by nature itself, the laws of his own mind, and a certain divine spirit. Accordingly, our Ennius called the poets holy men in their own right, because the bards who have been sent into our midst seem almost to be gifts from the gods.[71] Let the myths and the poets tell us, then, that there is a certain fountain where old men who immerse themselves regain their youth, and let it be the concern of others to investigate where in the world it might be found. But you have now poured forth in your poems to me streams from this finest of fountains so that, utterly oblivious of myself, I have dreamed that the things you imagined about me were in some way true.[72]

You do rightly then in striving to grace wisdom and the science of the

---

69. We have been unable to identify a source; possibly an invention of Nogarola's.

70. Alexander's love of reading and especially of poetry is chronicled in Plutarch *Alexander* 8.1–4, according to whom he always had a copy of Homer's *Iliad* under his pillow in his tent when he went to war.

71. The whole passage, including Cicero's notion of the opposition between reason and nature as the wellspring of poetry, the inspiration of poets coming directly from nature itself, poetry as divinely inspired, and the quote from Ennius (Roman poet b. B.C.E. 239–169)—all of the above—come almost verbatim from Cicero *Pro Archia* 8.18: "Atqui sic *a summis hominibus erudi-tissimisque accepimus, ceterarum rerum studi et doctrina et praeceptis et arte constare, poetam natura ipsa valere et mentis viribus excitari et quasi divino quodam spiritu inflari. Qua re suo iure noster ille Ennius sanctos appellat poetas, quod quasi deorum aliquo dono atque munere commendati nobis esse videantur.*" Cf. Nogarola (p.131): "*Nam quod a Cicerone dictum est, . . . qui a summis viris eruditissimisque accepisse se dicit ceterarum rerum studia et doctrina et praeceptis et arte constare, poetam natura ispa valere et mentis iure excitari et quasi divino quodam spiritu inflari. Quare iure suo noster ille Ennius poetas sanctos appellat, quod quasi deorum aliquo dono ac munere commendati nobis esse videantur.*" The italicized section is quoted verbatim by Nogarola.

72. " . . . *mihi* vero tu nunc carminibus tuis optatissimi huius fontis latices superfudisti, ut *mei* penitus oblita, quae de *me* finxisti, vera esse *mihi* quodam modo somniaverim." Our italics. Other than Nogarola's disregard for the usual sequence of tense in classical Latin (we would have expected the imperfect subjunctive in the *ut* clause instead of the perfect subjunctive), the passage is striking because of her repetition of the first person pronoun so many times in such a short sentence. Her emphasis on the importance of how she is viewed and portrayed by other people is also a typical theme in humanist letterbooks.

law with the sweetness of speech and with eloquence—the founder, perfecter, and matrix for all the virtues. And, as Cicero is our witness, eloquence has always been held in the highest esteem among every free people and in every republic that is founded on good customs. Come then, the histories bear witness to how much honor and utility your energetic work in defending the accused and pleading cases will confer on you. History tells us that Caesar was roused to imprison Quintus Ligarius as a condemned man, and when Cicero came to defend him he said to his friends, "The defendant is most certain to be condemned, but nothing prohibits us from hearing Cicero." When Cicero spoke, his very temperate and highly skillful oration affected Caesar's mind and spirit in such a variety of ways that it caused his face and color to change frequently and caused him almost to take leave of his senses to such a degree that his entire body appeared shaken and he dropped the books he held in his hands.[73] What is more, when men were sent by Marius and Cinna, the harshest of generals, to kill Marcus Antonius, they were so spellbound by his oratory that they returned their swords, which they had already drawn and were waving around, to their scabbards untouched by blood.[74] They say that Pisistratus had such power when he spoke that the Athenians, swept away by his oratory, made him their king, although from the opposing faction, Solon in particular, who was especially beloved in Athens, strove against him.[75] Solon's speeches were more healthy for the city, but the other man's were more eloquent, with the result that this city, so sagacious in every other respect, chose slavery over liberty. Therefore, Euripides used to say rightly, "Oratory can accomplish everything that a hostile sword cannot accomplish."[76] For eloquence is the companion of

73. The anecdote about how Cicero's moving defense of Ligarius and Caesar's response is Nogarola's nearly verbatim translation down to her quoting of Caesar and all the graphic details from Plutarch *Cicero* 39.5–6.

74. The story of Marius and Cinna's brutal entry into Rome in 86 B.C.E., their sending soldiers to kill the orator Marcus Antonius (the grandfather of Antonius of the second triumvirate and lover of Cleopatra), and his enchantment of the soldiers with his oratory are from Plutarch *Marius* 44.1–4. Nogarola's vocabulary and the aphorism about Antonius's eloquence are from Val. Max. 8.9.2. Note this vivid vocabulary: "strictos et *vibratos* gladios cruore vacuos vaginis reddiderunt." "Vibratos" swords (Val. Max. "vibrantes gladios") is much too unusual and graphic to be reduced to the stock "flourished" or "brandished."

75. The story of Solon's opposition to Peisistratus is paraphrased from Plutarch *Solon* 29.1–6; 30.1–6. Nogarola's vocabulary and also the aphorism about the choice of verbal facility over liberty are from Val. Max. 8.9. ext.1.

76. "Omnia oratio conficit quod hostile ferrum non conficit." Nogarola claims that Euripides said this, although we have not found the reference. The opposition between pen and sword is a commonplace in classical literature. There are plenty of resemblances to her supposed quote in Latin literature; see, for example, Cicero *Philippics* 5.38.

peace and tranquility and the daughter of the well-governed city, one might say.[77] But where am I going with all this? So you will know that what you do on your own you do rightly and you win the praise of all. As for me, I praise your poems themselves and your charming manner of writing to the point that I think you should be placed beside the Ovids, Theocrituses, and Virgils of this world. For these men are thought to have written pastoral poetry that was elegant and highly esteemed. That you praise me so highly in your poems, I admit, is for me the same as what happened to Themistocles.[78] But I do not believe those poems; really, I know that you have in no way been a flatterer but you have been deceived by my kindness. Farewell, and write something every day that is worthy of love and the Muses, and do not fail to do so, since glory is won by risking and doing; and, as it is said, it is not those who watch, but those who run, who win the crown.[79] Again, farewell.

77. Nogarola quotes almost directly from Cicero *Brutus* 45: "Pacis est comes otiique socia et iam bene constitutae civitatis quasi alumna quaedam eloquentia."

78. Both Plutarch *Themistocles* 24.4; 25.1–3; and Cicero *Brutus* 41–43 (the passage immediately prior to the one Nogarola just cited about eloquence) make the point that the historians distorted the facts of Themistocles' life to suit their own agendas.

79. We have been unable to locate the source of this quotation: "Coronae nec spectantibus, sed certantibus parantur." Nogarola believes (see chap. 4, n. 38) that the author is Cicero.

III

VENICE AND BEYOND (1 4 3 8 – 3 9)

The letters presented in the previous chapter show Isotta Nogarola breaking out of her immediate circle by approaching Guarino and the members of his school. The letters presented in this chapter show her reaching for and gaining the attention of a broader audience. If the main locus of the first set of Nogarola letters (chapter 1) was Verona and of the second Ferrara (chapter 2), those here look mostly to Venice, a more worldly and far vaster realm; two venture even further, to Modena and Florence. All of these letters are subsequent to the flurry exchanged in the early months of 1438.

Two events of 1438 should be noted as landmarks in Nogarola's development. The first was the mid-year marriage of her sister Ginevra, the companion of her early studies, to Brunorio Gambara of Brescia.[1] Once Ginevra departed from Verona, except for two letters to Damiano dal Borgo from Pratalboino in April 1440 and January 1441, any further literary activity she may have pursued has left no trace.[2] Among her descendants, however, is the noted poet Veronica Gambara (1485–1550),[3] a not unworthy legacy of the mental development of Ginevra Nogarola two generations earlier.

---

1. For Brunorio Gambara, see Abel, 1:xxxi and n. 48. Abel places the marriage in "mid-1438," but as he himself points out, Tobia dal Borgo in the first two months of 1438 points to wedding preparations (see chap. 2); and after that time, no further letters are jointly authored by Isotta and her sister.

2. Abel, 2:342–46.

3. For Veronica Gambara, the daughter of Francesco, son of Brunorio Gambara and Ginevra Nogarola, see Rinaldina Russell, "Veronica Gambara," in Russell, *Italian Women Writers: A Bio-Bibliographical Sourcebook*, 145–53. For excerpts from her works, see Richard Poss, "Veronica Gambara," in *Women Writers of the Renaissance and Reformation*, ed. Katharina M. Wilson (Athens: University of Georgia Press, 1987).

Ginevra's departure was a turning point for Isotta. Although readers to-day cannot recover her feelings at the time—did she wish to marry also? Or did she foresee that marriage for her sister meant (as it might mean for her) the abandonment of literary ambitions?—certainly the consequence of the marriage was that Isotta, if she was to continue to seek out humanist contacts, had to do so unaccompanied. She appears to have embraced that reality, or possibility, and ventured alone out into the world, intent on making a serious statement of her intellectual attainments and ambitions through the medium of the humanist letter.

The other significant event was Nogarola's encounter with Cardinal Giuliano Cesarini, who had journeyed from the Council of Basel, in which he was a key actor from 1431 to 1437, to Ferrara, to show his obedience to Pope Eugene IV at the council that convened there on January 8, 1438.[4] This encounter may have consisted of earlier communications. More likely, it was a face-to-face meeting, probably (rather than in Ferrara itself) in Nogarola's native Verona, as the cardinal journeyed southward from Switzerland, or perhaps in nearby Venice, where she and her family relocated during 1438. We know of it only from Nogarola's letter to the cardinal of March 29, 1438 (see below, no. 11), which reveals that he had praised her publicly and in-vited her to write and at the same time had shown his favor to her entire family. She writes in closing, thanking him for his courtesy and requesting patronage for her brother, intent on advancement in the church:

> It remains to say that on behalf of the Nogarola family I congratulate you, and thank you abundantly and enormously for showing us such kindness and love. You have been so generous that there is no one to whom we owe more than to you. And so humbly we pray you that you both continue and augment the friendliness, love, and charity you have already shown us; and first of all that you accept into your benev-olence as a father the care of my brother Leonardo, who is ready to be dedicated to the priesthood.[5]

The encounter with the Nogarola family, including its gifted daughter Isotta, would have been an extraordinary moment. The council then meeting

---

4. For Giuliano Cesarini (1398–1444?), an important papal agent in the crusade against the Hussites and the Turks, see DBI 24:188–95. On the Council of Ferrara-Florence, see especially Joseph Gill, S. J., *The Council of Florence* (Cambridge: Cambridge University Press, 1959); Gill, *Personalities of the Council of Florence* (Oxford: Basil Blackwell, 1964); and J. W. Stieber, *Pope Eugenius IV, the Council of Basel and the Secular and Ecclesiastical Authorities in the Empire: The Conflict over Supreme Authority in the Church* (Leiden: Brill, 1978).

5. From Abel, 1:156–57; see below, no. 11.

at Ferrara, one phase of a multiyear event that would move on to Florence and Rome, was important for its attempts to build bridges to the Greek (and Armenian, Jocobite, and Nestorian) communities and to reaffirm the foundations of papal authority for the next centuries. In these negotiations, the learned Cardinal Cesarini, already renowned for his role in the settlement of the Hussite rebellion and in attempts at the reform of the church at Basel, played an important role. As a cardinal, moreover, he had immense wealth and tremendous powers of patronage. That Nogarola was invited by such a personage to display her learning and eloquence in a letter that would surely circulate in prominent humanist circles was a notable achievement. The boost to her reputation acquired from the Cesarini encounter could only have encouraged Nogarola as she developed her determination to dedicate herself entirely to a literary career.

Her literary attainments continued to win the attention of eminent men and men senior in age and authority to those with whom she had corresponded previously. Less than a month before the date of Nogarola's letter to Cardinal Cesarini, the Sicilian humanist Antonio Cassario wrote to her a letter of extravagant praise.[6] He had recently returned from Greece and was staying at the house of the Venetian nobleman Giovanni Corner, bibliophile and patron, where, in the course of a discussion about leading literary figures, he had heard of her attainments and was amazed: "[F]or since I knew that men rarely receive such praise, I found it very difficult to concede that a woman might."[7] In addition, one of his companions had shown him a copy of her letters, bound in a collection of works by other contemporary humanists, and he found that her eloquence was even greater than he had been told.[8] Encouraged by his friends, although he hesitated, he wrote to her a letter of glowing praise (to which she either did not respond or we have no record of her reply).

On June 8, Niccolò Venier, a young Venetian nobleman, wrote from that city to praise the two sisters—the last time the two would be addressed

6. Abel, 1:137–45. For Antonio Cassario, see Abel, 1:xxviii and xxxi and n. 44; for Giovanni Corner, see King, *Venetian Humanism*, esp. 354–55.

7. Abel, 1:138 ". . . fit namque, ut quam viris laudem perraram cognoscam, puellae ut eam difficilius concedam."

8. Abel, 1:138–39: "Sed cum tandem ex his qui aderant unus ex epistolis tuis quasdam legendas mihi tradidisset—fuerant etiam cum illis aliorum alligatae nonnullae—et uno quasi aspectu pervolassem, sic mihi et ingenii tui copia et orationis cum color cum dignitas sese et ostendit et aperuit, ut res ipsa longe opinionem et famam anteiret et quae viderentur quam quae auditu ceperam multo essent digniora."

jointly in the extant letter collections.[9] He had heard much talk of her achievements, and although they had had no prior contact, he was moved to write her when their mutual friend, Tobia dal Borgo (see chapter 2), who was staying with him, urged him to do so. He had, moreover, just recently seen the two letters the sisters had written to Jacopo Foscari (see chapter 2) and was struck by their eloquence. He asked them apologetically to forgive the inelegancies of his own work and encouraged her to continue her studies. Nogarola responded, singly, soon afterward (see below, no. 12), encouraging him, too, to literary tasks and closing with a message that reveals that Venier was related to the Nogarolas: "I would like you to give my best greetings to Andrea, your brother and my cousin."[10]

Later that year (apparently by September 10, when Isotta writes dal Borgo from Venice),[11] the Nogarola family (including Isotta's mother Bianca Borromeo, and brothers Antonio and Leonardo, her sister Bartolommea, and the latter's husband, Jacopo Lavagnola) relocated to Venice because of the dangerous war, intensified by plague, then raging in Verona and its countryside. Isotta was already established in Venice when reports of her fame reached the humanistically trained nobleman, Niccolò Barbo,[12] who wrote to her on December 9, 1438. Barbo had been educated by George of Trebizond, and his correspondence, although not wide, includes exchanges with Guarino Veronese, Francesco Barbaro, and Antonio Beccadelli. He had heard so much from other learned men about Nogarola, he wrote, that he dared to write, although he feared she would scorn his rough literary style. However, he had recently seen copies of her work that had "come into his hands" and decided he would delay no longer to offer her praise and encourage her work.[13] Isotta responded to him after a brief delay (see below, no. 14).

To her polite reply, Barbo responded, on January 25, 1439. Now he sees indeed, in the letter he has just received from her, how great her achievement truly is. Just as one sees more clearly the glories of a ship as it sails into closer view, so now he sees hers; and he never could have guessed that anyone, and

9. Abel, 1:158–63; for Venier, see Abel, 1:xxviii and n. 42.

10. Abel, 1:169: "Plurimam salutem Andreae fratri tuo agnatoque meo nunties velim."

11. Abel, 1:209.

12. For Niccolò Barbo, see King, *Venetian Humanism,* esp. 328–29; and Abel, 1:xxx and n. 46.

13. Abel, 1:178: His autem proximis diebus elapsis cum perlegissem quasdam tuas quae ad manus meas pervenerant elegantissimas epistolas ac vehementer in iis admirarer ingenium tuum summamque dicendi facultatem decrevi omnino huic tuae ad summam gloriam magis ac magis in dies florescenti facundiae meis litteris aliquantulum congratulari . . ."

certainly not a woman, could have proved to be so extraordinary.[14] As she had urged him, he encouraged her to persevere in her studies and assures her of their continued mutual friendship—"and may you cherish me with a mutual love."[15]

These three encounters—the letter of Cassario and the exchanges with Venier and Barbo—have common features. All three figures wrote letters from noble Venetian houses (Cassario from that of his host, the nobleman Giovanni Corner). All allude to discussions with peers about literary affairs in which Nogarola's conspicuous attainments were mentioned (Ginevra's as well, in the case of Venier). All reported seeing and reading copies of Nogarola's works.[16] Together, they provide a rare glimpse of the activity of humanist circles in the early fifteenth century, where solitary labor, convivial discussion, and the exchange of texts combine to create a vital intellectual world—an early example, perhaps, of the society of the academy or the salon that would flourish in the sixteenth and seventeenth centuries. To this image may be added that of the circulation of people as bearers of ideas, observed in the next letter to be discussed, when one figure's journey from one city to another contributes to the creation of a new connection in a growing literary network.

During the latter half of 1438, Isotta initiated a relationship, at the suggestion of her brother-in-law Jacopo Lavagnola, who had just returned from Modena, with Feltrino Boiardo, grandfather of the more famous Matteo Maria Boiardo, author of the epic *Orlando innamorato* (1495). Boiardo may have seen Lavagnola in Modena, but in this period more generally, he was a humanist in the d'Este circle in Ferrara, with an official role at the church council then in progress.[17] Nogarola's letter praises Boiardo's political and intellectual achievements, deferentially invites him to correct her errors, and expresses her hope for their continued mutual friendship (see below, no. 13). If he responded, that letter is not known to be extant.

14. Abel, 1:193–94: "Antea etenim tuam dicendi mirabilem elegantiam tamquam navem quandam praetereuntem strictim aspexeram nec temporibus nostris tam lautam suppellectilem in muliere potissimum unquam inesse consideraram."

15. Abel, 1:198: "Vale mea summa spes et me mutuo amore diligas."

16. Nogarola's later correspondents Costanza Varano, Lauro Quirini, and Antonio Contrario would all first be introduced to her by seeing, in distant Pesar, Padua, and Rome, copies of her letters. In Contrario's case, it was an entire letterbook (*liber epistolarum tuarum*), in Rome: Abel, 2:140.

17. For the nobleman Feltrino Boiardo (late–fourteenth century to 1456), of the ruling family of Reggio, see Abel, 1:xxix–xxx and n. 45. For Feltrino's relationship to Matteo Maria Boiardo, *Encyclopedia of the Renaissance*, s.v. "Boiardo."

The final letter in this sequence was written, like the first discussed, to a cardinal of the church: the Venetian nobleman Francesco Condulmier, nephew of then-reigning pope Eugene IV and recently appointed (1439) to the bishopric of Verona (see below, no. 15).[18] Isotta's elegant letter praises the new bishop, congratulates the city of Verona on its good fortune, and recommends (as did her letter to Cesarini) her brother Leonardo.

The two letters to the two cardinals frame this *annus mirabilis* for Nogarola, extending from spring 1438 to spring 1439. Her name was now known in humanist circles—a prominence that can still be noted today by examining the indices of collections of humanist works in manuscript, where letters of Nogarola are found in close company with those of the major figures of Italian humanism.[19] The men with whom she corresponded in 1438–39 were no longer privileged youths of the smart sets of Verona or Ferrara. They were adults of significant literary fame: all but Cassario were of the nobility; and Cesarini and Condulmer, as cardinals, ranked in the highest circle of Renaissance society.

But Nogarola's venture out into the world would not be unmarred by difficulty. On June 1, 1439, her literary fame struck an anonymous, humanistically trained satirist as literary pretension. Calling himself "Plinio Veronese," the "Veronese Pliny," he addressed to a fictional friend an attack on the Nogarola family:[20] accusations of promiscuity, adultery, male and female homosexuality, even incest. Isotta received "Pliny's" special attention precisely because she had pretended to literary fame:

> Let us cease to wonder at all these things, when that second unmarried sister, who has won such praise for her eloquence, does things which little befit her erudition and reputation—although the saying of many wise men I hold to be true: that an eloquent woman is never chaste; and the behavior of many learned women also confirms its truth. . . . But lest you approve even slightly this excessively foul and obscene crime, let me explain that before she made her body generally available for promiscuous intercourse, she had first permitted—and indeed

18. For Francesco Condulmier, see Abel, 1:xxix and n. 44; also King, *Venetian Humanism*, 272, 321, 446.

19. See Kristeller, *Iter italicum*, the cumulative index (vol. 7), where there are sixty-seven references to works by Nogarola (those written to her are not included, and dual appearances within the same manuscript are not noted), most of which are in humanist miscellanies of the fifteenth to seventeenth centuries in which most of the other authors are renowned male figures.

20. The incident is described, with the text of the anonymous attack appended, in Arnaldo Segarizzi, "Niccolò Barbo, patrizio veneziano del secolo XV e le accuse contro Isotta Nogarola," *Giornale storico della letteratura italiana* 43 (1904): 39–54.

even earnestly desired—that the seal of her virginity be broken by none other than her brother, so that by this tie she might be more tightly bound to him. Alas for God in whom men trust, who does not mingle heaven with earth nor the sea with heaven, when she, who sets herself no limit in this filthy lust, dares to engage so deeply in the finest literary studies.[21]

Thus slandered in a publicly circulated text—it came to the hands of Niccolò Barbo, who defended her against the incest charge—Nogarola must have been deterred somewhat in pursuing her literary ambitions. Perhaps it was the effect of this episode to encourage Nogarola in an exclusive correspondence with her elder compatriot, dal Borgo, of whose correspondence between 1438 to 1441 nineteen letters are extant (in addition to four others exchanged between Isotta and dal Borgo's son, Eusebio). These will be the subject of the next chapter.

XI

Isotta Nogarola to Cardinal Giuliano Cesarini: Verona, March 29, 1438

Nogarola praises the great achievements of Cesarini, a prince of the church, who had encouraged her to write him (perhaps at a prior meeting in Verona or Venice). In closing, she asks for his favor toward the Nogarola family and especially her brother Leonardo, who was to become a priest.

*T*f (as we read) Cicero, the prince of eloquence, was overcome with fear whenever he began to speak, since he felt each time that not only was his intellectual ability under scrutiny but also his character and honor—for he was afraid he would either appear to be publicly admitting what he could not achieve (which is impudence) or to not be doing what he could achieve (which is negligence or bad faith);[22] then it is no wonder, most reverend father, if I myself fear and an awful tremor runs through my bones, and all the more so when I reflect that I was born a woman, who

---

21. Segarizzi, 53.

22. Virgil *Eclogues* 5:46–48:
    Tale tuum carmen nobis, divine poeta,
    quale sopor fessis in gramine, quale per aestum
    dulcis aquae saliente sitim restinguere rivo:
    nec calamis solum aequiparas, sed voce magistrum.

garbles words rather than pronounces them and who writes to you, whose knowledge of canon and civil law is so extraordinary and whose eloquence, power, and sweetness of speech are so great that the same thing is said of you that Homer said of Nestor—that from your mouth flows speech sweeter than honey.[23] But encouraged by your kindness, I have undertaken to attempt with my womanly capacity this task of writing, preferring to fail and to fall than not to do your will or follow your instructions, both because I know you will not condemn my scribblings but will kindly emend them and because all men, both of our own and later generations, will offer me both honor and praise when they learn that my writing, whatever quality it may have, did not displease your excellency.

For while I have always tried strenuously and zealously to be approved by great men, it has exceeded my wish that you should find me pleasing, or indeed, as it appears, worthy of admiration. If there is anything that could have happened to me in my life that might afford me greater praise or glory, I do not know what it would be; since it is the highest honor to please princes who delight in nothing base or vulgar but only in excellent things: and if it happens that anyone is exalted by them or honored by their words, then he achieves the greatest happiness. For you illustrious and lofty men occupy so high a rank that you love only those who are endowed with exceptional virtue. Accordingly, I thank you enormously for your kindness, you who love me and have judged me worthy of a friendship that in no way threatens my virtue. This being so, is it not permitted me to glory a little, since I have entered into this man's circle, in whom [I find] so much and so many kinds of virtue that not only your subjects but also foreigners rival one another in their love for you and encircle you with their ears, eyes, and, finally, their minds.

The Council of Basel bears witness, which you headed with such wisdom, modesty, humanity, polished gravity, which indeed you governed with such holiness that your leaving was accompanied by tears and sobs. In this matter you have surpassed the pious Cato, upon whom his soldiers bestowed, as he left the province at the end of the war, not only oaths, as was usually done, but tears, passionately embracing him, scattering their garments in the path on which he would walk, kissing his hands.[24] Such honor was given to none except emperors and to very few of those.

These indeed are the fruits, these are the rewards accruing to you because of the magnitude of your incredible mind, your immense knowledge of letters and of holy scripture, your eloquence, your divine memory, your

23. Homer *Iliad* 1.249.
24. Plutarch *Cato the Younger* 12.1–2.

excellent piety, your untainted honor, your domestic loyalty, your special humanity to all, and, finally, your regal splendor and munificence. I leave out for now your sanctity, kindness, worship of the immortal God, in which traits no monks exceed you, not even the most pious, so that you should really be named not only "most wise" but also "most holy." For your sanctity has held all these things—wealth, pleasures, riches, dignities—in contempt, although others strive for them with such zeal and ambition. So it seemed to Marcus Curius, the victor over the Samnites. For after his victory, when the Samnites came to offer him a great weight of gold and found him cooking turnips, he told them that he, a man who ate such fare, had no need for gold; it was, rather, better and more honorable to rule those who possessed gold than to possess it himself.[25]

For you have so lived through all the stages of your life that whenever you are thought of, a worthy image of some virtue presents itself to human minds. Xenocrates' great virtue was celebrated by all mortals to such an extent that they believed there was no human soul so violent, so cruel, so furious by nature that he would not be moved by a mere glance of Xenocrates to admiration and veneration.[26] I shall say nothing here about the great concern, effort, toil, and diligence with which you labored to win back the Hussites to holy faith and true worship;[27] to which end I believe you scarcely would have been able to soften their savage and pertinacious souls unless you possessed eloquence as well as wisdom. You have taught the whole world, by heaven, that it is no wonder forests and mountains obeyed the lyre of the poet Orpheus, which by its sweet modulation tamed wild beasts: "[T]he lamb offers its side to the wolf, deer play with the dappled tiger, stags have no fear of the Massilian lion's mane."[28]

For Cicero himself must cede to you and confess himself vanquished, whose enemies sneeringly called him "king," since none were condemned and none acquitted unless he condemned or acquitted them.[29] How much you excel in human and divine law! You have so mastered this knowledge

---

25. Plutarch *Marcus Cato* 2.

26. Xenocrates (396–314 B.C.E.), Greek philosopher, born Chalcedon, disciple of Plato who succeeded Speusippus as head of the Academy.

27. Cesarini was entrusted with the suppression of the Hussites in rebellion in the 1420s, and from 1431 to 1437, as a key figure at the Council of Basel, called for the reform of the church and settlement of the Hussite controversy. See DBI 24:188–95 and n. 4 above.

28. Claudius Claudianus *De raptu Proserpina*, lib. 2 preface, ll. 26–28:
   vicinumque lupo praebuit agna latus,
   Concordes ludunt varia cum tygride damae,
   Massiliam cervi non metuere iubam.

29. We are unable to locate a source for this anecdote.

that your contemporaries believe it originated with you, just as the ancient Roman citizens believed that jurisprudence, with the aid of Egeria, was born from Numa Pompilius.[30] We shall actually find very few men in whom, as in you, reason accords with action. For such exalted pinnacles of honor generally attract certain men, who are so puffed up with the glory of celebrity that, forgetting they are men and pondering neither their own worth nor the places they came from, they want to be judged by their pride and ostentation. But your behavior is far different, you whose virtue and magnitude of soul are apparent to all, you who have learned from your liberal studies to place little value in human things. No self-exaltation, no condescension, no haughty words do you evince; no suitable visitor, no human address is refused, and while there is no one so lowly that he is not allowed access to you, each person addresses you without an intermediary. You, therefore, most holy priest, must know that you have achieved a great joy and honor in becoming the most celebrated and reverend father lord Cardinal Giuliano. Therefore, you have won for yourself immortal glory in which you live now and will continue to live and take pleasure in after your death.

But I return to the praise you give me, which brought me great pleasure, since your praise of my virtues, if I have any, is their reward. For your highest goodness causes this, you who praise me as such a person as you want me to be, trumpeting it with such eloquent magnificence that you make me into a goddess, from a sewer to a castle.[31] And so I devote, give and bestow myself entirely to your governance, and beg you kindly to forgive me if I do not thank you worthily enough, but ascribe it, I pray, not to my will but to the insufficiency of my mind.

It remains to say that on behalf of the Nogarola family I congratulate you and thank you abundantly and enormously for showing us such kindness and love. You have been so generous that there is no one to whom we owe more than to you. And so humbly we pray you that you both continue and augment the friendliness, love, and charity you have already shown us; and

---

30. Numa Pompilius, the legendary king of Rome who immediately succeeded Romulus, is said to have been aided by his consort, the nymph Egeria. He established Roman ritual law defining the major priesthoods and the calendar of festal and ordinary days. See the *Life* by Plutarch.

31. Cicero *Pro Plancio* 40.95: "nunc venio ad illud extremum in quo dixisti, dum Planci in me meritum verbis extollerem, me arcem facere e cloaca lapidemque e sepulcro venerari pro deo; neque enim mihi insidiarum periculum ullum neque mortis fuisse." Trans. C. D. Yonge: "Now I come to your last assertion, when you said that, while I was extolling so highly the services which Plancius had done me, I was making a castle out of a sewer, and worshiping a stone taken from a sepulcher as a god; and that I had never been in the least danger of any one forming plots against me, or of death."

first of all that you accept into your benevolence as a father the care of my brother Leonardo, who is ready to be dedicated to the priesthood. Which if you will do, not only will you tie yourself to us for eternity, but also those born to us, and those who will be born thereafter. But since I feel that I have gone on too long I shall cease lest I bore you and let it be said of me what the philosopher Zeno said to one loquacious person: If you heard yourself with my ears, truly you would be silent.[32] Farewell, and consider me the daughter of your wisdom and charity. I commend myself to you.

XII

Isotta Nogarola to Niccolò Venier: Verona, probably after June 8, 1438

Nogarola politely responds to the young Venetian who had written her a letter of enthusiastic praise having heard of her fame and examined the letters to Jacopo Foscari that she and her sister Ginevra had written.

The letters I recently received from you delighted me enormously, for they display your excellent nature, your literary talent, that is, and your craftsmanship and discipline—in other words, your diligence and hard work. Indeed I am so moved when I think of your age and the feeling in your letters that this maturity you show seems remarkable and clearly beyond your years, nor am I afraid, provided that you do not sell yourself short, that you will not become a most excellent man. Therefore, be alert, please, accumulate and add something to your accomplishments every day and reflect on the fact that great rewards have been planned for you in your studies—for the trajectory of your life and career and for the glory and renown of your name. These are not possessions of the kind that a thief can pilfer, or ones that a public notice can remove, or those that come and go like the waves and the tides of the sea, like goods possessed by a succession of masters: these are goods no enemy can pillage. When Demetrius razed the philosopher Stilpo's city to the ground, he asked him whether he had lost any of his possessions. Stilpo replied to him, "I have lost nothing, since war wins no spoils from virtue."[33] For what else is there in which we can

32. We do not find this comment attributed to Zeno, but others, which also reprove loquacity, in Diogenes Laertius 7.21, 24. Zeno, Greek philosopher (ca. 490 to ca. 430), of the Eleatic school, a follower of Parmenides, famous for his difficult problems or "paradoxes."

33. The anecdote and aphorism from Stilpo is Nogarola's aphoristic adaptation of Plutarch *Demetrius* 9.5–6: the philosopher's answer to the inquiry as to who stole what from him during

take pride unless in those things we obtain from the study of the virtues?[34] For these possessions are ours, born of our work, care, and sleepless nights[35] and cannot be stolen from us in life or in death. This virtue contains a true and solid dignity in itself. This virtue will follow you wherever you go: it is preferred to the gifts of fortune and all other things. It is said that the mind of the sage is outside all fortune; it has also been said that no man is free except the philosopher. For this reason, history testifies, there was such a great desire for learning among our ancestors. So great was the philosopher Euclides'[36] passion for knowledge that when the Athenians decreed that if any citizen from Megara was caught setting foot in Athens he would be put to death, he managed to journey to Athens by night without getting into danger. Before evening came, he donned a long women's tunic, wrapped himself in a pallium of many colors, and veiled his head. He then went from his own house in Megara to Socrates' so that he could partake of the talk and wisdom of the philosopher. Before dawn, he made the twenty-mile trip back home again disguised in the same garb. Democritus, moved by a great desire for wisdom, after setting aside a moderate portion of his patrimony for his kinsmen, gifted the remaining portion to his native city, thinking that such enormous wealth would be a difficult burden for those of his heirs who might wish to pursue knowledge.[37]

If you obtain this virtue, as I hope you will, what riches are to be collected with the rewards of these studies! For see how much honor there is in

---

the sack of his city was, "Οὐδείς," εἶπεν, "οὐδένα γὰρ εἶδον ἐπιστάμαν ἀποφέροντα." ("No one," said Stilpo," for I saw no one pillaging knowledge.").

34. "Virtutum studiis": *studia virtutum* (studies in the virtues) is a key concept in Italian Renaissance humanism. It derives from Cicero's ideas on the cardinal virtues (*prudentia, justitia, fortitudo, temperantia*), which he linked inextricably to learning and studies in rhetoric and philosophy. On the connection between moral philosophy (*studia virtutum*) and oratory (*eloquentia*), see Cicero's *De inventione, De officiis, De partitione oratoria,* among other canonical texts for our humanists.

35. "Cura et vigiliis" (care and long nights of study): the same images Laura Cereta uses repeatedly to describe how she finds the time to study and write (Cereta, *Collected Letters*).

36. Nogarola's source is Aulus Gellius (123–ca. 165 C.E.) *Attic Nights* 7.10.2–4. Gellius studied in Athens; he is grouped with the so-called Silver Latin writers; his work is described as an archaizing collection of notes on grammar, public and private antiquities, philosophy, and literary criticism. Nogarola quotes almost verbatim this anecdote of Euclides of Megara (called elsewhere the Pythagorean or the Socratic to distinguish him from the mathematician). As usual, when she quotes her sources she makes changes only in verb forms and noun cases, deleting phrases she considers unnecessary or embroidering the text when she thinks explanation is called for. This is an especially interesting case since she uses the anecdote in three of her letters and it is a relatively rare story: it is not in Diogenes Laertius, *Lives of the Philosophers,* Plutarch's *Lives* or the *Moralia,* Valerius Maximus, or any of Cicero's works on rhetoric and oratory.

37. The story of Democritus's donation of his patrimony to his patria so that it would not be a distraction to his quest for knowledge is in Valerius Maximus 8.7.4.

these studies, such that no prince, no king has ever considered it a disgrace to be endowed with such knowledge and eloquence. By day, the emperor Theodosius was either training with his army or ruling in cases involving the affairs of his subjects; by night he reclined beside his lamp with his books.[38] Augustus always used to read and write when he was at war in Modena.[39] O pleasure and delight in such studies! How great they are, and how hard it is to tear our minds away! But lest I relax too much the reins of speech and, like a noisy goose, intrude upon the swans, I shall bring my writing to a close since, now that I have urged you on in the pursuit—which you must do for yourself—of the humanities and the liberal arts, I shall go. That you praise me so highly and exalt my name to the stars is the result of your own goodness, and I have and give thanks to you from the tenuousness of that talent which is mine.[40] Vale. I would like to give my best greetings to Andrea, your brother and my cousin.[41] Again, vale.

XIII

Isotta Nogarola to Feltrino Boiardo: perhaps Verona, 1438

Prompted by her brother-in-law Jacopo Lavagnola, Nogarola sends a letter of praise and invitation to friendship to the nobleman Feltrino Boiardo, an intimate of Niccolò d'Este of Ferrara.

38. Theodosius was Roman emperor 379–395 C.E., during the lifetime of Saint Jerome, whose letters frequently refer to his rule. Nogarola knew Jerome's letters well and frequently alluded to or quoted from them. We have not found the passage about Theodosius reading books during a military campaign or in his camp.

39. We have not found a passage describing Augustus (then Octavian) reading books when he was at war in Mutina. It is possible, as in the case of Theodosius (n. 38 above) that the topos about Alexander reading or being read to when he was encamped has been transferred in these two instances to other cultivated generals.

40. "Pro ingenioli mei parvitate": this self-deprecation is a frequent characteristic of female humanist prose. These are the precise terms in which Cassandra Fedele and Laura Cereta speak of themselves (see Cereta, *Collected Letters*; Fedele, *Letters and Orations*.) Note the diminution of *ingenium* (mind, literary talent, nature, inborn ability). See also King and Rabil, *Her Immaculate Hand*, passim.

41. This statement is the sole evidence known to us of the intermarriage between the noble Veronese Nogarola family and the noble Venetian Venier family, but such intermarriage was exceedingly common. See, for instance, the discussion of the marital career of Jacopo Antonio Marcello in King, *The Death of the Child*; and for the marriage patterns generally of the Venetian nobility, the studies of Stanley Chojnacki, *Women and Men in Renaissance Venice: Twelve Essays on Patrician Society* (Baltimore: Johns Hopkins University Press, 2000).

*W*hen I asked Jacopo Lavagnola, who recently returned from Modena, many questions about news of the city, he spoke at last of you as the city's crowning glory and honor.[42] Even though your fame flew to us from a single source, I have heard daily how great was your virtue, humanity, and eloquence. For he extolled your virtues at such length that they themselves testify to the fact that you have attained everything that men hope for and seek in life. When I heard these things from him, I so burned with a remarkable love of your mind and studies and character that I could not resist my desire to write you, even though I hesitated on account of my trifling abilities. But at his urging and suggestion I did not dare refuse this duty, and so I determined to make a pact with you that you would not mock my girlish letter bereft of ornament or charm, but that rather you will by your courtesy, urbanity, and accustomed kindness accept and cherish it. In so doing, you would imitate Artaxerxes, king of the Persians, who thought it no less kingly and humane to accept small things courteously and graciously than to give large ones.[43]

You were also born from most noble lineage that has extended through many generations from its ancient origin, adorned by many famous cavaliers who ranked high both in the city and on the battlefield, and yet you surpass all these not only in virtues, wealth, and magnificence, but even more in humanity, being dutiful to friends, courteous with your staff and household, humane toward all. Add to this the loftiness of your mind, your excellent knowledge of letters, the righ elegance of your style, your divine memory, your familiarity with many things, your great constancy, modesty, and integrity, by which virtues you have won the affection of the most illustrious princes, and especially the marquis d'Este,[44] who loves and treasures you, holding you no less dear among the other very great men in his circle than Caesar did Antony; when all the leading men of the city gathered to greet him on his return from Spain, Caesar stepped out ahead of them and accorded Antony the highest honor.[45]

To eloquence, moreover, in which you greatly shine amid many occupations and crises, you have applied yourself so industriously that you have attained the utmost perfection in eloquence. For you understand the impor-

---

42. For the Este supporter, nobleman, patron, and amateur humanist Feltrino Boiardo, see *DBI*, 11:210–211.

43. Plutarch *Artaxerxes* 5.1. Artaxerxes I (r. 464–425 B.C.E.), son of Xerxes I, whom he succeeded to the throne of Persia.

44. Niccolò III, who reigned 1393–1441.

45. Plutarch *Antony* 10.1.

tance of the excellence of style, a skill essential even in the midst of battle. When on the field at Durachium, Pompey's soldiers were reluctant to fight, he delivered an oration about liberty, about virtue, about the contempt for death, about glory—and speaking as long as the time allowed so inspired the soldiers that they longed for battle and that day drove all of Caesar's cohorts to flight.[46]

You also do well, most excellent man (as I have heard also from Lavagnola), to study history so zealously and ardently. Our ancestors called history life's teacher, for knowledge of the past fosters prudence and counsel, and the outcomes of matters similarly begun either encourage or deter us according to their origin. For history encourages a certain perfection of style, adorned [as it is] with every splendor, an opulence of words, a power of speaking, a wealth of anecdotes that illumine the oration and make it admirable. What more is there to say? All excellent orators gain their vitality and passion from history. In brief, you have pursued these interrelated studies, expertise in letters and the knowledge of things, which together promote those who have mastered them to high reputation and glory.

But why am I telling you these things, since your virtues have already won you immortal glory, in which you live and prosper? And so I shall stop; yet read this, and forgive my temerity if I have been so bold as to write you this inept letter; and if you find errors in grammar or style, may you in your prudence, I pray you, emend them. For I have been compelled to write both by your splendid virtues and my love and reverence for you, and because I know that I shall acquire honor and adornment if you include me among your friends, since (as you know) great honor derives from pleasing princely men. Farewell, and if you write me, as I believe you will, I shall treasure your letter always as a sign of our mutual love. Again, farewell.

XIV

Isotta Nogarola to Niccolò Barbo: Venice, between December 9, 1438 and January 25, 1439

Barbo had heard much praise of Nogarola and had recently read some of her letters and now writes to praise her and to encourage her literary studies.

---

46. We have been unable to locate the source of this anecdote.

$\mathcal{E}$ ven though I had decided many times that I would write something to you so I could pay the debt I owed you and did not do it, I beg you not to believe that I neglected this duty because of forgetfulness or arrogance, since I was unable to do it due to my commitments—my commitments, that it, to literary studies. Now since you have called me to writing, I have thought that it would be the conduct of an ungrateful, careless, and outrageous man[47] not to gratify your very fair wish in whatever way possible. But when I pay attention to these things—in what place and to what critics I read my letters—I am afraid the objection may be raised that Petronius Arbiter, a very learned man, appeared to have made very well and truly in jest. For he said, "After someone wove and put together a line of verse and tender emotion in a well-balanced period, he immediately thought he had arrived at the Helicon."[48] I also know that the Pythagorean rule was made for me, whereby the philosopher commanded his disciples to begin their studies by being silent for no less than two years, lest shamefully they should appear to commit errors, make mistakes, pursue fallacies, or stubbornly defend precepts they themselves understood too little.[49] And now you will be the best witness that I have undertaken the task of writing you at your prompting. And so you will receive a short and unpolished epistle from me which, if it does not give you the thanks you deserve for all your combined praises of me, I beg you to fault neither the letter nor my intention but rather the tenuousness of my talent, minuscule as it is.[50] Now I am not unaware that your incredible affection toward me forces you to write and believe those things about me that are not so much true as they are great. Nevertheless, I am pleased with your good intentions toward me and persuade myself that everything you have said to me and thought comes from a very kind heart. But how shall I express the happiness your letter brought me not only because I consider it a very great reward for my virtue (if I have any), but also because I think that what Cicero and other learned men have said is very true: "For on account of their virtue and integrity we love even those whom

---

47. " . . . ingrati, imprudentis audacisque *hominis* officium: we think her use of the word "hominis" ("the duty of an arrogant man . . . ," as opposed to that of a woman) should be noted here; certainly the already gendered "ingrati," which would have subsumed both sexes, would have made the specification of gender unnecessary.

48. On Petronius, the first-century C.E. author of the *Satyricon*, see chap. 1, n. 25 above. The passage about the Helicon is a quote from the *Satyricon* 118. Kristeller, *Iter,* 6:387b) documents Nogarola's ownership of a codex of the *Satyricon,* which bears her coat of arms.

49. On Pythagoras's rule on silence and the sources, see above, chap. 2, n. 68.

50. Again almost the same self-deprecating phrase: "ingenioli mei parvitate adscribas."

we have never seen![51] For my esteem for learned men "increases from hour to hour, as far as the green alder shoots up when spring is young."[52] Do we not read in the ancient histories that certain men surveyed the provinces, approached new peoples, crossed the seas so that they would come to know those men face to face whom they had only known in books?[53] We read that certain noble men came from the outer limits of Spain and Gaul to hear Titus Livy dripping with the milky fountain of eloquence. It was not to the contemplation of Rome that these men were drawn; it was the fame of this one man that brought them there. That age held an amazing miracle that would be celebrated by all subsequent ages so that those who entered sought a great city outside the city. Do we not see that those who were endowed with virtue as though they were gods flourished among other men? When Cato was led back from exile and entered the city with his fleet, all the magistrates, the priests, the entire senate, and the majority of the plebs came to meet him, and so both banks of the Tiber were filled, and his arrival did not differ much from a triumph.[54]

I could recount more stories here of famous men, but I would bore you to distraction since their stories are equally well known to you and me and I know that I have already gone on too long. For if I were allowed to dwell on each individual figure, I would want to gild their glory with too much praise. But it is certainly not fitting for my sex to enter into such weighty tasks best left to the most learned men,[55] since even for them such labor sometimes seems more daunting than Mount Aetna. And rightly so. For who has enough eloquence and genius to give virtue a worthy eulogy? And so I shall close, once I have begged you to devote all your time and care to the study of literature, which alone can make you immortal. With me, really, you should be lenient if I do not give thanks worthy of your love and praises of me, since I have decided not to speak further, much less to emulate your trumpeting

51. Cicero *De amicitia* 28: "Cum propter virtutem et probitatem etiam eos, quos numquam vidimus, quodam modo diligamus. Changing the word order and vocabulary slightly, Nogarola writes: eos etiam quos nunquam propter virtutem et probitatem amamus."

52. Nogarola's "Nam tantum meus in quoscumque doctos in horas crescit amor, quantum vero novo viridis se subicit alnus" is an almost exact quote from Virgil *Eclogues* 10.73–74: "Gallo, cuius amor tantum mihi crescit in horas,/quantum vere novo viridis se subicit alnus." In Abel's text "vero" is an error for *vere*, the correct ablative form of ver, veris (spring). This translation quotes from G.P. Goold's translation of the eclogue in the Loeb Library edition (Cambridge, Mass.: Harvard University Press, 1915.), 94. See also chap. 2 at n. 63; chap. 4 at n. 30.

53. See chap. 2, n. 21 on Apollonius's travels.

54. Nogarola's description of Cato's triumphal return to Rome from exile appears to be an adaptation of Plutarch's account of Cato's arrival in Antioch in *Cato the Younger* 13.1–2.

55. " . . . *viris* peritissimis": again, and note the context.

of me, but I do see that I cannot respond to your words. I have and will continue to give the greatest thanks to you—as long as I am in possession of a memory and have life in these limbs. Vale and surpass yourself in increasing your virtue. From Venice.

XV

Isotta Nogarola to Cardinal Francesco Condulmier: Venice, 1439

Nogarola writes to praise the career and character of Francesco Condulmier, a cardinal and recently appointed bishop of Verona. She congratulates Verona on its good fortune in its new bishop and commends her family and especially her brother who is beginning his clerical career, to the cardinal.

T remembered having read, most reverend father, that Cicero said he preferred simple prudence to foolish loquacity,[56] and since I agreed with that view, although many men urged me to write to you, I decided to remain silent, thinking that it was not fitting for one of my sex to assume responsibilities that should be left to important men. Yet this most difficult and imposing task I have assumed, I confess, impelled not by my strength, nor my power of speech, nor glory of eloquence, but alone I have conceived it in my mind and soul, as Augustine says,[57] according to the will of God, compelled by your charity, which urges and provokes me thus to speech, although I am both ignorant and unlearned, so that while I do not know how to speak, I cannot hold my tongue. You then, in your humanity, will accept this barren letter, adorned with no ornament or charm, in place of a more suitable reward for your excellence, offered by me, a woman and profoundly a stranger to this kind of task as I am to gold and luxuries. You will accept it in a kingly and friendly spirit, most reverend father, as you do all things, since you wisely understand that neither gold nor silver, nor any of the things that are given, constitute the gift, but only the will of the giver. You will receive it indeed, as I have said, as a sign of my reverence for you, my love and my joy, which I along with our city feel on account of your advent as bishop no less than the city of Rome experienced at the advent of Cato whom, when he returned from his exile and entered the city,

---

56. Cicero *De Oratore* 3.142: " . . . malim equidem indisertam prudentiam quam stultitiam loquacem."
57. This is too vague an attribution to Augustine to be attributed to any particular text.

all the magistracy, the whole senate, all the priests, and most of the people so thronged to meet that both banks of the river Tiber were filled with the crowds.[58]

Therefore, I have come to congratulate you and our city. For since you especially excel in faith, integrity, constancy, moderation, fairness, prudence, justice, love, in which virtues the worthiness of any action consists, our city will serve as an arena, a place in which you will give a magnificent and devout demonstration of your excellence, as you always do everywhere, and you will demonstrate it in such a way that the expectation of your dignity and excellence will surpass your fame, and admiration will surpass the expectation, and you will promulgate the treasures of your precious mind, your magnanimity, integrity, and devotion in such a way that our entire city—deeply stirred by your performance—and its entire clergy will increase each day the path of righteous living.

For if the deeds of our forebears and ancestors confer useful examples of worthy living, how much more your presence will benefit us, since all will profitably see and contemplate you circulating well and blessedly through all types of people, protecting the good, assisting the needy and the paupers of Christ, lifting up the oppressed, controlling the fractious, visiting holy places. Since you have done these things from a tender age, it is no wonder if the Roman pope, if the College of Cardinals, if the Roman Church has wished you to be cardinal and our bishop, camerarius and vice-chancellor, and has judged you most worthy, finally, to be the legate against the Turks for the sake of the Christian faith and holy religion. Truly, what a responsibility, what a burden you have undertaken with a joyful expression, a still more joyful spirit, and the highest ardor and zeal in your devotion to Christ! Neither the hardships of the journey, nor the heat or cold of the region, nor the perils of the sea itself or the war could deter you. Have you shown reluctance to risk your life and suffer death, so long as you can be of aid or assistance to the Christian faith and the church militant? And rightly indeed. For he easily disdains human things and even life itself who rightly, who piously, who truly follows Christ.

O happy city, which has acquired such a pastor, guardian, bishop, and a most splendid resting place, in whom with your troubles put aside you may take refuge, to whom your anxieties may be entrusted, to whose loyalty and integrity your welfare has been committed, and so committed that the Veronese people should wish, should pray to God and entreat with solemn

---

58. Plutarch *Cato the Younger* 39.1.

promises that this dignity of yours be eternal not only for you but also for them.

I omit the many statements in praise of your virtues that exceed what should be said by me in this place—your excellent mind, your experience in many spheres, your kindness, your pleasantness, your love for and benevolence toward learned men—since this is no place to linger, lest I should appear to have taken up the task of writing for the sake of flattering you, lest I should myself have committed something I thought should be castigated in others, or lest I should exceed the bounds of an epistle with the garrulous tongue of a woman, especially since I realize that too great loquacity in women was detested by our ancestors. Therefore, I shall put an end here, most reverend father, if I may offer thanks to your excellency, your majesty expressed in your kindness to us all in our family with love and charity and commend to you both myself and my brothers, and especially Leonardo,[59] who by your aid, your guidance, and your auspices has dedicated himself entirely to God. Accept him therefore, in whom now the signs of your love are reflected, in your protection and guardianship. If you do this—you will do it, however, because of your humanity—I do not doubt that one day he too will be a benefit and an ornament of our church. Farewell.

59. For Leonardo Nogarola, Isotta Nogarola's brother, see volume editors' introduction, n. 4.

I V
DAMIANO (1 4 3 8 – 4 1)

From 1434 to 1439, the literary career of Isotta Nogarola is documented by frequent letters, written by herself and by correspondents, which attest to her growing fame in the humanist circles centered on Venice and Verona. Thereafter, the record is spotty—although Nogarola's major works belong to the later period. A transitional series of letters dates from 1438 (the early ones coincident with the letters reviewed in chapter 3) through 1441, all exchanged between Nogarola and her elder compatriot Damiano dal Borgo (ca. 1390–1465/1466), a member of an important Veronese patrician family, yet inferior in status to the Nogarolas.[1] Dal Borgo's younger kinsmen, Tobia dal Borgo and Ludovico Cendrata, have already been encountered (see chapter 2).

Amid the eighteen mostly brief letters exchanged between Nogarola and dal Borgo are, in addition, four more Nogarola exchanged with dal Borgo's young son Eusebio. Three of the twenty-two letters (in total) date from the second half of 1438, during which the Nogarola family relocates in Venice; fifteen are securely from 1439, with one from 1439 or 1440; two more are from 1440; and a last from 1441. Although there are no later letters exchanged between the two, dal Borgo continued to know Nogarola and her family well, as appears from a 1461 letter—a full twenty years later—of the Venetian Ludovico Foscarini to dal Borgo (see chapter 6).

The Nogarola–dal Borgo correspondence has features that distinguish it from the polite and formal letters discussed in the preceding chapters.

---

1. Abel, letters 29–50, 1:206–69. For dal Borgo's career, Abel, 1: xxxi–xxxix and nn. 52, 53. We have based the hypothesis of a birthdate of ca. 1390 on a first official appointment in 1420. Abel informs us that Damiano's son Eusebio, with whom Nogarola has correspondence twice in 1439, will die in 1440; a sole son, Marcello, survives.

Although the two exchange descriptions of their literary labors and encouragements to study, these are not the main object of their correspondence. Dal Borgo conveys information in his letters—about Verona, about persons known to them both. Nogarola reveals her state of mind—variously intense or troubled. Even the descriptions of study are more personal and, to a modern ear, more genuine than the stylized portrayals found in more typical humanist letters. After the first months of 1439, moreover, their correspondence is exclusive: Nogarola writes no other letters that survive from early 1439 until 1451. Did she withdraw from her epistolary exchanges with important men of 1434–39, at first into an exclusive exchange with dal Borgo and then into silence, in response to the anonymous attack levied against her in late 1438 (see chapter 3)?

The Nogarola–dal Borgo correspondence is transitional, therefore, in that it marks the boundary between Nogarola's early literary career, in which she writes frequent and polite letters to patrician humanists introducing herself and displaying her talents, and a later career, in which she writes fewer works in accord with her scholarly and personal interests. Not only will the pattern of her life change over the period of this correspondence, but her tone changes as well. The quality of relationship Nogarola has with dal Borgo, while it remains puzzling, is more intimate by far than that displayed in the Veronese author's earlier letters. In many regards, it foreshadows the equally puzzling relationship between Nogarola and Foscarini (see chapter 6), among the most intriguing in the annals of humanist correspondence.

This account will simply review the correspondence *in seriatim*.

On August 20, 1439, dal Borgo wrote Nogarola, from Verona, to thank her for attempts to alleviate his pain caused by the death from plague of his brother and daughter—his daughter, whom he wished to educate as Nogarola had been, so that she might delight him in his old age.[2] Dal Borgo's style is complex, and his contorted sentences are at times difficult to untangle, but the tone of this letter is sincere and intimate. He addresses his correspondent, at one point, as "Isota amantissima" ("most loving Isotta"), a surprising characterization to be used by a married man of an unmarried woman in this age of exceptionally circumscribed sexual and personal behavior. He has written to Lavagnola, Nogarola's brother-in-law, about the military calamities of the day, should she care to write a history about them. The plague continues to rage, approaching its fortieth day, "and it does not cease to kill."[3]

---

2. Abel, 1:206–9.

3. Abel, 1:209: "Hec pestilentia male nobiscum agit, nam singulo die XXX. et XL. ferire et necare non desinit."

On September 10, not quite three weeks later, Nogarola responds (see below, no. 16) with an elegant consolatory letter that is both personal and correct, full of classical and Christian sentiments and allusions. She acknowledges, too, at the end, the news he had sent of the war in progress and closes warmly: "Do write frequently, for you will make me very happy."

After a lapse of some months, two brief letters of dal Borgo's written December 4, 1438, and January 2, 1439, give evidence of an ongoing, rather informal relationship.[4] In the first, dal Borgo comments on the waning of the plague, which gives him hope the Nogarola family will soon be returning to Verona. In the second, he refers to a report to Veronese officials (under the Venetian governor) of the war in Brescia by a citizen of that city and an oration that he, dal Borgo, had been asked to compose in response—more likely, an official report of the news relayed by the Brescian. He sends that work to Isotta, for her comment and correction—a striking request, given that he is the senior by age and gender. Both letters are addressed (and later letters similarly) "to his most dear [or most illustrious] and revered virgin, the lady Isotta Nogarola, beyond all others most affectionately."[5] Nogarola replies immediately in January 1439 to dal Borgo's missive (see below, no. 17), praising his account of Brescian events, "which whenever I read it I think that I am reading Sallust, Livy, Justin, so have you eloquently and learnedly described the deeds of the Brescians and that savage war." She thanks him for his high opinion of her and closes affectionately, as in her previous letter: "I pray you not to stop writing to me, since your letters please and delight me."

That same month, Eusebio dal Borgo, the young son of Damiano, addressed to Isotta some verse in schoolboy Latin,[6] and a letter, to which Isotta promptly responded with praise, fulsomely calling the few halting lines "carmina . . . suavissima" (see below, no. 18). She closes—and closes with a message to the young poet's father, asking him to send her the copy of her letter to Cardinal Cesarini (chapter 3, no. 11). This request is a sure

---

4. Abel, 1:215–16, 217–18.

5. Abel, 1:216, 218: "Carissime [clarissime] et spectate virgini domine Isote de Nogarolis sue preter ceteras colendissime." In the second of these letters, dal Borgo's closing words include greetings to Nogarola's mother, her brother Antonio and his wife, and her sister Bartolommea, his beloved *comater*, or "godmother," and her husband Jacopo Lavagnola. Given that their ages were close, or even that dal Borgo was older, it would be curious if Bartolommea were his godmother; this term may indicate some other linkage, which was nevertheless acknowledged and real, between the two families, and may help explain dal Borgo's familiar tone. Alternatively, *comatri* may be amended to *compatri*, "my compatriot;" cf. Abel, 1:226, where dal Borgo sends greetings to Lavagnola and Bartolommea both, "amantissimis compatribus meis." But then why, in the earlier case, would dal Borgo refer to only Bartolommea as a *compater*?

6. Abel, 1:221.

indication, if one were needed, that there was correspondence between these two figures beyond the letters that survive in our manuscripts.

On January 28, dal Borgo writes to Nogarola, expressing gratitude for her correction of his history and promising that he would find and send the requested letter to Cesarini.[7] Between these two messages, he describes in brief his wife's premature delivery of an infant girl and the illness and, it seems, death of both, "on which account I am exceedingly sad."[8] The letter is affectionately addressed as before.

The next letter from Nogarola, written in February or March 1439 (see below, no. 19), seems not to be a response to the previous. Nogarola describes how dal Borgo delights and inspires her, and urges him to continue writing. On March 31, dal Borgo writes to praise Nogarola and to encourage her return to Verona[9] to which she responds, in April (see below, no. 20), that she is gratified by his praise of her and urges further correspondence.

Dal Borgo's long letter of May 5 follows rapidly and is unique. Here, dal Borgo is in love with Nogarola.[10] Calling himself "the secret companion of your studies, whom you are setting on fire with your love," he affirms his loyalty: "I am so drawn to you by the kinship of our studies and the harmony of our minds that no division or discord could turn me away."[11] He wishes to awaken her ardor and, in order to do so, tells her a provocative and admonitory story from Pope Gregory the Great's moral dialogues on the early saints of Italy. It describes a woman who, widowed young, gave herself to God.[12] Overcome by illness, the doctors pronounced that the only cure was to return to sexual contact with a man—a prescription she refused. As a result of that refusal, the unhealthily accumulated heat of her body caused her to sprout a disfiguring beard. An astonishing, indeed bullying message to be conveyed to the unmarried daughter of a lofty patrician family by a

---

7. Abel, 1:224–26.

8. Abel, 1:225. Coniunx mea urgente tusci ante maturum fetum peperit puelam, que nec valet, nex puerpera, quare admodum tristis sum. . . ."

9. Abel, 1:229–30.

10. Abel, 1:233–39. "In love" is one explanation for the intensity and innuendo of this letter. Another might be that dal Borgo is under some form of extreme pressure, or that he experiences some form of hostility toward her (because of what she represents, or his anxieties over his own household), that explains the oddness of his rhetoric. He attributes his anger and depression to his frustration over the present conditions in Verona (*ex innato maerore pestis et urgentis belli*, 238). In any case, this letter is another and particular instance of their intense and sometimes heated correspondence, features unusual in humanist letters between a man and a woman.

11. Abel, 1:233–34; "Iam enim tantum comunione studiorum nostrorum et animorum concordia in te conversus sum, ut nec divisio nec discordia quevis me diversum agere possit."

12. The story is told at length in Abel, 1:234–37.

respected associate! The missive is addressed as early ones to Nogarola (see above), with the addition of an adverb: *amantissime* ("most lovingly") is added to *colendissime* ("affectionately").

In the works that survive, which clearly omit at least one letter in this sequence, Nogarola does not respond directly to this urgent, almost hectoring missive of dal Borgo's. Perhaps it alarmed her and deterred her from writing. She writes again at some point between May 5 and September 10, 1439 (see below, no. 21) a light and cursory letter excusing herself for not having written sooner: that failure is "neither because I have forgotten our friendship, nor because I am impeded by business, since my entire business is involved in the study of letters." Isotta has become a scholar, investing herself in study, not so as to shine among the young litterati of her set but as a vocation. He had asked her to write, so she does; but there is no mention in this letter of any "harmony of minds" that might unite the pair. If Nogarola discouraged dal Borgo's forthright claims in his letter of the previous May, that encounter seems not to have warranted her complete withdrawal from the relationshp, as this and subsequent letters suggest.

Not at all light-hearted is dal Borgo's letter of September 10, 1439, in which he rejoices at Nogarola's news that the family, and the child Ludovico, her brother, has survived the plague.[13] His tone is both playful and passionate in a letter of November 21,[14] in which he assures her of his admiration and their enduring friendship (although with somewhat less urgency than in his letter of the previous May): "You have blessed me, therefore, in having seized me by your love to such an extent that I could by no stroke be wrested from it, and so you have fastened to hold me firm for so long as you shall live, and I in turn, holding fast, give myself to you."[15]

Later in the same month of November, dal Borgo's son Eusebio again sent some lines of verse to Nogarola,[16] upon which she bestowed an elegant response within days (see below, no. 22). Soon thereafter, on December 3, she wrote to dal Borgo (see below, no. 23), commending his son, "first because I saw his extraordinary talent, and second because I easily learned from him how much you love me and I realized how much you value me. . . . I hope I can be worthy of your opinion of me!" Can it be that her last state-

---

13. Abel, 1:242–43.

14. Abel, 1:244–46.

15. Abel, 1:245: "Beasti itaque me quod adeo tuum in amorem corripuisti, ut nullo violenti distractu dirripi possim, sicque quod vixeris firmum tenere pepigisti et ego me tibi vicissim trado tenacem."

16. Abel, 1:247–48.

ment here alludes to her awareness of his professions of powerful and enduring friendship in his previous letter, from which she keeps herself aloof? She writes somewhat cryptically: "It remains only to say that your messenger Antonio Furlano brought your letters to me, and he will take care to do what pleases you, even if I am unwilling."

On some date between December 3, 1439, and April 18, 1440, Isotta sent dal Borgo the last letter she would contribute to this epistolary sequence (see below, no. 24). It is playful and sharp, a retort to his repetition (in a letter that evidently has not survived) of the statements in classical literature that women talk too much. She replies, with copious examples that make her case, that it is not that they talk more than men, but that they are more learned and indeed more effective than men. In closing, she crows a bit at her *tour de force*, since she has used the standard figures of the parade of women worthies to demonstrate not the equality but the superiority of women: "But since these things are true, I must ask you to tell me whether women are superior to men in verbosity or rather in eloquence and virtue? For if you confess yourself beaten, I shall rejoice and I shall congratulate you for having surrendered to me, a not insignificant victory."

If that is Nogarola's last word for dal Borgo, dal Borgo has more for her in letters dated April 19, 1440, November 30, 1440, and January 19, 1441. On the first of these dates, he writes angrily that she has not answered his letters: "The closer I approach you, the further you flee from me and avert your stopped-up ears;" he has come to Venice to see her and hopes she will not repel him (who brings a splendidly bound book as a gift) as she has his letters.[17] The second, following his journey west from Verona toward the lands around Brescia, reports at length on the ravaged countryside and wartorn lives there, including those of Brunorio Gambara and his wife Ginevra, Nogarola's sister, and their young child. Ginevra, just two years after marriage, and the experiences of childbirth and war, was completely changed: "Oh, how much she has changed from that Ginevra whose splendor outshown the stars of heaven!"[18] The last, brief letter, from Verona, also speaks of wartime conditions and contacts with Ginevra.

The epistolary trail of the relationship between dal Borgo and Nogarola

17. Abel, 1:259–60; 1:259: "Quanto tibi propius accedo tanto longius me fugis et obtussas aures avertis." Abel explains that the family had in fact temporarily removed to Padua (1:xxxvii), which would explain Nogarola's silence.

18. Abel, 1:262: "heu quantum est mutata ab illa Zenebra, nitore cuius hebetabant lucentia sidera celi." It is around this time that Ginevra sent dal Borgo a letter, from Pratalboino, in April 1440 (Abel, 2:336–38) and another in January 1441 (Abel, 2:339–42). Both ask him to greet for her the members of her family she has not seen and to deliver letters and messages.

is shifting and intense. Sometimes their letters have the courtly quality of humanist exchanges between persons who do not know each other intimately or do not reveal such intimacies in their quotation-strewn Latin showpieces. But at points, especially on dal Borgo's part, the Latin texts become the vehicle for the description of traumatic events and the expression of powerful emotions unusual for the age, and especially unusual between an adult man and an unmarried woman. Perhaps the medium of Latin prose, fenced all about with humanist conventions, permitted these two at least to breach to some extent the walls of rank and gender.

XVI

Isotta Nogarola to Damiano dal Borgo:[19]
Venice, September 10, 1438

Adducing classical and biblical examples (the latter for the first time in her letterbook), Nogarola urges dal Borgo to cease grieving, although his grief is understandable, for his brother and daughter in the plague then raging in Verona. She is grateful for his praise of her and assures him of her friendship; and as a compatriot she expresses concern for the calamities befalling their region as a result of the war between Venice and Milan.[20]

I got your letter in which I received your explanation of why you were so slow to tell me about your sorrow; you reinforced what you said with such worthy examples and so elegantly that I had to believe you—although I was unwilling. For I know that you are shocked and call me iron-hearted and cruel because I urge you to stop your weeping and give up your futile grieving for your loved ones. For to allay your sorrow I offer something

19. See King, *Venetian Humanism*, 10, 46, 376. Dal Borgo (also Burgo) also corresponded with Nogarola's friend Ludovico Foscarini, who admired his writings. See Foscarini's letters to dal Borgo of 1453 and 1461 in Abel, 2:84–87 and 159–60 (nos. 63, 81) respectively.

20. The wars in which Venice, sometimes aided by Florence, strove for supremacy in northern Italy against the dukes of Milan in the 1430s and 1440s are described in the chronicles of this period and in specialized studies of particular figures. See, for instance, the letters of Francesco Barbaro written from Brescia in the 1430s in his *Epistolario*, ed. Claudio Griggio, 2 vols. (Florence: L.S. Olschki, 1991); and the wartime ventures of Jacopo Antonio Marcello, for which King, *The Death of the Child*, chaps. 3 and 4. In September 1438 (when this letter was written), Francesco Sforza, condottiere of Duke Filippo Maria Visconti of Milan's army, lay siege to Tolentino, setting fire to farms and ravaging the countryside around the small city—the calamity to which dal Borgo here refers. The Tolentinans fought courageously, but in early October reports were already circulating that Sforza's troops had entered the city, pillaged its shops and homes, and were brutalizing the male population and raping the townswomen; on this see Francesco Filelfo's letter of October 1438, in Diana Robin, *Filelfo in Milan*, 45–47.

that will impel you to think otherwise of me and to approve my advice—and that is the example of heroes and saints. You have given me the examples of Job,[21] that holy man who grieved so long over the death of his son, and our Jesus, who bitterly wept over Lazarus,[22] and yet you wonder how it can be that I forbid you to mourn. But this is an easy response to these things, and one that you have understood less well because you are preoccupied with sorrow. Our most blessed Jerome[23] writes in his epistle to Tyasius that Jesus wept not over Lazarus's sleeping but over his rising, for he believed he was returning to the toils of the world.[24] And so we know it was not the death itelf of his friend he mourned, but that confused unbelievers were urging him to return Lazarus to a life of pain. Job and other men who lost their sons and brothers and mourned them believed that their dead were in hell, since, as the apostle said, death ruled from Adam to Moses, even over those who did not sin.[25] For it is permissible to mourn for the dead, but for those whom Orcus[26] has swallowed up, where punishment is an eternally boiling conflagration, not for those, as with your loved ones, whom Christ welcomes and who are in the company of a band of angels. But more to be mourned are those who linger too long in this tabernacle of death.[27] Do not lament their fate and ignore the troubles of this world.[28]

21. The book of Job is a favorite text of Nogarola's: the story of the good, God-fearing man's prosperity, his loss of everything in recompense for no wrongdoing on his part, and God's restoration of Job's prosperity.

22. See John 11:17–44 on the death and resurrection of Lazarus; 11:35 on Jesus weeping.

23. Saint Jerome (Latin: Eusebius Hieronymus, b. 345 C.E. in Stridon, Dalmatia; d. 419), early church Father. See chap. 8 for a full discussion.

24. "Iesum non doluisse Lazarum dormientem sed resurgentem": The image of Christ's seeing Lazarus as "sleeping" ("dormientem") rather than dead is important; Jerome in his letter puts all the emphasis on Christ's grief over Lazarus's *return* to the world; to him, death is only sleep, a temporary state. See *Jerome: Selected Letters*, trans. F. A. Wright (Cambridge, Mass.: Harvard University Press, 1933), Letter 60 to Heliodorus, 276: "Ipse salvator ploravit, quem sucitaturus erat."

25. Direct quote of Rom 5:14.

26. Orcus, the Roman god of death and also the land of the dead: a name rich in classical associations from Ennius to Petronius and typical vocabulary for a humanist who talks of Dante's Christian hell (*inferno*) in one breath and Virgil's classical Orcus in the next. Note that Nogarola invokes Orcus and the inferno but does not mention heaven.

27. "Sed magis dolendum est eos diutius in *hoc tabernaculo mortis* habitare" (our italics): this a strange image but is resonant of 2 Corinthians 5:1 and 2 Peter 1:12, 13 where *tabernaculum* (tent or temporary structure for worship) is a metaphor for the body. See also 1 Corinthians 3:16–17.

28. "Noli eorum sortem dolere et mundi calamitates relinquere": There is ambiguity in the Latin. *Noli* would generally govern both infinitives: "do not lament their fate and do not abandon the calamities. . . ." But an ellipsis of *necesse est* could be understood with the second infinitive: "do not lament and do relinquish the calamaties of this world." Everything hinges, we think,

But, "Think," you will say, "that I was their father and brother." But when I think that you grieve because of this, I do not forbid you to weep and I forgive you your tears. Yet seek moderation in your sorrow, and I warn you, and I will repeat it again and again, do not torment yourself with grief. Remember that you are a man: you must preserve your gravity and maintain your constancy. For it is shameful for you not to bear wisely the common and uncertain terminus that not one of us can avoid. And think, when this terminus comes to those who have exchanged life for death, that now it has been done for the best. Think that "nothing new has happened to you," and that, as Cicero also says, "we were born under the condition that our lives would be subject to all fortune's barbs; nor should we deny that we must live under the condition to which we were born."[29] Because of this, do not torment yourself if you want us to be well. I swear by God and the holy angels, whose company your daughter enjoys, that I have been equally troubled to the extent that I myself have deeply needed the consolation I wanted to give you. So much the law of friendship seems to demand. And so, make now an end to mourning and grieving; spare yourself and spare your friends who grieve over your sorow. Spare the dead themselves who do not wish this from you, and believe me, you can do nothing more honorable than this.

All that is left for me to say is that I give you enormous thanks for the accolades you have given me. If you decide, however, to follow my advice because of your love for me, this will be very pleasing to me, for there could be nothing more agreeable at this time than that I should learn that you have borne this our sorrow, yours and mine, courageously and with wisdom. Because on the back of your letter you implore me not to lessen my love toward you, I want you to know this one thing: "it grows from hour to hour, as fast as the green alder shoots up when the spring is young;"[30] and also,

---

on her choice of the word *calamitates*: mass, public disasters, not a personal tragedy. So we read the second infinitive as dependent on *noli* (" . . . and do not relinquish"). Note that at the end of this letter she asks dal Borgo to share with her his obvious involvement in the "calamities of our republic" (calamitates rei publicae nostrae). *Calamitas* is a rather specific word in Latin, usually used to describe a specific military disaster in which thousands lose their lives.

29. Cf. Cicero *Epistulae ad familiares* 5.16.2: "Homines nos ut esse meminerimus ea lege natos, ut omnibus telis fortunae proposita sit vita nostra, neque recusandum, quominus ea, qua nati sumus, conditione vivamus . . . Nihil accidisse nobis novi cogitemus;" and Nogarola (212–13): "Cogita nihil novi tibi accidisse, cogita nos ea conditione, ut inquit Cicero, natos esse, ut omnibus telis fortunae praeposita sit vita nostra, neque recusandum essem quo minus ea qua nati sumus conditione vivamus." Nogarola has carefully recalled Cicero almost verbatim here, and so it has been placed within quotation marks; her readers would have recognized the locus.

30. Virgil *Eclogues* 10, 73–74: "Gallo, cuius amor tantum mihi crescit in horas / quantum vere novo viridis se subicit alnus"; cf. chap. 3, no. 14 to Niccolò Barbo. In neither place does she

"sooner, each wandering over the other's frontiers, shall the Parthian in exile drink the Arar, and Germany the Tigris, than that look of his shall fade from my heart."[31] Vale.

The bravery of the Tolentinans, whose circumstances you relayed to me in your letter, has pleased me very much. I beg you to write me more often telling me how it goes there and also about the calamities of our republic—but God will bring an end also to these things. Do write frequently, for you will make me very happy. Again, farewell. From Venice.

XVII

Isotta Nogarola to Damiano dal Borgo: Venice, January 1439

Nogarola praises dal Borgo for his history of events in Brescia, and assures him of her friendship.

I rejoice in God, and thank Him, that my mind is so admired by you, that I might be she to whom that glowing praise in your most elegant and ornate composition could be given, which whenever I read it I think that I am reading Sallust, Livy, Justin, so eloquently and learnedly have you described the deeds of the Brescians and their savage war.[32] And wisely indeed has Andrea Mocenigo[33] assigned to you the task of composing that history, since he knew your eloquence and wisdom to be so great that you could worthily fulfill the request of that eloquent man. For all who see your writings to me and know me to be so highly regarded by you form a lofty opinion of me, since, as you know, great praise is bestowed on those whom praiseworthy men praise. And so I thank you for your praise of me and will

---

cite Virgil, but the language—suddenly bursting into hexameter verse—is so foreign to Nogarola's idiom that it has been put in quotation marks to indicate that it would have immediately sounded like a quote to her contemporaries.

31. Nogarola quotes verbatim here (substituting *tuus* for *illius* in 1.63) from Virgil *Eclogues* 1.61–63: "antepererratis amborum finibus exsul / aut Ararim Parthus bibet aut Germania Tigrim / quam nostro illius labatur pectore vultus." See *Virgil: Eclogues, Georgics, Aeneid I–VI*, trans. H. Rushton Fairclough, rev. G. P. Goold (Cambridge, Mass.: Harvard University Press, 1999, 29).

32. Sallust, Livy, and Justin (2d–3d centuries C.E.) are the canonical Roman military historians, although Justin is comparatively obscure.

33. For Andrea Mocenigo, the Venetian nobleman who was appointed captain of Verona in 1436 and provveditore in campo (supervisor of the Venetian mercenary army) in 1438, also centered at Verona, see Abel, 1 n. 54.

give thanks so long as I live. I pray you not to stop writing to me, since your letters please and delight me. Farewell.

Marginal distich in ms. R: From this scrap of paper the manly virtue of a woman/ springs forth; farewell, rare woman of Italy.

XVIII

Isotta Nogarola to Eusebio dal Borgo.[34]
Venice, January 1439

Nogarola praises Eusebio, Damiano's son, for his poem, and encourages his further efforts. She asks him to relay a message to his father: she requests the return of her letter to Cardinal Cesarini, which is in his hands.

*Y*our very sweet poems that were recently brought to me delighted me greatly, and when I think of the feeling in them, I cannot fail to admire them. While you gave up almost all other pursuits, you compared yourself to this one man and you practiced so that you would attain skill at versification. For our Ennius called the poets holy men because they seemed to have been entrusted to us as though by some gift from the gods.[35] Along the same lines, Cicero has said that the poets derive their power from nature itself, whereas men in all other pursuits rely on skill and perseverance.[36] Because of this, I beg you not to stop writing, but as he [Cicero] himself said, it is not those who watch, but those who run, who win the crown."[37] Vale.

By the way, I am asking you to convey my message verbatim to your father, that he should send me a copy of the letter I wrote to the Cardinal

---

34. See n. 1 above.

35. Nogarola quotes varbatim and paraphrases from Cicero *Pro Archia* 8.18, reversing the order of Cicero's *sententiae:* "Atqui . . . accepimus, *ceterarum rerum studia* et doctrina et praeceptis et *arte constare, poetam natura ipsa valere* et mentis virbus excitari et quasi divino quodam spiritu inflari. Qua re suo iure *noster ille Ennius sanctos appellat poetas, quod quasi deorum aliquo* dono atque *munere commendati nobis esse videantur.*" These are Nogarola's words (122–23): "Nam *noster ille Ennius poetas sanctos appellat, quod aliquo deorum munere commendati nobis esse videntur,* et a Cicerone dictum est *poetam natura ipsa valere, cetera vero arte et studio constare.*"

36. From the *Pro Archia;* see n. 36.

37. We have been unable to locate the source of this quotation: "ut inquit ille, nec spectantibus coronae sed certantibus parantur." Nogarola, however, appears to believe that the author is Cicero. The same sentence appears in her 1438 letter to Tobia dal Borgo (see above, chap. 2, no. 10, n. 79).

Sant' Angelo[38] if possible. I gave him a copy that he said he would give to the Veronese governor[39] because he wanted to read it. Vale, Again. From Venice.

XIX

Isotta Nogarola to Damiano dal Borgo: Venice, February or March 1439

Nogarola tells dal Borgo that she enjoys receiving his letters and promises to write more often.

I rejoice whenever it is time to write to you, not only because when I receive your letters the style of speaking itself, elaborate in both its images and ideas, gives great pleasure while I read, but also because sorrow, so great that it does not subside easily, never invades my mind; rather, when I write to you and think about you, I revive and become myself once more. And so, lest I be deprived of the sweet conversation of your letters, I give you my promise and, because of my extraordinary affection for you, willingly grant your request, that whatever may enter my mind, however trifling, I shall write you about it. Ah, then, most learned Damiano, rouse yourself and exert your mind, virtue, eloquence, that I may have many of your letters, since I gain from them not only utility but immortal glory. Your duty it will be to write me often and show me the right way, so that I may the more boldly follow you and join in this race. Farewell.

XX

Isotta Nogarola to Damiano dal Borgo: Venice, April 1439

Nogarola urges dal Borgo to write and will write often in turn; she thanks him for singing her praises and hopes he will continue.

I want my letters to annoy you sometimes not because of their clumsiness—may Jupiter forbid it!—but their frequency. I do not know if

38. The cardinal she refers to (Cardinalis Sancti Angeli in her letter) is Giuliano Cesarini, to whom she writes in chap. 3, no. 11 and whom she met at or en route to the Council of Basil in 1438.

39. The "Venetian governor" is probably Andrea Mocenigo, mentioned in dal Borgo's letter of January 2, Abel, 1:217–18 (no. 82), and Nogarola's response, no. 17.

this could ever happen since your kindness and goodwill are so great—and so great in fact that not only I but the other citizens who have experienced it (and most have, so help me God) are witnesses, but the whole city sings these verses of Virgil's:

> What happy ages brought you? What great parents gave birth to you?
> As long as the rivers run in the narrows, as long as the shadows wander
> across the mountains and the pole feeds the vaulted heavens, your
> honor, your fame, and your praises will forever remain.[40]

As the immortal God is my witness, Damiano, there is no one to whom I am more indebted than you. You adorn and ennoble me so extraordinarily, and you never tire of loving and glorifying me.

There is no one who, when he sees how extraordinary your love is for me, does not feel and think that I am marvelously endowed with virtue. But since this is the case, I should give great thanks to God that I am part of your circle of friends, while I have gained acclaim under of the shade of your studies and have been confirmed by your testimony. Come therefore, praise me, commend me with all your powers, since nothing you can do will please me more than this. Vale.

XXI

Isotta Nogarola to Damiano dal Borgo: Venice, between May 5 and September 10, 1439

Nogarola assures dal Borgo that she has not written not because she is no longer his friend, but because she is deeply engaged in her studies. She writes now and will write more in the future.

I am anxious indeed when I think of what excuse I might give you as to why I have not written to you more often, since I do so neither

---

40. Virgil *Aen.* 1.606–609:
> Quae te tam laeta tulerunt
> Saecula, qui tanti talem genuere parentes?
> In freta dum fluvii current, dum montibus umbrae
> Lustrabunt, convexa polus dum sidera pascet,
> Semper honos nomenque tuum laudesque manebunt.

Nogarola's citation corresponds perfectly with the modern edition (*Virgil: Eclogues, Georgics, Aeneid I–VI*, 304). The translation, however, is ours.

because I have forgotten our friendship nor because I am impeded by business, since my entire business is involved in the study of letters. But this has worried me when I consider that you are the kind of man to whom nothing is suitable unless it is important or extraordinary. But now since I have diligently honored all the obligations of friendship, I thought I must not leave this duty undone. For you have frequently asked me to write more often. And so I have decided that it would be unlike me not to respond to your wishes. As Cicero says, "it is not only difficult to oppose the demands of friendship—especially in a worthy cause—but it is also wrong."[41] Since this is the case, I send you this letter so that I may do what I have often promised. Farewell. From Venice.

XXII

Isotta Nogarola to Eusebio dal Borgo: Venice, toward the end of November 1439

Nogarola praises Eusebio for his poem and discourses on the importance of the liberal arts.

*Y*our poems, in which I could easily see your literary talent and your affinity with your father's nobility, gave me great pleasure. And when I think about the feeling in those poems, I am delighted and impressed. For I see that the beginnings of your youth and nobility promise so much for you that I can see you will grow to be an absolutely excellent man. Indeed, you should be extolled and celebrated to the skies. For what young man do we see in this age endowed with such virtue and yet so drawn to literary studies by his own inclination and without any outside prompting? I think no one. But I venture this opinion privately, so as not to ask it publicly. Indeed, such talent comes from a divine mind. You are doing the right thing. For what shall I say is a pursuit more brilliant than literature? We have read how passionately our ancestors loved learning, for they believed that the supreme father of the universe had never given them anything better.

The philosopher Euclides[42] had such a desire for knowledge that, when the Athenians decreed that if any citizen from Megara was caught setting foot into Athens he would be put to death, he managed to journey to Athens

---

41. Cicero *De Amicitia* 26: "Studiis *enim generorum*, praesertim in re bona, *cum* difficile est, tum *ne* aequuam quidem obsistere."

42. The anecdote about the Socratic philosopher Euclides of Megara from Aulus Gellius 7.10.2–4 is also quoted in full in Nogarola's letters to Niccolo Venier (chap. 2, no. 12) and in her oration in praise of Saint Jerome (see below, chap. 8, no. 30).

by night considering the danger of no importance.[43] Before evening came, he donned the long tunic of a woman, wrapped himself in a robe of many colors, and veiled his head. He then went from his own house in Megara to Socrates' so that he could partake of the talk and wisdom of the philosopher. Before dawn, he made the twenty-mile trip back home again disguised in the same garb. And rightly so, for what else is there in which we can truly take pride unless it is in preparing ourselves for studies in the virtues? And so I urge you, even though only the smallest urging is needed, to use every effort, all care and diligence, in the pursuit of virtue, and I want you to know this one thing: that I care for you so much that now I actually appear to love you, whereas before I merely esteemed you; I accept you with my whole heart, and my love for you seems to grow daily. Farewell, and do not fail to write something. From Venice.

XXIII

Isotta Nogarola to Damiano dal Borgo: Venice, December 3, 1439

Nogarola thanks dal Borgo for his confidence in her, shown by his having his son Eusebio send her his work for comment. She praises his fatherly virtues.

*T*wice I have delighted in the poems of your darling Eusebio, first because I saw his extraordinary talent, and second because I easily learned from him how much you love me and I realized how much you value me. I thank you, who so highly rate my mind and virtue that I may be one who can give proper praise to the noble first efforts of your son. I hope I can be worthy of our opinion of me! But I speak not just for myself, who has little expertise or judgment in this matter; but I have no doubt that he should be celebrated and extolled to the skies by any eloquent and virtuous man. And indeed Cicero points to this maxim: "The greatest inheritance that descends from [parents] to their children and far greater than any patrimony is the glory of virtue and of great deeds, and to disgrace this must be judged a crime and [dishonor]."[44] Because he understood this with supreme reason, Eusebio has immersed himself in letters since he knew that he would obtain glory

---

43. Note the idiom *nihili facere* with the genitive of worth (*nihili*): to consider of no importance.

44. Cicero *De Officiis* 1.121: " . . . optima autem hereditas a *patribus* traditur liberis, omnique patrimonio praestantior, gloria virtutis rerumque gestarum: cui dedecori esse, nefas et *impium* iudicandum est."

for himself and for you his father by no other means except by learning, the queen of all the other virtues. Therefore, I will not fail to praise him with the greatest accolades—and I think he should rank first among eulogists along with Hesiod![45] How could you not rejoice and name yourself fortunate to have such a son and thank God? But so that you will not think the purpose of this letter is more to flatter than to tell the truth, I end here and ask you to keep me informed of the health of our lord Io. Fed.[46] and take care that you and your household fare well, which will be most pleasing to me. It remains only to say that your messenger Antonio Furlano[47] brought your letters to me, and he will take care to do what pleases you, even if I am unwilling. Farewell. From Venice December 3, 1439.

XXIV

Isotta Nogarola to Damiano dal Borgo: Venice, April 18, 1439 or 1440

Dal Borgo had commented on the legendary loquacity of women, but Nogarola responds sharply with a demonstration that women exceed men in virtue and excellence and is pleased by her triumph over him.

*Y*our letter yesterday disturbed me a great deal, for I learned from it that you trust the words of our comic poet who claims a silent woman has never been found in any age,[48] since you say women are more loquacious than men. But this, I say, is the result of a few women behaving in a way that makes all of us women appear to deserve such an indictment. This is something I thought you would never say: first because you were writing to me when you surely knew I would take offense, and second because night and day you are reading about how many women surpass not only other women but also men in every kind of virtue and excellence and,

---

45. Hesiod, one of the oldest known Greek poets, was author of *Theogony* (on the origin and genealogy of the gods) and *Works and Days* (advice of living a life of honest work). See *The Oxford Classical Dictionary*, ed. Simon Hornblower and Antony Spawforth, 3d ed. (New York: Oxford University Press, 1996), 700.

46. We cannot identify this figure.

47. We cannot identify this figure.

48. Plautus *Aulularia* 124. The same text is cited above in her letter to Ermolao Barbaro (see chap. 1, no. 1); see no. 26.

we claim, in eloquence.[49] Just look at Cornelia, the mother of the Gracchi,[50] and Amesia,[51] who in pleading a cause before the Roman people, delivered a brilliant oration in a crowded assembly hall. Think of Affrania, the wife of the senator Lucinius Buco, who pled the same kinds of causes in the forum.[52] Did not Hortensia repeatedly do the same?[53] Did not Sappho's[54] poetry flow with wondrous sweetness? In how many verses by learned men have we heard sung the fame of Portia, Fannia,[55] and the rest of the female race? Look at Camilla, whom Turnus attended, as the poet tells us, with so much honor.[56] Did not Thomiris, queen of the Scythians, slay Cyrus, king of the Persians and his whole army, so that not even a herald survived?[57] Did not the Amazons increase their republic without men? Did not Marpesia, Lampedo, and Orythia subdue the greater part of Europe and occupy a number of cities in Asia without men?[58] For so powerful were these women in their extraordinary knowledge and virtue in war that it seemed impossible for Hercules and Theseus to capture the Amazons' arms for their king.[59] Penthesilea fought like a man in the Trojan war among the bravest Greeks; the poet testifies thus: "A raging Penthesilea blazes among the armed men."[60]

49. " . . . Plures feminae non modo mulieres sed etiam viros in omni genere virtutis . . . Volumus in eloquentia aspice Corneliam . . ." A period seems to be missing after "eloquentia."

50. On famous Roman republican women, Nogarola's source is Valerius Maximus; on Cornelia, mother of Gracchi, see Val. Max. 4.4.

51. On Amesia or Maesia oratrix see Val. Max. 8.3.1.

52. On Affrania or Afrania oratrix see Val. Max. 8.3.2.

53. See again Val. Max. 8.3.3 on Hortensia, the oratrix made famous in the Renaissance by Boccaccio's *De Claris Mulieribus*, a text Nogarola does not cite in this tale. She is also not working with Plutarch's "Mulierum Virtutes" from the *Moralia*.

54. On the epithet "dulcis" for Sappho's verses, Aulus Gellius's 19.9.4 remark about her songs as "erotica dulcia et venusta" indicates a well-established tradition about Sappho that survives into the second century C.E. She is not mentioned in the *Lives* of Plutarch or in Valerius Maximus.

55. On the bravery of Portia, the conspirator Brutus's wife, Nogarola consulted Val. Max. 3.2.15; on Fannia's courage she paraphrased Val. Max. 8.2.3.

56. On Camilla the sources are Virgil *Aen.* 11 and Giovanni Boccaccio *Famous Women*, chap. 39.

57. The story of Queen Thomiris's (or Tamyris) relentless pursuit and destruction of Cyrus and his forces is told in Val. Max. 9.10. ext.1 and Boccaccio *Famous Women*, chap. 49.

58. The stories of the Amazon queens Lampedo and Marpesia and her daughter Orythia and their conquest of European as well as Asian cities are told in Boccaccio *Famous Women*, chaps. 11–12 and 19–20, respectively.

59. Boccaccio *Famous Women*, chaps. 19–20.1: "[Orythia] adeo militaris discipline sans laudas extulit, ut arbitraretur Euristeus, Micenarum rex, durum posse bello eius obtineri baltheum; ob id aiunt debitori Herculi tanquam maximum iniunctum ut illud afferret eidem." This is surely the passage Nogarola was reading, about the difficulty of obtaining the arms of the Amazons.

60. Virgil *Aen.* 1.491: "Penthesilea furens mediisque in militibus ardet."

But since these things are true, I must ask you to tell me whether women are superior to men in verbosity or rather in eloquence and virtue? For if you confess yourself beaten, I shall rejoice and I shall congratulate you for having surrendered to me—a not insignificant victory. Vale.

V

THE BOOK-LINED CELL
(1 4 4 1   T O   E A R L Y   1 4 5 0 s)

In 1441, at the age of twenty-three, Isotta Nogarola returned to Verona, where she lived for the rest of her life. She chose—and her family apparently permitted her to do so—neither of the two choices available to young women of her social rank: she did not marry, and she did not enter a convent.[1] Instead, she remained in her mother's household (shared with her brother Antonio in the 1440s and '50s and with her brother Ludovico in the 1450s and '60s) until the latter's death in 1461 and thereafter perhaps in Foscarini's household; it was inconceivable that a woman in her situation might live alone. Although her most important works are written during this period and attest to her continued reading, thinking, and productivity, she has left, to our knowledge, no works describing her life in the anomalous condition of a permanently unmarried woman.

Her contemporaries, however, do tell us a little. This chapter looks at the letters of five contemporaries (only one of which, that of Lauro Quirini, is published here), which portray Nogarola from 1441 into the mid-1450s as a scholar and, as two of them perceive her, a holy woman. The next chapter looks at her relationships with one figure in particular whose words deepen and make more complex our understanding of her life at home alone amid her books.

All five of our witnesses are aware of and approve of Nogarola's dedication of her life to study. That decision she had already forecast, sounding a new note, in her letter of mid-1439 to Damiano dal Borgo (see above, 000): she had not written him, she explains, "neither because I have forgotten our friendship nor because I am impeded by business, since my en-

---

1. The problem of limited career options for women is discussed above in both the volume and series editors' introductions.

tire business is involved in the study of letters." Two of them explicitly, and two others in passing, also commend her for her commitment to religious or "spiritual" or "higher" studies. Two allude to devotional and ascetic behavior resembling that engaged in by a female type familiar in the era: the holy woman, alone while in the world, whose works of self-sacrifice were deemed salvific to those about her. Both professional clerics and canons of the cathedral at Verona, they comment not only on "holy books" (which might include the works of the Christian Fathers, whom Nogarola certainly studied, which were often found in the libraries of humanist scholars, as well as saints' lives, mystical guides, and other devotional works), but also objects: crosses, images.

Did Nogarola enter into a religious, as well as a scholarly retreat, in 1441? Did she do so willingly, or was that role imposed upon her by cultural expectations? Or was the construction of Nogarola as a holy woman the fantasy of male observers (perhaps charged with a certain component of sexual desire) who could not otherwise understand the circumstances in which an unmarried woman, alone, studied and wrote? The written record cannot yield certainty on these issues, or illumine our understanding of Nogarola's own thoughts during those years in her *libraria cella*, her "book-lined cell," as contemporary Matteo Bosso named it: was it a library? or a convent cell?

The first of the five witnesses to Nogarola's middle years was, in fact, a woman—the humanistically trained Costanza Varano (1428–47), herself an author of some few humanist works.[2] A descendant on both sides of northern Italian warrior noble clans and a casualty of the signorial political structures of the era, Varano was raised in Pesaro following the murder of her father and eviction from the city of Camerino. She was subsequently married to Alessandro Sforza (brother of Francesco Sforza, who became duke of Milan in 1451). Her letter to Nogarola says nothing of this political turmoil, but praises the Veronese woman for her learning and her exquisite letters (which Varano had apparently seen in Pesaro). Although she does not urge upon Nogarola a religious life or a commitment to virginity, she does note that in choosing the scholarly life, her Veronese contemporary is opting for the goods of the spirit over those of the body and predicts that her scholarly

2. Abel, 2:3–6 and 7–8, for letter and poem, respectively. The letter, but not the poem, is translated in King and Rabil, *Her Immaculate Hand*, 55–56; the same volume prints other works by Varano: a second letter to another learned woman, Cecilia Gonzaga, 53–54; and orations to Bianca Maria Visconti and the people of Camerino, 39–41 and 42–44. The letter and poem are also printed in the edition of Varano's works by Lamius and in Bettinelli, cited in "Book-Lined Cells," 83 (from *Her Immaculate Hand*). For Varano, see Abel, xliv and no. 58; and Margaret King, "Thwarted Ambitions: Six Learned Women of the Renaissance," *Soundings* 59 (1976): 280–304.

achievement will constitute a greater "fruitfulness" than the fruits the body might produce—meaning the children who would be born from marriage, a condition that Nogarola has renounced: "For nothing could be more expedient and fruitful for women than to forget the needs of the body and to reach out strenuously for those goods which fortune cannot destroy."[3]

The long letter of the Venetian nobleman Lauro Quirini (ca. 1420 to ca. 1475/79) advising Nogarola on an advanced course of study is the second witness to the Veronese scholar's middle years.[4] A humanist and philosopher (capable of reading Aristotle in the original Greek) and, at the time of this composition, a student of law, Quirini would write important philosophical and political works as well as orations and other occasional pieces before his retirement in 1452 to Candia (Crete), where he lived for nearly thirty years more as a landed proprietor and entrepreneur. The advice to Nogarola is characteristically ill-tempered in its criticism of intellectuals Quirini finds limited or wrongheaded, but highly generous in its treatment of the learned Veronese woman. He had heard about her from her brother Leonardo, another Paduan student; and the Venetian nobleman Giovanni Dolfin had brought to Padua a volume of her letters that had impressed him.[5] He treats her, accordingly, exactly as he might a male colleague; and indeed, he might as well be addressing one, since he indicates that by her high intellectual achievements Nogarola has in fact become a man: "you have overcome your own nature:"

> For that true virtue, which is proper to men, you have pursued with a unique diligence—acquiring not just a mediocre excellence, as most men do, but that which befits a man of whole and perfect wisdom . . .[6]

The substance of Quirini's recommendations is also unusual. After a recitation of the familiar great women of antiquity, Quirini urges Nogarola to study the most advanced and difficult philosophical authors and issues,

3. Abel, 2:5: "Nihil enim conducibilius ac magis frugiferum dominabus esse potest, quam posthabitis corporis commodis ad ea tendere summo conatu quae non possit labefactare fortuna."

4. Abel gives the possible dates of this letter as 1443–48 and 1451/1452; the 1440s are far more likely. For Quirini, see King, *Venetian Humanism,* 419–21 and *ad indicem.*

5. For Leonardo, see introduction, n. 4; Giovanni Dolfin is unknown to us, but see King, *Venetian Humanism, ad indicem,* for Giorgio and Pietro Dolfin.

6. Abel, 2:12: "Iure igitur es tu quoque, Isota praeclara, summis laudibus prosequenda, quippe quae naturam, ut sic dixerim, tuam superasti. Virtutem enim veram, quae virorum propria est, singulari industria es consecuta, nec eam quidem mediocrem, ut plerique virorum, sed ut integerrimae perfectaeque sapientiae virum decet . . ."

notably Aristotle (partly available in sound Latin translations) and the commentators available to her in Latin (Boethius and the Arab philosophers,
whose works were translated into Latin). Although, as he assumes, she may
be unable to read philosophical texts in Greek, he is hopeful that there
will be Latin translations of all the Aristotelian works and the other Greek
thinkers. He warns her against scholastic authors and commentators, commending only Thomas Aquinas. The curriculum that Quirini urges upon
Nogarola is that of a university student of philosophy, a difficult one for even
the most advanced students. "Give your whole heart then . . . to philosophy
alone, for I want you to be not semilearned, but to have knowledge of all
the good arts . . . [i.e., humanistic studies], as well as the science of human
and divine things [i.e., philosophy and theology]."[7]

Quirini, evidently, unhesitatingly approves of Nogarola's intellectual
pursuits and urges her to continue and even to extend them to more esoteric
subjects. He is not concerned with her body, her virginity, her family, or her
affections: simply the higher training of her mind.

The last three witnesses all wrote in the early 1450s, at undetermined
times: Andrea Contrario (before 1410 to 1473),[8] Matteo Bosso (1428–
1502),[9] and Paolo Maffei (b. ca. 1380).[10] Contrario's long letter is a classic
humanistic epistle revealing little about Nogarola's life, which Contrario
knew only from the reports of others. He had been moved to love her when
recently, in Rome, there had come into his hands some of her letters; and
reading these reinforced the reports of her extraordinary achievements that
he had previously heard about from "many great and illustrious and most
studious men" in Venice or Padua.[11] After six hundred years, in which the

---

7. Abel, 2:21–22: "Proinde huic uni rei, toto, ut aiunt, pectore incumbe, volo enim te non semi-
doctam esse, sed cunctarum bonarum disciplinarum peritiam habere . . . et humanarum atque
divinarum rerum scientiam noscere."

8. Abel, 2:133–42. Abel dates this letter, written from Rome, tentatively as 1451–52 or 1457–
62. Its contents suggest the early date. For Contrario, see Abel, 1:xliv and n. 59; King, *Venetian
Humanism*, 352–53 and *ad indices*.

9. Abel, 2:127–32. Abel gives the range of dates for Bosso's letter, written in Verona, as 1451–
56, but it was probably closer to 1451. Bosso refers to Nogarola's brother Antonio as part of
the household, a situation that would not have been true after the Nogarola property disputes
of 1453; see below, chap. 6. See on Bosso's career, see Abel, 1:lxiv–lxv and n. 74.

10. The letter in Abel, 2:23–27. For Maffei, see Abel, lxvii–xxviii and n. 78.

11. Abel, 2:133: "Facilius intelligi quam explicari potest, Isotta illustris, quam acriter ad te aman-
dum permotus sim, postquam proximis diebus Romae praeter opinionem pervenere ad manus
meas nonnullae tuae epistolae dignae profecto expectatione tua, quibus lectis avidius facile per-
spexi, quod iam pridem, credo Venetiis vel Patavii, complures magni et illustres viri studiosissimi
rerum tuarum non sine tua ingenti laude et gloria de te mihi narrare solebant."

classics had been neglected, it is astonishing that a woman has been able to recover their spirit so completely in her smooth and lucid Latin. You are to be celebrated "since you . . . are the ornament not only of our sex and your city, but indeed the adornment of the whole of Italy and the splendor of this age. . . ."[12] Contrario, the professional humanist stationed in remote Rome, makes no mention of any religious dimension of Nogarola's studies.

The Veronese canon Matteo Bosso (who entered the religious life in 1451, not long before this letter was written) expresses his reverence for Nogarola, "holy and venerable sister in the lord," and refers to their long experience of friendship.[13] He is concerned that she is a woman, always a danger to a man intent on serving God because of the power of the flesh. It was not so when he was *parvulus*, a schoolboy:

> I used to come to you after school and my lessons, and pass the time with you and with your most noble and wise mother where I would sit in your book-lined cell (*libraria cella*) and happily hear you gently singing sweet hymns and the rhythms of the psalms.[14]

Now, however, converted to the religious life, he must not even think of women, nor engage with them in friendship, since "innumerable men have been made captive by woman, and among them the wisest and holiest."[15] Nevertheless, he cherishes her—"Your mind, your learning, the beauty and splendor of your intact body, your abstinence, frugality, prayers, and other virtues I shall always revere and carry about engraved upon my mind"—and her worthy and eloquent works, whose purity is such they do not lead him to think of the sex of the author: "So also as I read your works and letters I think of nothing less, indeed, than of Woman; so does their dignity hold me, weighty with charm and eloquence."[16] Fearful of women, of even the

---

12. Abel, 2:138: "Iuvat certe, Isotta clarissima, et decet de te magnifice loqui, . . . quum sis non modo amplissimo generi tuo atque patriae decus, sed etiam totius Italiae ornamentum atque huius seculi splendor. . . ."

13. Abel, 2:127: "sancta et venerabilis in domino soror . . ."

14. Abel, 2:128: "Ad te e ludo scholaque ibam, tecum quoque et cum nobilissima ac sapientissima tua matre nugabar librariaque in tua cella et assidebam, ubi dulces hymnos et psalmorum numeros te suave canentem laetus audiebam."

15. Abel, 2:128–29: "Nunc autem ad religiosam vitam habitumque conversus duxi mea quantum fragilitas potest . . . de foemina non cogitare, ne amice quidem versari, a qua captos innumeros et eos profecto sapientissimos atque sanctissimos lego."

16. Abel, 2:131: "Tuum ego ingenium, tuam docrinam, decus splendoremque intacti corporis tui, abstinentiam, frugalitatem, orationes, caeterasque virtutes semper venerabor tuas et insculptas mente gestabo. . . . Sic quoque editiones et epistolas lego tuas, ut nihil profecto tum minus quam de foemina cogitem; ita me tenet earum dignitas et cum lepore et eloquentia pondus."

thought of women, of the words wrought by the ends of a woman, still he loves and admires her.

Finally, the elderly Veronese canon Paolo Maffei (who had entered the religious life in 1425) while ambivalent—he opens by addressing Nogarola as "a most learned woman" and closes asking her for her prayers—tends also in his letter to portray his subject as a religious figure. Maffei had composed a book for her but could not send it yet, because he was unable to find a scribe. In the meantime, he had advice to offer:

> Meanwhile, dedicate yourself entirely to God, and hurry to prepare for Him a pleasant domicile in your virginity, as there is nothing more excellent, after the worship of God, than adhering most firmly to a perpetual virginity. . . . [17]

In doing so, although many holy women could be named as models, she should especially think of Mary:

> But for you the virginity of Mary, who brought God to earth, is put forward as an exemplar of perfect holiness. . . . And so let Mary be for you, O Isotta, the unique model of living, of morality, of the worship of God, of the cultivation of virtue, so that, since she is of women the most beautiful of the beautiful, the most holy of the holy, indeed the most holy of all men and all angels too, you must try as much as it be possible to imitate and to enact her image in your mind and body.[18]

For Maffei, evidently, Nogarola was a holy woman who, despite her ample erudition, must follow the time-worn path of female holiness: the imitation of the virginity of Mary.

These two clergymen, respected figures in their own right, share, predictably, the vision of a woman's role constructed by the Latin church and prevailing since at least the fourth century. It may have been a vision shared, too, by many people of Nogarola's generation and even possibly by Nogarola herself. The three secular authors represented here, while they do not, and could not, hold modern views of woman's capacity and continue to

17. Abel, 2:24: "Interim vindica te totam deo et iocundum in tua virginitate domicilium praeparare festina, firmissime retinens post dei cultum . . . celibatu perpetuo nihil esse praestantius."

18. Abel, 2:25, 26: "Tibi vero Mariae virginitas ad exemplar totius sanctimoniae proponatur, quae deum traxit ad terras. . . . Quare sit Maria tibi, o Isota, singularis forma vivendi, componendi mores, colendi deum, sectandi virtutes, ut quoniam ipsa est pulchrarum pulcherrima sanctarumque sanctissima mulierum, immo et vivorum omnium et angelorum, eiusce simulacrum in tua mente et corpore quantum possibile fuerit imitari, exprimere coneris."

see high achievement in women as exceptional, nevertheless fully endorse a program of secular studies for Nogarola. Certainly, Quirini's muscular curriculum of advanced philosophical studies seems more plausibly to describe Nogarola's own concerns than the injunctions to virginity of Bosso and Maffei. So, too, do the invitations of Varano and Contrario to pursue humanist interests. Whereas in this chapter these alternate views of ideal women's roles have been presented, in the next chapter, the two extremes of possibility will be embodied in one figure, that of the Venetian nobleman, statesman, and humanist Ludovico Foscarini.

XXV

Lauro Quirini to Isotta Nogarola:
Padua, 1445–48? 1451/1452? [19]

Quirini has heard of Nogarola's interests, has read her letters, and has been urged by her brother Leonardo, a fellow student at the university of Padua, to guide her further studies. He writes enthusiastically, praising her achievements and urging her to the most serious philosophical studies.

Some sort of almost boorish shyness,[20] remarkable Isotta, greatest glory of the women of our age, has restrained me to this day from writing to you, whom, although silently, I have certainly cherished most affectionately. But now I have determined to be guided by that old proverb, "Fall once rather than hang forever." For when that excellent man Giovanni Dolfin came to Padua from Verona, and among the many notable momentos of the city showed me your letters now collected in a volume, and I read them through with the greatest pleasure, I could not contain my delight and my admiration for you. Moreover, your brother Leonardo, a brilliant young man now devoting the greatest diligence to the study of the greatest philosophers, has long since asked me to write something to you, for since you are presently giving serious attention to dialectic and philosophy, as he told me, he wished me to give you reliable and friendly advice especially about which authors should guide you in these higher disciplines. Several other friends also exhorted me to write to you. And further, the glorious and honorable fame that you have already deservedly enjoyed for a long time

---

19. The present translation is based on the translation and notes originally published in King and Rabil, *Her Immaculate Hand* no. 19.

20. Cf. Cicero *Ad Fam.* 5.2.1.

compels me—even if I were unwilling—both to revere you and to send you this letter. I hope you will accept and recognize it as coming from a friend with the most kindly intentions.

This letter asks of you nothing else than that you pursue in the most splendid way, until death, that same course of right living that you have followed since childhood. And if you find this letter dry and uncultivated, forgive me: for here we are especially interested in that philosophy that does not value an ornamented style.[21] Therefore, let your delicate ears put up with sometimes dry figures of speech, I beg you. You have been trained in the polished and exquisite art of rhetoric and are accustomed to elegant discourses and melodious style and so rightly can demand the most ornate eloquence; but we semi-orators and petty philosophers are content for the most part with a sparse and inelegant style. For your own learning I salute and congratulate you. And should we not greatly rejoice that you can be named among those admittedly few but certainly famous women when we see that the ancients gloried in the learning of such outstanding women? Let us at this time pass by in silence the women of both the Greeks and the Romans—among whom the most notable are the Sibyls; Aspasia, the teacher of the great Pericles; Sappho; Proba, who wrote the *Cento;* Amesia; Hortensia; and Cornelia, the mother of the Gracchi—who were learned only in the arts of poetry and rhetoric and whose fame was widespread.[22] It will be sufficient to focus on one.

Synesius, a distinguished philosopher, had as his teacher Hypatia, whom he exalted with such praise and such declarations as to demonstrate that all the philosophers of that time enthusiastically admired her.[23] Rightly, therefore, should you also, famous Isotta, receive the highest praises, since you have indeed, if I may so speak, overcome your own nature. For that true virtue that is proper to men you have pursued with remarkable zeal—not the mediocre virtue that many men seek, but that which would befit a man of the most flawless and perfect wisdom. Thus Cicero rightly said, "You young men have a womanly spirit, but that woman has a man's spirit."[24] Therefore, dissatisfied with the lesser studies, you have applied your noble

---

21. That is, Aristotelian philosophy.

22. For the ancient female prophets known as Sybils, see Giovanni Boccaccio *Famous Women,* chap. 24; for Aspasia, see Plutarch *Life of Pericles* 24.1–7; for Sappho, "Boccaccio, chap. 45; for Proba, chap. 95; for Amesia, see Val. Max. 8.6.1; for Hortensia, see Boccaccio, chap. 82; for Cornelia, see Plutarch *Life of Tiberius Gracchus* 1 and *Gaius Gracchus* 4.

23. The Neo-Platonic philosopher of Alexandria Hypatia (ca. 375–415), whose pupils included Synesius, bishop of Ptolemais, with whom she corresponded.

24. Cicero *De officiis* 1.18.61.

mind to those highest disciplines, in which there is need for keenness of intelligence and mind. For you are engaged in the art of dialectic, which shows the way to learning the truth. Having mastered it, you may become engaged skillfully and knowledgeably in a still more splendid and fertile field of philosophy [i.e., metaphysics]. Therefore, just like a teacher moved by the sight of a passionate and committed student, I shall teach you, a virgin deserving of praise.

I want, therefore, my Isotta, because of the fineness of your mind—in which I take great pleasure—and the familiarity resulting from our correspondence, to address you as though I were your brother and to demand as my right not only that you avoid and shun these new philosophers and dialecticians as men without knowledge of true philosophy and dialectic but also that you spurn all their writings. For when they teach dialectic they do not follow the long proven method of this ancient discipline, but they introduce I do not know what kinds of childish sophisms, inextricable arguments, and unnecessary digressions and thus obfuscate the clear and distinct order of this discipline. In order to appear to know much, they distort everything, even the most obvious, with a kind of futile subtlety and, as the comic writer says, they "look for knots in a bulrush."[25] For this reason, tied up in these complexities, they cannot aspire to true and solid philosophy. And so in that field also, while they want to be seen as perceptive debaters, by wrestling too much with the truth, as the old saying goes,[26] they let it slip away. For just as dull-witted negligence gives birth to heedless ignorance, so overprecise investigation cannot satisfactorily discover certain truth, as Labeo's opinion in civil law elegantly states.[27] But on account of all their elaborate argumentation they are judged to be both subtle philosophers and perceptive debaters, and even though true science is concerned with being, these sophists pertinaciously and contentiously quarrel about nonbeing (of whom Aristotle declared that they do not dispute but chatter),[28] with the result that the mind can scarcely—and a well-trained mind cannot at all—understand them. There is also an additional important reason for their ignorance: the texts of Aristotle, which contain true and elegant philosophy, some neglect

25. That is, to find difficulties unnecessarily. See Plautus *Menaechmi,* 2.1.22; Terence *Andria* 5.4.38.

26. Publius Syrus in Aulus Gellius *Attic Nights* 17.14.4.

27. Antistius Labeo was a renowned legal authority under Augustus, many of whose opinions are embodied in the *Corpus Iuris Civilis* [Body of Civil Law] compiled under Emperor Justinian in the sixth century.

28. See *Metaphysics* 1.5.986b17–31.

from ignorance, whereas others, greedy for glory and ambitious for honor, not at all understanding this most profound and deep of philosophers, rashly set about writing commentaries on his works. And so in trying to divide the divine Aristotle subtly [into topics for their expositions], they mutilate him instead, in elucidating they obscure him, in uncovering [his meaning] they bury it. Now that I have hooted these men off the stage, I shall briefly teach whom you should follow.

Read studiously, then, the glorious works of Boethius Severinus, unquestionably a most intelligent and abundantly learned man.[29] Read all the treatises he learnedly composed on the dialectical art and the commentaries he wrote on Aristotle's *Categories* and his twofold work on Aristotle's *On Interpretation*, the first following the literal sense, the second according to the understanding of a higher sort.[30] In these you will be able to examine the views of nearly all the most reliable Greek commentators. I marvel enormously at the mortals of our time who abandon a man so learned, so excellent, so eminent in the disciplines of the good arts, and I do not know whom . . . but it is better to be silent, lest I incite against me the vulgar crowd of philosophers who may imagine that I am plotting against them in this letter. After you have mastered dialectic, then, which is the method of knowing, you should read diligently and carefully the moral books of Aristotle, which he writes divinely, in which you may unfailingly recognize the essence of true and solid virtue.[31] And if you also, as you should, act upon his excellent teaching in your life, he will lead you as no one else can to the height and extremity of the good. Then, after you have also digested this part of philosophy, which is concerned with human matters, equipped with your nobility of soul you should also set out for that ample and vast other part [i.e., divine matters], which is threefold.[32] Here you should begin especially with those disciplines that we call by the Greek term mathematics, which offers knowledge of such certainty (even though it is very difficult) that many philosophers, and these the most serious, think we can know nothing with certainty

29. Boethius (ca. 480 to ca. 524), philosopher and statesman, friend and advisor of the German king of Rome Theodoric, later accused of treason and executed—having while in prison composed the *Consolation of Philosophy*, a fundamental text of the Western tradition.

30. For Boethius's works on the dialectical art, see *Introductio ad Syllogismos categoris* (PL 64:761–94); *De Syllogismo categorico libri duo* (PL 64:793–832); *De Syllogismo hypothetico libri duo* (PL 64:831–76); *Liber de divisione* (PL 64:875–92); *Liber de diffinitione* (PL 64:891–910). For this commentary on Aristotle's *Categories*, see PL 64:159–294; on Aristotle's *On Interpretation*, PL 64:293–392.

31. Reference here is to the works of Aristotle he classified as "practical," related to knowledge as a guide to conduct, including the *Nicomachean Ethics* and *Politics*.

32. Meant here are the disciplines Aristotle classified as theoretical, that is, having to do with knowledge for its own sake: mathematics, physics, and metaphysics. See *Metaphysics* 6.1.

unless mathematicians have demonstrated it. Thereafter, strive unceasingly and determinedly to pursue that philosophy that we call natural, in which we are taught about living things and bodies in motion [i.e., biology and physics]. Finally, you should delve into metaphysics, which the Peripatetics [the followers of Aristotle] call the divine science, so that you may be able to know God and the three substances. This is the right path and splendid order of truth, which permitted the ancient philosophers who pursued it to arrive, as we see, at such a degree of excellence that we do not hesitate to call them divine.

Then, if you had knowledge of Greek letters, I would teach you those masters to follow who would lead you to the peak of all things. But since you lack only this (although it is certainly a great good that you lack), pay no attention to these modern Latin philosophers whom we discussed a little earlier, who deal in the debris of philosophy, but diligently and carefully follow the Arabs who very nearly approach the Greeks. You should constantly and assiduously read Averroes, admittedly a barbarous and uncultivated man, but otherwise an exceptional philosopher and rare judge of things.[33] Even though on your first reading you will perhaps despair of understanding him, yet if you work hard you will find him easy. But if you wish quickly to understand the Philosopher [i.e., Aristotle], then read Thomas Aquinas often, who provides as it were the entryway to the understanding of Aristotle and Averroes.[34] But though you may touch lightly on the Commentator [Averroes], reject all the others. Thus, you should frequently read not only his commentaries and treatises, but also Avicenna on natural philosophy and the *Summa* of Al Ghazali.[35] These Arabs will be able to train you in the true discipline of the Peripatetics until we have sufficient leisure and opportunity to translate the Aristotelian works into Latin, to compose commentaries, and to arrange those things that Aristotle wrote confusedly into a simpler system, explaining and unraveling his majestic phrases and involved obscurities.[36]

33. The Islamic philosopher Averroes (1126–98) from Cordova in Muslim Spain, who wrote commentaries on Aristotle and was called "the Commentator" by Christian philosopher Thomas Aquinas, who called Aristotle "the Philosopher"; both terms appear below.

34. Thomas Aquinas (1225–1274), Dominican theologian, author of the *Summa theologica* and *Summa contra gentiles*, foremost among the medieval "scholastics" who synthesized Aristotelian philosophy with Christian doctrine.

35. The Arab Islamic philosopher Avicenna (980–1037) was an early Aristotelian whose work influenced the Latin West. The Islamic theologian Al Ghazali (1058–1111), from Iran, was known in the West for a version of his *The Intentions of Philosophers*.

36. Although Leonardo Bruni (1370–1444) made humanist translations of part of Aristotle, it was only late in the quattrocento that humanist translations of all of Aristotle were completed.

You should also make use of those studies, moreover, that you have splendidly embraced from your youth, and especially history, for history is as it were the teacher of life,[37] which somehow makes the wisdom of the ancients ours and inflames us to imitate great men. For why did our ancestors study history so zealously unless they thought it to be nothing other than the example of a good and holy life? Historians have preserved for us every trace left by antiquity. I pass by Cicero in silence, who must be our daily bread; often I have been tired, but never satiated, when I have laid him down.

It remains for me to exhort you to the performance of virtue and to the excellent studies of letters. But since I realize that you are inflamed by both of these with a certain wondrous desire, I may close this letter once I have said one last thing. I regret very much, my beautiful Isotta, born of Apollo, raised by the divine Mercury on nectar, and taught by holy Muses,[38] sorrowfully, sorrowfully, I say, I grieve that we have so lacked the benefit of a long acquaintance. We must strive, amid a multitude of responsibilities, to be able in some way to recover that lost pleasure. I promise you, therefore, with Attic faith[39]—in the event you would not believe me without this vow—by wind and earth I swear to you that I preserve your sweet memory within the secret places of my heart.

These things, goddess Isotta, of great virtue and honesty, I have freely written, moved by conscience, by duty, and by that marvelous affection I feel toward you, which affection, once I know that you have accepted it gladly and willingly, I shall maintain as long as you wish. Love, indeed, longs for a beloved. Therefore, you should love Lauro,[40] among many other reasons particularly for this, that it is always green, for which reason the pagans consecrated it to Apollo, your god of wisdom. But we will exchange more jests at another time when it suits us both, with honest wit. Take care of yourself so that you may be well, and study so that you may be wise and nobly imitate Hippolytus, considering philosophy your delight and the center of all else you love.[41] For nothing is more lovely than philosophy, nothing

37. See Cicero *De oratore* 2.9.36.

38. These allusions are all to the life of the mind. Apollo is the god of light and mind; Mercury (Greek Hermes) was viewed as the mediator between human and divine minds; the Nine Muses were divinities thought to preside over the various arts and sciences.

39. That is, sincerely; see Velleius 2.23.4.

40. The author's name, Lauro, means "laurel" (the tree), an evergreen whose never dying leaves signify Quirini's unchanging devotion to Nogarola. The laurel wreath, moreover, was (and is) the reward bestowed upon poets—hence contemporary poet "laureates."

41. The youth Hippolytus, son of Theseus, spurned all sexual relations, including those offered by his father's wife Phaedra, and is here offered as model to the studious Nogarola.

more beautiful, nothing more lovable, as our Cicero said;[42] to which I add, perhaps more truly, that there is nothing among human things more divine than philosophy. For this is the one most holy discipline that teaches true wisdom and instructs in the right mode of living. Those, consequently, who are ignorant of philosophy go through life not only having achieved no good but even having committed evil. Accordingly, give your whole heart, as they say,[43] to philosophy alone; for I want you to be not semilearned, but to have knowledge of all the good arts, that is, to know the art of good speaking and the discipline of correct disputation, as well as the science of human and divine things. Farewell, and I entreat you, love me. At Padua.

---

42. Cicero *On Duties* 2.2.5–6; also *Tusculan Disputations* 1.26.64–65.
43. Cf. Cicero *Ad fam.* 10.12.2.

VI

FOSCARINI (1451–66)

In 1451, a new Venetian governor arrived in Isotta Nogarola's town of Verona. It was an important position, to which the Venetian government appointed important men. The new arrival was a prominent statesman and humanist, the nobleman Ludovico Foscarini (1409–80).[1] Foscarini was a formidable figure, who held government office and performed diplomatic missions uninterruptedly from 1437 to 1474; among these, to focus on the dates when he is known to have been in contact with Nogarola, he was *podestà*, or governor, of Verona in 1451 and Brescia in 1453; ambassador to the Diet of Mantua in 1459; lieutenant-governor of Udine in 1461; ambassador to Rome in 1464; and ambassador to Bartolommeo Colleoni, captain general of Venetian forces, at his castle at Malpaga in 1465–66. He was the author of several orations and a hagiographical work on the martyrs Victor and Corona and of a volume of 302 letters. He received his doctorate in both laws at Padua in 1434 (and always identified himself, at the foot of his letters, "doctor of civil and canon law") and was friend or patron to many humanist contemporaries.

To this eminent man, Nogarola wrote a gracious letter of welcome (see below, no. 26), much as twelve years earlier she had written one for Cardinal Francesco Condulmier upon his entry to the bishopric of Verona (see chapter 3, no. 15). Foscarini had already expressed his admiration for Nogarola, which apparently had reached her through intermediaries. She writes, therefore, because it would be ungrateful not to acknowledge his benevolence. She alludes to her pattern of life as a solitary scholar who had turned from secular to sacred studies, and she praises Foscarini, first for his many

1. For Foscarini, see esp. King, *Venetian Humanism*, 374–77 and *ad indices*.

prior magistracies, and second for his commitment to study and especially to sacred literature. It is the last letter known to us written by her hand.

It is by no means the last contact Nogarola had with Foscarini. During the course of his year's term in Verona he visited her often in her mother's house, in the presence of her mother and brother Antonio—company without whom it would have been inconceivable, in this social world and in this cultural milieu, for an unmarried woman of thirty-three and a forty-two-year-old aristocrat of vast experience to meet. On these occasions, they spoke intently about books and ideas, as Foscarini reports in a later letter, from 1453: "We used to talk about all these things until that last hour of the night, in the presence of your illustrious brother. . . ."[2] Although in his journeys he had experienced innumerable delights, things luxurious to touch and magnificent to see, "nowhere have I dined more pleasantly than with you, where I heard your words redolent with piety, brimming with wisdom, adorned with loveliness, spiced with laughter, which greatly increased in me the desire to return again and again.[3]

These were not occasions for mere pleasantry, as Foscarini wishes to make clear. He is drawn to her not because she is a woman but a holy woman. Their intense, longed-for conversations were about religious experience and Christian philosophy. To my mind you exceed all other holy persons or philosophers, he wrote in the same letter, "when I recall what you said about piety, about the immortality of souls, about your illness, about your contempt for life when you chose, like Paul, to be dissolved and to become one with Christ."[4] In another letter of late 1453 or early 1454, Foscarini recalls again having been in her "book-lined cell": "In my memory I recall that little room of yours (cellula), which everywhere was redolent of sanctity."[5]

During the year of Foscarini's Veronese governorship, Nogarola engaged

2. Abel, 2:37: "Quae omnia usque ad extremum noctis tempus praesente clarissimo milite fratre tuo collocuti sumus." From Abel letter no. 56, 2:35–38.

3. The whole passage at Abel, 2:35–36: "Vidi ego in his meis proximis itineribus magnifica imperia, marmorea tecta, auratas trabes, Siricam suppellectilem, famulorum astantium greges, locupletissimos apparatus, fertilissima convivia, puellarum ludus, virorum contentiones et cetera omnia, quae inter voluptates numerantur. His expletus satiatusque necubi quam apud te iocundius cenavi, cum audiverim verba religione redolentia, sapientia redundantia, venustate ornata, facetiarum sale condita, quae maxime nos ad eosdem lares redeundi cupiditate incendunt."

4. Abel, 2:37: "Neminem religiosum tibi antepono, philosophos contemno, cum memoria repeto, quid de religione, quid de animorum immortalitate, quid de aegritudine tua, quid de vitae contemptu dixeris, quando optabas cum Paulo dissolvi et esse cum Christo."

5. Abel, 2:122: "Memoria repeto cellulam illam tuam, quae undique sanctitatem redolet." From Abel, letter no. 76, 2:122–26. This letter was written from Venice, Foscarini having returned from his Brescian mission by way of Verona.

him in a discussion of an issue not merely important in Christian theology but fundamental for the understanding of the female condition in premodern Europe: whether it was Adam or Eve who had sinned more when Adam, counseled by Eve, ate fruit from the tree of the knowledge of good and evil and both were punished by expulsion from the Garden of Eden. They may have exchanged written communications on this theme, or perhaps even held a public debate, as is implied by the words of Matteo Bosso (see chapter 5): "And recently that disputation you had with the Venetian nobleman Ludovico Foscarini, governor of our city, . . . in which it was argued whether there was graver sin in father Adam or in Eve, and in which you took the part of Eve, but he Adam, I have read with holy pleasure . . ."[6] Subsequently, Foscarini urged Nogarola to create a dialogue based on their statements, which is translated in the next chapter (see chapter 7). It is a fitting monument to the relationship between these two complicated and conflicted personalities equally committed to a humanist and a Christian worldview.

After 1451 until her death in 1466, what we know of Nogarola beyond her own sparse words we learn from Foscarini's letters. They leave an erratic and sometimes perplexing record. He wrote her twenty times in the course of 1453 (nearly twice per month), when, after a year back in Venice, he was stationed as governor of Brescia, further to the west in Venice's northern Italian empire. During that period, it appears that Nogarola was corresponding with him regularly. His subsequent letters to her of 1461 and 1466 also attest to their continued relationship. But her letters to him have not survived, and their disappearance is suggestive. Although she was in regular contact with the Venetian statesman for the last fifteen years of her life, we have only one letter from her hand—the very first, before their friendship ripened—as a witness to that relationship. It is unlikely that these letters have vanished by accident; it is far more plausible that either Nogarola herself, or her kinsmen on her death, destroyed these writings that displayed such intense feeling.

Foscarini's letters to Nogarola may also not be complete (while his own political and literary career otherwise continues uninterruptedly throughout this period). His letters to her of 1461 and 1466, and to Damiano dal Borgo and Ermolao Barbaro in, respectively, 1461 and 1464, document his sustained contact with Nogarola over the interval from 1454 to 1466, the

6. Abel, 2:131: "Atque nuper altercationem illam tuam cum Aluisio Foschareno patricio Veneto et urbis nostrae Praetore . . . qua contenditur utrius peccatum gravius extiterit, patris Adae an Evae, et in qua tu Evam, ille Adam tuetur, cum voluptate sancta perlegi . . ." For Bosso, see chap. 5.

year of her death. The materials that are extant, therefore, illumine some aspects of the Nogarola-Foscarini friendship more than others. Their absence is glaring and suggests that the intensity of their relation was such that prudence required their suppression.

The comfortable and mutually satisfactory friendship established between the two humanists in 1451 was interrupted by Foscarini's absence in Venice during 1452. When he returned to Verona in 1453, the city had just greeted the arrival of a new bishop: the same Ermolao Barbaro, now forty-three years old, whom Nogarola had written in 1434 when he was a young protonotary and student at Padua (see chapter 1, no. 1). Nineteen years later, he was a mature and authoritative figure who would in 1455 publicly oppose the study of the secular classical tradition (although he approved the study of religious classics).[7] Upon his arrival in Verona, now famed as a holy woman devoted to sacred studies, Nogarola welcomed him with an oration (translated here; see chapter 8).

Barbaro must have quickly assessed the Nogarola-Foscarini relationship and, even before Foscarini reappeared, determined it must end. It is this decision that provoked Foscarini's first letter of 1453 and put in motion the epistolary relationship that ensued when the possibility of their meeting in person had been stymied by (as Foscarini implies) a puritanical and intrusive bishop. Acknowledging the bishop's authority, and on his urging, Nogarola delivered a second oration that year in praise of Saint Jerome (translated here; see chapter 8, no. 30)—the ancient scholar and saint who was renowned especially as the author of the archetypal Christian work in praise of virginity but whom Nogarola views in a different light.

Knowledge of Barbaro's intervention in the Nogarola-Foscarini friendship comes from Foscarini's first 1453 letter, a statement of despair.[8] He had been looking forward to renewing his friendship with Nogarola when he returned to Verona (presumably en route to his new office in Brescia), especially since she had indicated in her letters to him that she would be even more outgoing toward him than in the past, "especially since you promised that in the future you would be more generous and more kindly toward me, and invited me to think what you might, on holy days, all things in their order hear, read, and say, if I were to return to you." But Barbaro must have confronted him, possibly in Nogarola's very house; and Foscarini had promised, apparently, to cease his visits—promises he then regrets:

7. Barbaro's *Orationes contra poetas* of 1455; see *Venetian Humanism,* 157–61.
8. Abel, no. 56; 2:35–38.

I am in torment, because now I must either fail the Bishop with regard to the promises made in your house, or deny myself the pleasure I was so much anticipating; especially since you had promised me you would be even sweeter and more generous when I return to you, and that you would remember and tell me, step by step, everything that you hear and read in your holy days. It is painful not to keep faith, painful to be denied those most precious, most honest, most fruitful, and most avidly awaited desires.

And painfully he concludes, "I know what I should do; what I shall do I know not."[9]

In his next letter, which is translated here as a lone eloquent sample of Foscarini's authorship (see below, no. 27), the Venetian reflects on her as scholar, friend, holy woman. She has exceeded her sex (that tag so often used of learned women and used previously by Lauro Quirini; see chapter 5, no. 25), winning renown as a humanist, and as an orator as well, based on her journey the previous year to Rome, on the occasion of the jubilee, when she delivered an oration (now lost) to Pope Nicholas V.[10] She could have had her pick of husbands: "Given the fame of your family . . . and your outstanding fortune, possessions, and beauty, you could have chosen from all Italy a husband at will."[11] Instead, she has chosen holiness: "You have devoted all that you are to sanctity;" "you long for nothing but Christ."[12] She studies constantly, and lives austerely: "You lead your life and spirit amid hard work and long hours devoted to study; desire you do not understand, pleasures you do not recognize, luxury has no allure for you."[13] She does not leave her house: "You do not know what it is like to stroll through your noble city."[14]

---

9. Abel, 2:37–38: "Quas ob res crucior maxime, aut pontificem promissionibus in domo tua factis aut me tam expectata iocunditate carere oportere, potissime cum te liberaliorem suavioremque futuram pollicita sis ac memoriae mandaturam, quid sanctis diebus audies, leges et omnia ex ordine dicturam, si ad te redierimus. Grave est fidem fallere, grave summis, honestissimis, fructuosissimis avidissimeque expectatis, desideriis carere. Quid optem scio; quid faciam, nescio."

10. Abel, 2:50: "Cum recto . . . et securissimo animo Roman piissimae peregrinationis causa petiisti, quo consilio, qua auctoritate, qua dicendi copia, quanta cum pontificis et fratrum admiratione locuta es!"

11. Abel, 2:41: "Poteras ex omni Ytalia generis claritate . . . dignissimis matronis refertum ac illustratum fuit, fortuna, facultate, forma, tuo arbitrio virum deligere."

12. Abel, 2:42: "Te sanctitati devovisti tota quanta es;" 2:40–41: "nihil praeter Christum concupiscis."

13. Abel, 2:43–44: "Vitam et spiritum inter labores et studiosissimas vigilias ducis, libidinem non intelligis, voluptates non cognoscis, amoenitate non delectaris. . . ."

14. Abel, 2:44: "per nobilissimam tuam urbem vagari nescis. . . ."

She brings honor to Verona and to her family, whom he knows well. She compels him to love her.

Forged between a woman just past thirty and a man just past forty, the Nogarola-Foscarini relationship was certainly intense; and while it was not explicitly sexual (impossible under the circumstances described), it was colored by sexual feeling. Over the next months, the two friends try out different versions of their understanding of the relationship, which seems to range from one of heterosexual love to a Platonic connection based on shared intellectual commitments to a Christian one involving a saintly female and adoring male worshiper.

The intensity of the relationship is seen in one episode, where Foscarini responds to Nogarola's distress when his expected letter did not arrive. He had most faithfully sent the letter by the hands of a trusted intermediary: "You accuse me of neglecting you, since amid your miseries you waited in vain for the solace of my letter." He had in fact written, entrusting the letter to his agent "to deliver to you, wherever you might be, and I send with this letter my signed instructions to him." She may not believe his protestations; but "you will not deny the proof of a witnessed document!"[15]

At the same time, while admonishing her not to berate him, Foscarini assures Nogarola of his loyalty and defines the basis of their friendship: "Let there be between us a contest of learning, probity, character, in which our most honorable love begins and grows . . . ; in this we triumph nor can we be overcome."[16] She must not berate him for not writing, since he had written, but recall their friendship, and write when she can. She must

> preserve our friendship eternally, and not grow lukewarm in our most delightful exercise of writing. If you have the time, your writing at greater length will please me greatly; if you lack time, I shall make your brief letters long by rereading them often, since there is nothing I read with greater pleasure, nothing more often and more deeply read than what you write with such elegance and sanctity.[17]

---

15. Abel, 2:52: "Negligentiae vitium ascribis, quoniam inter miserias mearum litterarum solatium frustra expectaveris. Scripsi litteras, Clementi Tedaldino ad te, ubicunque esses, deferendas dedi, cuius manu testimonium his inclusum mitto. Si mihi, si verbis, si scriptis, si testibus non credis, publico tabellioni fidem non deneges." From Abel letter no. 58, 2:52–58.

16. Abel, 2:53–54: "Sit inter nos doctrinae, probitatis . . . morum contentio, quibus honestissimus amor coepit excrevitque nulla utilitatis spe, nulla vouptatis cogitatione, sed virtutis opinione; in his vincamus nec superari patiamur."

17. Abel, 2:56: "Da operam potius, quod optima morum nostrorum opinio, quae principium ad benivolentiam dedit, amicitiam in aeternum servet et delectabilissimum nostrum scribendi

For his part, Foscarini cares intensely for the intellectual and spiritual passions that they share. He cannot be distracted by trifling pleasures and can only find satisfaction in mental satisfactions: "Wealth, power, honors and the other gifts of fortune I do not neglect, but neither do I count them, as the unlearned multitude does, as the only goods. But without the adornments of the best minds . . . I could not live."[18] He values a relationship based on shared spiritual aspirations more than any other, and for that reason will always cherish and love her:

> I was always one more joined in love to those engaged in literary stud-
> ies than to those who were joined to me by any tie of blood or descent,
> and I embrace you, the ornament of our age, with such love, that I
> would consider myself most happy if it could be matched by you and
> if you could respond either with equal or even much less feeling. And
> because I know that you desire those studies, and pursue and excel in
> them in which I also most greatly delight, . . . I could not fail to love
> your celestial qualities most enthusiastically. . . . But to conclude in a
> word, believe that you are cherished as much by me as any human
> excellence can be justly loved by any mortal man.[19]

Foscarini had sent the letter that Nogarola accuses him of having left unsent; but Nogarola for her part, sometimes refused to write, a betrayal Foscarini bears patiently. Nogarola alludes more often to her need to work without distraction. At one point, she writes to explain that she will not write; he accepts her explanations and assures her of his affection.[20] At another, she has made a vow to not write him letters for two months; he is saddened, but understands: "I have accepted your decision, and I shall bear

---

studium non tepescat. Si ocium superest, quanto latius scribes tanto mihi gratius erit; si in nego-
tio fueris, breves litteras tuas saepissime legendo longissimas efficiam, quoniam nihil iocundius,
nihil saepius, nihil amplius lego quam quae tu ornatissime et sanctissime scribis."

18. Abel, 2:54–55: "Divitias, potentias, dignitates et cetera fortunae munera non negligo nec
multitudinis indoctae iudicia sola bona censeo. Sed optimarum mentium ornamenta . . . in terra
sine veritate, auctoritate vivere non possem."

19. Abel, 2:57–58: "Ego ille semper fui, quicum omnibus qui litterarum studiis detinentur me
maiori benivolentiae vinculo . . . quam cum illis qui quacunque necessitudine sanguinis vel
generis coniuncti sunt, et te nostrae aetatis decus tanta caritate conplector, quod me felicissi-
mum iudicarem, si id tibi constare posset et aut paribus aut aliquibus licet longe inferioribus
affectibus responderes. Et quia scio te eas doctrinas appetere et in his versari et excellere, quibus
ego summopere delector . . . non possem caelestes mores tuos non summopere amare. . . . Sed
ut uno verbo concludam, tantum te a me coli tibi persuade, quantum virtutem mortalem ab
homine mortali fas est."

20. Abel letter no. 69, 2:101–2.

what I have accepted, which I know is what you wish."[21] Not that he can persuade himself that there is anything wrong in their writing; or that it would be a gift pleasing to God that they cease.[22] In the meantime, he asks for her prayers, just as he always prays for her even if she does not wish him to; and he will not cease reading and rereading her works to others or to him: "This you cannot prevent, this you cannot wish, this you cannot by your vow prohibit."[23] He is delighted when she resumes writing and assures her that if the task of writing him or reading his letters is ever tedious to her he will cease.[24] He reports that on receipt of one of her letters he stayed up all night reading it: "I received your letter yesterday evening, which I read so thoroughly that night that my eyes did not see sleep."[25]

These letters sometimes depart from the discussion of the relationship between the two correspondents and deal with the daily business of life. Nogarola suffers from a chronic ailment, about which Foscarini often inquires solicitously. When her physician dies in the course of the year, it is a double tragedy: "Oh, two most troublesome things, that my friend and Isotta's doctor has perished!"[26] She had nursed the dying doctor, and Ludovico imagines her ministering to him with food and drink: "Oh, the unique solace of death, to have angels standing guard!"[27] He urges her to choose a new physician wisely; doctors are often frauds or invasive experimenters. There is another loss, too, the same year—Nogarola's brother-in-law Jacopo

---

21. Abel, 2:112: "Dixit praeterea te vel voto vel iuramento firmasse per duos proximos hos menses ad nos non scribere. Acceptum habeo acceptumque fero, quicquid tibi gratum esse cognosco." From Abel letter no. 72:112–14.

22. Abel, 2:113: "Nunquam tamen mihi persuadere potiussem te nobis litteras dare tanquam rem prophanam existimare aut munus deo gratum fore credere vovere a scribendo desistere."

23. The whole passage at Abel, 2:113–14: "Tu interea me saepe tuis piis orationibus adiuva, quando quidem ego semper te etiam invitam ad sidere deferre, tua scripta ad alios vel ad me prius edita videre non desisto. Hoc interdicere, hoc vovere, hoc iuramento prohibere non poteris." There follows a discussion of his having recently seen a book of her works at the house of a friend in Asolo, including her letter to Cardinal Condulmier (see chap. 3, no. 15), which all the company there present praised.

24. Abel, 2:116–17: "Si tamen te in tuis ad nos scribendis litteris labor, in nostris legendis, quas si sine superbiae macula negare non valeo brevissimas praeter consuetudinem et voluntatem meam efficere semper conabor, fastidium gravat, sicuti frequentissimae Damiani 'Burgensis tui litterae testantur, malo vota mea omnia evanescere quam te ulla molestia gravari. . . ." From Abel letter no. 73, 2:115–17.

25. Abel, 2:120: "Datae sunt mihi hesterno vesperi litterae tuae, quas totiens legi, quod proxima nocte somnum oculis non vidi meis. . . ."

26. Abel, 2:59: "O res duas molestissimas, et amicum mihi et Ysotae medicum perisse!" From Abel letter no. 59, 2:59–68.

27. Abel, 2:60: "O singulare mortis solatium, angelos astantes habere!"

Lavagnola, who had become a prominent Veronese officeholder, and who now died while abroad—the same Lavagnola who had years before more than once introduced Nogarola to prospective humanist correspondents (see the introduction and chapters 1–3). He cannot console her, Foscarini writes, because he too is overcome: "So great is my sorrow that no words, either Latin or Greek, can express it."[28]

Foscarini is there for Nogarola, too, when during this same wrenching year a dispute breaks out among her brothers—his good friends—over their long dead father's estate, which was only now to be divided.[29] Foscarini is distressed and at first urges Nogarola to settle the dispute. She might even contribute some of her own wealth to do so; God would provide, and then her brothers would thank her as though she were the founding ancestor of their family. When Nogarola, as it seems, responds that the controversy distracted her from her studies, Foscarini wrote with the contrary advice—she should stay out of the dispute altogether. Foscarini then wrote Damiano dal Borgo, whom he apparently knows well. This is the same dal Borgo with whom Nogarola had corresponded in 1438–39 (see chapter 4), who has remained throughout the faithful supporter of the family with which he is somehow related. Dal Borgo must see that the dispute is settled, safeguarding the position of the two Nogarola women, mother and daughter. He must act boldly and call the brothers to their senses before the controversy grows greater.

So it must have happened, although not without a lawsuit in which Nogarola's mother was able to protect her rights and an inheritance for her daughter.[30] Moreover, the women shifted their residence from the household of Antonio, with whom they certainly lived in 1451, to that of the youngest brother Ludovico, with whom they are living in 1457 when Isotta's mother Bianca Borromeo makes her will. That will further provides for Isotta's material well-being. Remarkably in this age, she made explicit property provisions for Isotta (as she did for her son Ludovico, who was also named "universal heir," he who would inherit all not specifically detailed in the will). Not only was Isotta left productive land and the rights appertaining, but upon Ludovico was laid the burden of providing her at her place of habitation

28. Abel, 2:88: "Tantus enim nos dolor urget, quod neque Latina nequa Graeca idiomata sufficiunt." From Abel letter no. 64, 2:88–91.

29. This issue is the subject of two letters to Nogarola and one to dal Borgo: Abel letter nos. 61, 62, 63; 2:73–87.

30. See Abel, 1:lx–lxi and nn. 71–73 for the legal controversy and no. 83 for Nogarola's mother Bianca Borromeo's will.

(which was unspecified) with stated quantities of grain and wine each year, at his expense. To her other children, male and female, Bianca left only nominal legacies (but still slightly more to the male). Other mothers, like Bianca, would bestow their dotal wealth, theirs at last to dispose of freely at their deaths, on preferred offspring, and often on women servants, neighbors, and distant kin. But Bianca's great wealth enabled her to make truly substantial bequests in favor of her daughter at a time when daughters frequently received only a dowry from the patrimonial wealth of their fathers.

There also occurred in the same year of 1453 that saw separation, illness, death, and domestic conflict, a quasi-comic event when an obscure figure, Antonio Cugnano, apparently sent Nogarola a proposal of marriage. She promptly consulted Foscarini, who responds crossly, "I really would have preferred that Antonio Cugnano had approached you, a holy virgin about things other than marriage, or that you had not appointed me—who adores you and does not know how to displease you—as judge."[31] She had written him an intelligent letter, which would have been acceptable had it been written by her sister Ginevra, a matron. Irritated, he reminds Nogarola that she has chosen to dedicate her virginity to God: "You are the intact and uncorrupted ornament of the Christian life, and however great is your zeal for eternal glory, so much greater should be your care to preserve divine grace."[32] She should not even entertain the possibility of marriage: "You pursue the good of continence, you flee all things that are evil and harmful. It is not fitting, in my judgment, that a virgin should weigh the benefits of marriage, nor even think about that lascivious liberty, that libidinous way of life."[33]

During the course of the year, the relationship between the two humanists seems to stabilize at the Christian pole of possibility—she will be the holy woman, and he will faithfully adore her. She proposes to him that he, too, take up the religious life. In one letter, he explains why he cannot—she must serve God, he must serve Caesar:

> For [our] duties are greatly different. I am troubled by the dangers, the mistakes, the calamities of the Brescians, you delight in the expectation of a tranquil future. I must be on guard against deception, you are

31. Abel, 2:96: "Maxime voluissem, quod Anthonius Cugnanus alias quam de nuptiis quaestiones ad te, sanctam virginem, accivisset, vel me, qui adulari nescio et displacere . . . censorem non constituisses." From Abel letter no. 67, 2:96–97.

32. Abel, 2:99: "Tu es integrum atque incorruptum Christiani ordinis decus, et quanto sublimiorem gloriam expectas tanto maior sit tibi servandae caelestis gratiae cura."

33. Abel, 2:98: "Continentiae bonum sequeris, perniciosa quaeque et infesta fugias. Non decebat meo iudicio virginem de nuptiis disputare, sed nec cogitare illam lascivientium morum liberatatem, libidinosa convivia." From Abel letter no. 68, 2:98–100.

nourished by the deep understanding of the knowledge of the highest things. I most cautiously watch out for evil, you most simply treasure the holy. I must pursue my daily business even in my dreams, you ascend to heaven by those steps that the divine clemency has considered worthy of you. . . . I serve the body, you the soul . . . I know that my thoughts have no consequence, I fear lest I be conquered, or fail in the administration of the city committed to me, or that the enemy invades my province; you cannot be vanquished, what you love cannot be taken away, and you glory in the many companions you will have when you come to the divine kingdom.[34]

He responds in a second letter to the same question:

You ask in your letter that I put aside all my official duties, my public and private affairs and that I feel and choose as you do, as befits friends who together wish and do not wish the same things. I would enormously desire to obey your Christian admonitions, but there is a long way, a long stretch of sea to be sailed between us. You follow the examples of the holy fathers, I do nothing of the sort. Those who struggle to pursue your kind of saintly life have progressed by hunger, thirst, cold, nudity, labors, vigils, fasts, and prayers, serving God in the hermitage, in the cloister, and in the home; forgetful of themselves they have disdained honors, wealth, patrons and clients, duties. You follow these models, you imitate them. I am immersed in secular affairs and am seen to perform best in my responsibilities when I limit my concerns to the business of the law.[35]

34. Abel, 2:95: "Haec tamen officia plurimum distant. Ego periculis, erore, dolore Brixiensium commoveor, tu futurae quietis expectatione delectaris. Ego ne fallar invigilo, tu acutissime intelligens in summa rerum cognitione nutriris. Ego cautissime nequissimos observo, tu simplicissime sanctissimos colis. Ego vitam meam in somnia converto, tu gradibus, quod tibi divina clementia constituere dignata est, ad caelum tendis. . . . Ego corpori, tu animae servis . . . Ego cogitationes meas evanescere cognosco, timeo superari, in administratione urbis meae fidei commissae falli, hostes provinciam ingredi; tu vinci non potes, quod amas non auferetur, et plures comites in divini regni successione habere gloriaris."

35. Abel, 2:103–4: "Petis per litteras tuas, ut desideriis forensibus, publicis et privatis derelectis idem quod tu sentiam et optem, sicut amicos decet, quorum idem est velle et nolle. Maxime cuperem posse Christianis admonitionibus parere, sed longa via, longum nobis maris iter arandum. Tu in sanctorum patrum exemplis versaris, ego nihil ago. Qui ad vivendi genus, quod sanctissime ducis, se accommodare studuerunt, per famem, sitim, frigora, nuditates, labores, vigilias, ieiunia, orationes progressi sunt, in heremo, in claustro, in domo deo servientes, sui obliti honores, divitias, clientelas, necessitudines contempserunt; hos sequeris, hos imitaris. Ego inter secularia negotia mergor et tunc in magistratibus optimus videor, quando iurisconsultorum legibus me contineo." From Abel letter no. 70, 2:103–7.

On a third occasion, she reports she has had a dream that he is struggling with his conscience over this issue.[36] He responds, delightedly, that she has mystically seen exactly what occurred—so now, adding to her resumé another feat for which holy women are famous, she is a prophetess, too! He had gone into the garden behind the house, far from the sounds of the household, and thought to himself,

Omnipotent Lord, our reader, when shall I deny myself food, I who nourish my whole family abundantly? When shall I put on a hairshirt, when I have a superfluity of [some kind of textile?] and purple? When shall I suffer fire, iron, the cross for Christ, I whom legions of doctors surround even when I am not sick? When shall I put aside the insignia of command, I who scarcely dare to go out without an army? When shall I find peace in a perpetual pilgrimage? How can I find safety among these eager evaders of truth and zealous corrupters of virtue? When shall I make myself first pleasing to God, if mortals praise me, if I please men?[37]

But once again, he cannot renounce his commitments in the secular world and cannot join her in a paired holy existence such as Héloise constructed with Abélard.[38]

Foscarini's term in Brescia came to a close. He visited Nogarola in Verona on his return to Venice. Afterward, with his last letter to Nogarola in the 1453 sequence, he sends a little gift, a holy object for her to cherish along with the others he knows she has, because he has seen them, and they were lovely, in her book-lined cell:

36. Abel, 2:108 (letter no. 71) for Nogarola's dream, reported to Foscarini, in which she (in Verona) sees what has happened to him (in Brescia): "Promisisse me memini studia caelestia tua non impedire, sed cum litteras tuas de somnio legissem, non potui me continere, quia maxime mirandum est, quod locus, tempus et cogitationes meae Brixienses tibi Veronae notae fuerint."

37. Abel, 2:109–10: "Domine redemptor noster omnipotens, quando me cibo fraudabo, qui familiam omnem locupletissime nutrio? Quando hispida veste tegar, cui bissus et purpura undique superfluit? Quando ignes, ferrum, crucem pro Christo patiar, quem etiam non aegrotantem medicorum legiones circumstant? Quando fasces negligam, qui vix audeo sine exercitu exire? Quando in perpetua peregrinatione quiescam? Quando inter veritatis evertendae ac virtutis corrumpendae studiosissimos et ingeniosissimos artifices securus esse potero? Quando deo prius gratus ero, si me mortales, laudant, si hominibus placeo?" From Abel letter no. 71, 2:108–11.

38. For the twelfth-century drama of Abélard and Héloise, the once-lovers and later colleagues as committed heads of religious communities, see Abélard, The Story of His Misfortunes, trans. Betty Radice (London: Folio Society, 1977); The Letters of Abelard and Héloise, trans. Betty Radice (Harmondsworth: Penguin, 1974); also M. T. Clanchy, Abelard: A Medieval Life (Malden, Mass.: Blackwell, 1997).

In my memory I recall that little room of yours (*cellula*), which everywhere was redolent of sanctity. I think of the sacred relics I touched . . . which I scarcely dared to look upon. I put before my eyes your pictures of the saints, veils artfully embroidered with crosses and decorated with images of the saints with which you bless yourself with holy water, and all the many other things which required a long time to be placed before me, which seemed to give me a foretaste of paradise.[39]

The next extant letter from Foscarini to Nogarola is dated 1461, eight years after the last. There must have been other exchanged between them: the text of the letter implies that the relationship had not suffered interruption in the interval. Moreover, Foscarini was again posted to Verona during 1456, during which time it is likely that their friendship resumed, although there are no letters left to document it. In 1459, Nogarola had written a letter to Pope Pius II (translated here; see chapter 9, note 31), the year of the Diet of Mantua (which Foscarini attended as Venetian representative) where discussion was held about the threat of Ottoman expansion following the capture of Constantinople in 1453. Two years thereafter, leaving behind her munificent gifts, Nogarola's mother died. Isotta was now alone. Her mother had been her principal companion for the more than twenty years since her sister Ginevra married and left home in 1438. She had permitted Isotta to stay, unmarried, in her household—a most unusual decision, complementary to Bianca Borromeo's earlier decision to provide for the humanistic education of her daughters.

Nogarola describes her grief in her own letter of consolation to the Venetian nobleman Jacopo Antonio Marcello who had recently lost his eight-year-old son (translated here; see chapter 10). It is also revealed in Foscarini's 1461 letter to dal Borgo, whom he commands to have Nogarola sent to join him in Udine, where he was stationed as lieutenant-governor, at the northeastern edge of the Venetian terraferma, "See that the illustrious virgin Isotta Nogarola comes to us, where she may both carry your letters and put aside her grief and mourning dress and enjoy the fruit of our most pleasant company. . . ."[40] It appears that she did, in fact, go. It is hard to

39. Abel, 2:123–24: "Memoria repeto cellulam illam tuam, quae undique sanctitatem redolet. Cogito sacras reliquias manu nostra tactas . . . vix prospicere audebam. Pono ante oculos picturas illas, quae sanctos referunt, vela arte elaboratissima crucibus, beatorum imaginibus insignita, quibus aqua te sancta benedicis, et cetera omnia nostris longe anteponenda, quae mihi paradisi degustationem quandam attulisse visa sunt." From Abel letter no. 76, 2:123–26.

40. Abel, 2:159: "Ut autem tabellarii fidem non timeas, da operam, quod clarissima virgo Isota Nogarola ad nos veniat, quo et epistolas tuas deferat et deposito luctu atque squalore

picture the circumstances, in 1461, that would have allowed such a journey to happen.

Just as extraordinary is the new configuration of relations among Nogarola, Foscarini, and their old nemesis Barbaro, who as a newly installed bishop had put an end to their intimacy. In 1464, Barbaro was expelled from Verona by a rebellious faction and took refuge in the village of Bovolone, some fifteen miles outside the city. From there he had written a treatise (which Abel reports to have seen) against his persecutors, dedicated to Nogarola.[41] Later that year, although we have no response from Nogarola to Barbaro, Foscarini had read Barbaro's work and commended him upon it; and he sends greetings from Isotta Nogarola, still, it appears, in his household: "I add the pious prayers of Isotta Nogarola, who is the model of innocence and sanctity, than whom no one in our age lives a purer life, from whom God learns about the merits of virginity and the holy profession of virtue."[42] Foscarini and Nogarola have found a way to live together. Given the strict rules of their social world, they can do so because she is a virgin dedicated to God, and he, on that account alone, adores her.

By 1466, dal Borgo was dead and Barbaro was reinstalled in Verona. From the Colleoni castle at Malpaga, Foscarini writes Nogarola the last letter of his collection, consoling her on her sickness, assuring her of his return, reminding her of her promise—their nature, unstated.[43] Later that year, she died.

What is to be made of the friendship between Isotta Nogarola and Ludovico Foscarini? In our own era, it would have been a love affair. In the fifteenth century that was impossible—not that there were no love affairs

---

fructu iocundissimae consuetudines nostrae uti possit, sicut gravissimo iurisconsulto Montorio Mascarelo ferme pollicita est et suus in universam familiam nostram amor cogere debet et lacrimarum suarum medicina exposcit." From Abel letter no. 81, 2:159–60.

41. Barbaro's work is described at Abel, 2:179–80. Barbaro's letter to Nogarola of February 19, 1464, is a mere sentence and does not mention the treatise. For Barbaro's difficulties with the Veronese, see James S. Grubb, *Provincial Families of the Renaissance: Private and Public Life in the Veneto* (Baltimore: Johns Hopkins University Press, 1996), 213.

42. Abel, 2:182: "Accedunt piae preces Isothae Nogarolae, quae est innocentiae et sanctitatis exemplum, qua nullus nostris temporibus integrior vivit, quam deus exaudire consuevit virginitatis meritis et divinae professione virtutis." From Abel letter no. 84, 2:181–82. Abel tentatively gives the return address of this letter as Malpaga and the date as 1464. In 1464, Foscarini was with the pope in Rome or Ancona and apparently Nogarola was in his household at the time. Kristeller, *Iter*, at 4:199b cites ms. London, British Library, Royal 8 A III (membr. XV), of 28 folios., which contains works of Ermolao Barbaro, Isotta Nogarola, and Ludovico Foscarini, dated 1464. We have not seen this manuscript, but it likely contains the letters discussed here and perhaps others casting light on this incident.

43. Abel letter no. 85, 2:183–84.

but that persons of this social rank, engaged in these pursuits, could not psychologically have broken so with the norms that defined them. Instead, they shared a relationship that endured fifteen years, from Foscarini's arrival in Verona in 1451 until Nogarola's death in his household in 1466. It was a relationship sustained by their mutual love of words and ideas, based on her role as a holy woman, and his tireless, unflagging, demanding support of her in that role. In the end, it does appear that—enmeshed though they were in a complex social system, physically distanced, equipped with a humanist language that was expressive in many ways but dealt only clumsily with mutual intimacies—they were in love.

XXVI

Isotta Nogarola to Ludovico Foscarini: Verona, 1451

In her thirty-three years, the scholar and holy woman Isotta Nogarola had seen famous men come and go to leadership positions in Verona—among them the cardinal Francesco Condulmier, as bishop, whom she had previously written (see above, 80–82), and the military leaders Jacopo Antonio Marcello and Andrea Mocenigo, both of whom make an appearance in this correspondence. The new arrival is Ludovico Foscarini, the Venetian nobleman sent to assume the supreme civil position in Verona of governor, a position he has performed before in other cities, alongside his many other official and diplomatic assignments. He is also, she notes, a scholar and an expert in civil and canon law. She greets him properly with a self-deprecating letter whose erudition belies the pose of modesty.

*K*now yourself!" That famous saying of Socrates,[44] whom the ancients thought most wise, which has been repeated often up to the present day, has frequently deterred me from writing, since it has encouraged me to recognize the frailty of my intellect and the inelegance of my speech. My sex, too, and my current way of life also urge me to be silent, and all the more so now since I have all but abandoned these studies and others call me that will better prepare me to live with God in the age to come and to restore order to my present life. But since I know that I am so greatly loved and praised by you, I decided that to remain silent would constitute the great sin of ingratitude—and I am aware that the most holy and learned men greatly detest this vice, and above all Augustine, really the prince of sacred letters, who wrote, "Ingratitude is a burning wind that dries up the

---

44. A well-known saying attributed to Socrates; we have not located the precise source.

goodness of all things."[45] And Cicero said that as he looked back on all that was past, "For my part, I consider no faculty to be so essentially human as the power of recognizing the obligation not merely of a kindly act, but even of anything that betrays a kindly thought."[46] And so I have decided to send you this letter, although it is crude and admittedly written only by a woman, preferring to be judged impudent and garrulous rather than ungrateful; and I am sure that you will receive it happily, joyfully, out of your civility and good will toward me, as testimony of my reverence and gratitude to you, you who, men say, are the kind of man who wants to attain true glory and the goodwill of men and not by pretense or insincere talk.

In you there is no ambition, no foolish pretension, but you have always remained constant in every part of your life: you have changed neither your speech nor your face nor your brow; this was what, as that man says, people remarked of Epaminondas,[47] that he among other virtues was diligent in truthfulness to the point that not even in jest would he utter a falsehood. Fortunate indeed our republic, had it always been ruled by such a governor and father! Wherefore Plato celebrated such rulers, and Cicero commented, "[M]ost blessed are those republics, if their rulers are either wise or seekers of wisdom."[48] In you truly nobility of blood, wisdom, virtue, greatness of soul, justice, kindness, mercy so greatly flourish that our citizens deem you to be and celebrate you as another Lucullus,[49] whom all the provinces extolled, celebrated, and revered with enormous praise; he was the most sought after of all, and contemporaries thought that city most fortunate that happened to be ruled by such a man. So Vicenza[50] considers itself, which you governed with such wisdom, prudence, justice, and kindness that the Vicentines love

---

45. We have not located the source of this statement of Augustine's.

46. Cicero *Pro Plancio* 33.81: "Equidem nil tam proprium hominis existimo, quam non modo beneficio, sed etiam benevolentiae significatione alligari." Cicero *Pro Archia, Post Reditum in Senatu, Post Reditum ad Quirites, De domo sua, De haruspicum responsis, Pro Plancio*, trans. N.H. Watts (1923; reprint, Cambridge, Mass.: Harvard University Press, 1993), 513.

47. Epaminondas, the fourth-century B.C.E. Theban general and statesman celebrated for his brilliant victory over Sparta, exemplified the virtues of self-denial, simplicity, and scorn for worldly goods. We have not located a source for this reference. Plutarch's *Life of Epaminondas* is lost, but it is frequently quoted in other classical works.

48. Cicero *Epistulae ad Quintum Fratrem* 1.1.29: "atque ille quidem princeps ingeni et doctrinae Plato tum denique fore beatas res publicas putavit, si aut docti et sapientes homines eas regere coepissent aut ii qui regerent omne suum studium in doctrina et sapientia conlocassent hanc coniunctionem videlicet potestatis et sapientiae saluti censuit civitatibus esse posse."

49. Lucius Licinius Lucullus Ponticus (ca. 110–56 B.C.E.), Roman general who served under Sulla, known for his self-indulgence. See Plutarch's *Life of Lucullus*.

50. Foscarini served as governor of Vicenza in 1446–47; King, *Venetian Humanism*, 375.

you no less than the Sicilians loved Timoleon of Corinth,[51] who reigned with the approval of all, for he preferred to be loved rather than feared. Ferrara, too, and Genoa and Florence,[52] and innumerable other glorious cities among the others that now flourish, when you served there as ambassador considered you worthy of respect, praise, and admiration. Indeed, you have won so many honors and awards that you seem not so much to gain glory from them as to confer glory upon them.

Add to this that unique and splendid achievement and honor of yours, and truly yours (because birth, ancestors, and those things that we have not done ourselves, these I scarcely call "ours"), that is, your deep understanding of human and divine law and knowledge of the sacred scriptures;[53] in the study of which they say that you excel to such an extent that you appear to follow in the footsteps of the very wise emperor Theodosius,[54] who by day deliberated justly in matters concerning his subjects, while at night he pored over books by lamplight; or in the footsteps of Gallus,[55] who came close to death in his attempts to measure heaven and earth, who often, having begun to write something at night, was surprised by the dawn, or by nightfall if he had begun in the morning. In this way, your studies minister to you, in this way they instill your soul and lofty mind with strength. These impel you to those things that I have called your faithful comrades and counselors— books, that is, with which your household glows and shines, a truly splendid furnishing and a pleasant family, which, as they say, does not bawl or howl; which is not greedy or hungry or insolent; at a nod they speak, and at a nod they are quiet; for from them only what, and as much as you wish, will you hear.

---

51. Timoleon of Corinth, died after 337 B.C.E. Greek statesman and general who defended the Sicilians against would-be tyrants and established a just constitution.

52. Foscarini served as ambassador to Genoa in 1449–50. Although he held no specific magistracy known to us in Ferrara or Florence prior to the date of this oration, his positions as *podestà* of Ravenna in 1438 and ambassador to Bologna in 1445–46 would plausibly have given him occasion to visit those cities; King, *Venetian Humanism*, 374–75.

53. Foscarini was indeed very learned, having received, after early humanistic training, a doctorate in arts at Padua in 1439 and in both canon and civil law in 1434; King, *Venetian Humanism*, 377.

54. Possibly Roman emperor Theosodius I (347–395), who in 380 established the Nicene Creed (325) as the standard for a Christian orthodoxy to be required of all subjects; while he appears not to have been a learned man, he was an enthusiastic student of history. Alternatively, Roman emperor Theodosius II (401–450), under whose aegis the set of laws known as the Theodosian Code, the most important compilation before Justinian's, was published in 438.

55. Possibly the Roman soldier and poet Gaius Cornelius Gallus (ca. 70–6 B.C.E.), a friend of Augustus and Virgil.

But what am I doing, I who am praising you with my babbling words to such an extent that I seem to strive to imitate them? I shall put a stop to words, lest by saying too much I appear to affirm the opinion of those who assert that nowhere in the world can a silent woman be found. In truth, I have dared to send you this letter not, as I said from the first, so that I might demonstrate to you, a most learned and eloquent man, the strength of my intellect or my ability to write, of which I have none, but so that you might understand from it rather that you are loved, treasured, and revered by me. Accept this letter, therefore, in your name, for the sake of your love for me, who am most devoted to you; more, accept me in it, since your native kindness allows you to reject no one. Since there is no other way in which I might excel to accord with your excellence, it may be permitted that I, since God does not listen to sinners, may in all my prayers remember you, and this I promise and pledge always to do. Farewell.

XXVII

Ludovico Foscarini to Isotta Nogarola: Brescia, early 1453 [56]

Nogarola and Foscarini became friends and correspondents, developing a close relationship that the new bishop of Verona, Ermalao Barbaro, cuts short on his arrival in 1453. Here a chastened Foscarini pictures Nogarola as a scholar and recluse, affectionately describing her as a woman surpassing all others: "But of you and with you I cannot be silent, since in Isotta, whom none surpass in virtue, that sex greatly pleases, which is otherwise burdened by the frailty of lesser women." [57]

The elipses in the translation are in the Latin text and result from lacunae or fragmentary or illegible passages in the original manuscripts.

You praise, most worthy virgin, my devotion in admiring your virtues that very nearly approach the divinity of the heavens; I, rather, am astonished by and detest those who do not celebrate them. If the most worthy matrons of our age will permit me to say so, I believe that you, excelling all others, have exceeded your sex, first of all in your obedience to your saintly mother, from whom you first learned the patterns of

---

56. The present translation is based on the translation and notes originally published in King and Rabil, *Her Immaculate Hand,* no. 20.

57. Abel, 2:49: "de te autem et tecum tacere non possum, quoniam in Ysota sexus ille paululum aliarum debilitate pressus maxime placet. . . ."

your most holy life. Her you hear, her judgment you never dispute, whatever she commands and ordains you believe to be beneficial, and you consider it sufficient authority if there is something your pious mother wishes. Ready always in soul, mind, body, you obey her will . . . , and your other near ones you have embraced with such affability that they are most happy who can spend a little time with you.

All desires you have crushed in seed, you have condemned the lush wealth that even the wisest men have often regarded too highly; you have learned from the laws of Lycurgus who prohibited gold and silver to the Spartans, believing that by that single edict he had extirpated the root of all crimes.[58] You have chosen not a necessary but a voluntary poverty; besides food and the most urgent necessities, you have desired nothing at all from your most ample patrimony. I see the golden robes of your family, their full wardrobes and frequent changes, while you always wear the same dress, neither shabby nor ornate, which brings you closer to your creator. Devoted to Christian thoughts, you disdain both our public and our private responsibilities. You have renounced pleasure and shunned delights, you constantly attend to learning and prayer, you long for nothing but Christ. You are most wealthy in poverty, and in those riches, I say, in which Epicurus correctly taught all to be rich, saying, "If you wish to make a man rich, do not add money but subtract desire."[59] Since, then, you do not desire gold, nor seek it, nor pursue it, nor pray for it, since you need little and are content with little, you lead your life without anxiety, richer than any queen; although placed on earth, you are like the angels, speaking or thinking nothing except what pertains to the glory of God. Dress, word, gesture, mind, and works are in accord, and at death you will fly to heaven light and unclothed, unburdened by the weight of wealth or sins.

Given the fame of your family—which has given birth to and been honored by a continuous succession of great-spirited men and worthy matrons—and your outstanding fortune, possessions, and beauty, you could have chosen from all Italy a husband at will. Since all your celebrated sisters—to whom in no respect are you inferior—became worthy of illustrious marriages, can we not imagine what your future would have been, in whom shine the outstanding and rare gifts of all past, present, and future women? . . . Oh, how much better is the career you have chosen! You have devoted all that you are to sanctity. Religious devotion alone is stable; it is not lost, it does

58. Lycurgus was the legendary founder of the Greek city of Sparta and its constitution; for this incident, see Plutarch *Life of Lycurgus* 9:1–2.

59. Possibly a paraphrase of similar statements in Diogenes Laertius *Epicurus* 10.130, 144.

not change. Amid the great and turbulent storms and wretched calamities of the city, the earth, the times, it maintains you pleasantly in the quietest province of the mind—since all things prosperous, peaceful, and welcome come to those who love the Lord, and all those things adverse, wretched, and bitter to those who spurn him. For although the counsels of evil men may at the moment be tempting, it is always better to act upon those of the good—advice not found in the poets' songs, but in the judgment of wise men. Your stupendous and incredible humanity lies in this, that you yield to all, although you surpass all in virtue. I shall not dwell on your virginity, concerning the excellence of which the books of holy men are full. I say nothing of your modesty, temperance, and other glories, which in the judgment of the best men are numbered as virtues. Rather, since you are unique, you should be offered unique honor.

Given to us by the highest God, raised by a wise mother, you were born to all types of the greatest virtues that all have been instilled in you, assuredly as a gift from God rather than by the generosity of nature, above all because you never insist on your own glory; and yet, however much you scorn praise, that much more does it abundantly accrue to you. You follow Christ, you have offered yourself as a purest living sacrifice and pleasing to God.[60] Your serious demeanor, your judgment seem beyond your years and sex. An enemy of idleness, you have never failed yourself, nor piety, nor learning. By adding and heaping virtue on virtue, you have employed all the diligence of the greediest merchants in your enterprise of letters and Christian life. You lead your life and spirit amid hard work and long hours devoted to study, desire you do not understand, pleasures you do not recognize, luxury has no allure for you. You do not know what it is like to stroll through your noble city. From no literary labor do you seek respite, amid no vigils do you seek sleep. Pastimes, applause, which many women avidly pursue, you do not even take the time to think of. From heaven you have come—to which it is clear you will easily be admitted. And since you understand rightly that goodness derives from and is adorned by learning, as much time as virgins of your age give to arranging their faces you give to your divine soul in the cultivation of the liberal arts in studies.

And you do well. Moses did not turn to holy contemplation until he had disciplined his mind with studies.[61] Daniel first was educated among the Babylonians in the doctrine of the Chaldaeans before he advanced to divine

60. See Rom 12:1.
61. See Acts 7:22.

things.[62] When Zeno asked how he might lead the best life, Apollo advised him with a famous reply: by revering the dead.[63] Heeding such admonitions, you have always wisely devoted yourself to letters, to those studies . . . which, I maintain, render you learned and good. And although you read the poets in your youth with excellent teachers, you have chosen . . . to master those disciplines that most nourish your soul; and more zealously than the Epicureans were said to have pursued . . . the delights of the body, having delighted in rhetoric, in which you greatly excel, you then turned to sacred writings. Not with a superficial learning, but by diligent and acute study, you have omitted nothing at all that you knew pertained to conducting your life in the present and to obtaining glory in the next. And however much you read, you understood much, and I believe you have acquired more by sacred prayers from the holy spirit. . . . For otherwise you could not feel so deeply, speak so elegantly, write so richly, to the admiration of all.

I often peruse the histories of the most oustanding women. Ancient Rome, which extended its empire to the ends of the earth and its spirit as high as Olympus, produced none equal to you.[64] Your writings from as long ago as your adolescence and an even younger age exist, which manifest a rare mind and extraordinary knowledge. When I am in your presence and hear you speaking, I recognize such maturity of counsel, such wisdom, and such authority of learning, that I feel these qualities cannot simply be the emanations of a brilliant intellect and the reading of great books; rather, they come from that most Holy Spirit that blows where it will.[65] That Holy Spirit rules you, having impressed your body into its service, stained by no filth of lust, resplendent in its virginity, adorned not by finery but by virtue; it brightens your words and instills your demeanor with the most worthy emotions and permits you in no way to be slandered or held in suspicion, even by the most evil men. And this spirit so inhabits your heart[66] . . . that you do not so much live in the desire to possess it with mind, intellect, and senses, but rather it lives in you.

The ancient men who sang the praises of Sempronia and Cornificia[67] would have extolled you to heaven with praise, since you have rendered poetry and every kind of human study in speaking and disputing most familiar

---

62. See Daniel 1:17–20.

63. Zeno, not Geno as in text; we do not find the source for this anecdote.

64. See Virgil *Aen.* 6.782.

65. See John 3:8.

66. Lacuna in text.

67. See Boccaccio *Famous Women* chaps. 74, 84.

to you. Equipped to read sweetly and write easily in all the liberal disciplines, you surpass learned men in pronunciation, bookish men in celerity and elegance. I have often seen you, as you know, speak extemporaneously with such glory that I suspect there was nothing ever more worthy and sweet. What can be more glorious, what more magnificent, than to hear you pleading in a way most worthy of majesty, gracious with noble modesty, bright with distinction, severe with authority, in teaching dignified and in diligence most sound? What woman, then, was ever more learned than you—or could be, who from the school of childhood up to this age, by learning and by teaching, have committed to memory more books than many learned men have seen? What kind of liberal learning is there in which you are not versed? Oratory, poetry, philosophy, theology declare that there is no study you have neglected that can adorn the mortal mind.

To you, therefore, I do not promise praise equal to your merit. Those who erected a bronze statue to Sappho, the woman from Lesbos,[68] should have erected it to you, since in this age there is more wisdom in you than all women in all ages even impudently could claim. I always except those whom our religion worships and whom we revere with pious prayers. Solomon, who praised the Queen of Sheba, would have paid you a visit once he had espied the peculiar wisdom of your noble family and had found out that you considered as delights, not gold or embroidered robes, but Cicero, Virgil, Jerome, Augustine;[69] and he would have judged you the most outstanding of all, who are nourished by virtue and literary leisure, unconcerned with pleasures, and, unimpeded, follow the highest good.

Your Verona rejoices in her marble monuments, theaters, basilicas, mountains, rivers, paintings, and, in short, in every most exquisite ornament of the people. It admires your famous ancestors, it venerates your noble brothers, it reveres your prudent mother, it gazes in stupor upon the incredible beauty of your sisters, and it triumphs in you, most divine virgin, as though you were its true and matchless light, splendor, and ornament, for you are known to surpass ancient and modern forms of virtue. As many times as I bring you to mind, I seem to see Catelina Crichastina and other most holy and learned virgins.[70] The heretics who suspect that the stories of

68. Sappho of Lesbos (b. ca. 612 B.C.E.), one of the most famous Greek lyric poets; see Boccaccio *Famous Women* chap. 45; and literature cited in the volume editors' introduction, n. 21.

69. It was in fact the Queen of Sheba who praised Solomon, in the biblical account: 1 Kg 10; 2 Chr 9. Cicero and Virgil are classical Roman authors; Jerome and Augustine are Latin Fathers of the Church. In effect, Nogarola is said to imitate the best of both pagan and Christian traditions.

70. Not identified; perhaps a local holy woman in an era that greatly celebrated female "living saints."

their virtues are false will believe in devotional books once they understand that you with constancy and learning and every illustrious kind of virtue have in your time as much exceeded them as they in their times are said to have excelled other women. Normally, I love fine minds but refrain from frequent association with them. But of you and with you I cannot be silent, since in Isotta, whom none surpass in virtue, that sex greatly pleases, which is otherwise burdened by the frailty of lesser women. Even the worst men make so much of your religion and learning that you are judged to have been born for the glory of our age.

I am forced, therefore, to love you—to return to the point from which I have digressed at length—by the certain evidence of what I know and what I have seen, because there is no earthly body that houses a soul of more brilliant virtue. In saying this, I do not deceive nor am I deceived. Concerning no other woman have so many and such glowing reports been circulated; there is no place in Italy so deserted that the fame of your name has not reached it. When with righteous . . . and confident soul you went to Rome on that holiest of pilgrimages, with what great authority, wisdom, and elegance did you speak, arousing the great admiration of the pope and his cardinals.[71] Great are those who among the great are esteemed as great.[72] Here let me say no more, nor propose other examples, since now both for me and for all posterity you will always be a highest example. Nor will anyone doubt how great you were, who already for a long time—not by my writings, but by your own merits—have been famed beyond the stars.[73] The letters of learned men, which are delivered to you from various and diverse places, have increased your authority, and your responses are awaited and circulated more avidly than the counsels of the Sibyls[74] once were. Cardinal [Giuliano] Cesarini judged nothing more worthy in his whole long journey than meeting you and concluded that nature, virtue, and learning were at your command.[75] For

71. See Abel, 1:clvi–clvii and his n. 61 on Nogarola's trip to Rome in 1450 in a pilgrimage company, he infers, of pious men and women, and her delivery of an oration. "The brothers" are most likely the other prelates there assembled. Foscarini is the only contemporary witness we have of this event.

72. Apparently a reference to Aulus Gellius *Attic Nights,* 14.3.2.

73. See Virgil *Aen.* 1.379.

74. Sibylla, in Greek legend, was an aged woman prophetess; in Roman times, she multiplied into several sibyls, whose oracles were recorded in a body of literature called the *Sibylline Books,* which the Romans often consulted for guidance in public affairs and which were stored in the Temple of Jupiter on the Capitoline Hill.

75. Giuliano Cesarini (1398–1444), a prominent ecclesiastic and papal diplomat, made cardinal in 1430, attended the Council of Basel in 1431; see Joseph Gill, S.J., *Personalities of the Council of*

that reason, you may rejoice in the Lord, since you so greatly excel by birth, are outstanding in majesty, flourish in letters, are conspicuous in virtue— which should be praised in every sex, but in a woman is much more, because it rarely occurs and thus is judged more worthy and more admirable. I would write much more, if this discourse had been intended to undertake all those matters that the magnitude of your merits deserves. But since I accidentally embarked on this speech because I wished to praise you, you may not accept the things I have said, since . . . to enumerate your matchless virtues would require several volumes and an age of talk. Farewell.

Florence and Other Essays (New York, 1964), 95–103. Nogarola's letter to Cesarini of March 29, 1438 (see above, chap. 3, no. 11), indicates that they had met and that he was a patron of her brother Leonardo.

VII

THE GREAT GENDER DEBATE (1451)

M atteo Bosso's letter to Nogarola, discussed in the previous chapters noted that she and Ludovico Foscarini publicly debated the question in 1451 of whether Adam or Eve had committed the greater sin when they ate of the Tree of Knowledge and were expelled from Paradise. "And recently I read with holy pleasure," he wrote, "that debate you had with the Venetian nobleman Ludovico Foscarini, governor of our city, a most excellent man of great authority and one cultivated in letters, in which it was argued whether there was a graver sin in father Adam or in Eve, and in which you defended Eve, but he Adam."[1] A debate had occurred, and Bosso had read a work recording the debate. Whether this learned debate was held in a public forum or a smaller venue or whether it was based on a conversation or exchange of letters revised and circulated by Nogarola in manuscript is not known.[2] In any case, the substance of the argument and its supposed occasion created something of a sensation. After all, the themes aired were sex, sin, nature, and theology, and the participants were a married man who was the new governor from Venice and a single woman who was Verona's most brilliant woman humanist. Was the lingering talk about the debate the last

1. Abel, 2:131–32: "Atque nuper altercationem illam tuam cum Alvisio Foschareno patricio Veneto et urbis nostrae Praetore, viro praeterea optimo atque gravissimo et egregie litteris culto, qua contenditur utrius peccatum gravius extiterit, patris Adae an Evae, et in qua tu Evam, ille Adam tuetur, cum voluptate sancta perlegi . . ." For an analysis of the Nogarola *Dialogue*, see now also Allen, *The Concept of Woman: Volume II: The Early Humanist Reformation, 1200–1500* (Grand Rapids, Mich.: Eerdmans, 2002), 944–55.

2. Letters are extant in at least three manuscript versions that may have been copies of actual correspondence between Foscarini and Nogarola: Florence, Biblioteca Nazionale Centrale, cod. xxxviii, 142, fols. 117–33; Naples, Biblioteca Nazionale, cod. V.B.35, fols. 27–42; Rome, Biblioteca dell'Accademia Nazionale dei Lincei e Corsiniana, cod. 839 (43 D 8), fols. 67v–75.

straw for Foscarini's friend and compatriot from Venice, Ermolao Barbaro, when he arrived in Verona as the city's new bishop two years later?

Sexual innuendo would be expected in a conversation between a man and a woman on the nature of sin. Barbaro, however, who had as much as forbidden Foscarini to visit Nogarola,[3] could hardly have been pleased that his friend, now the governor of Brescia, had remained in constant touch with her that year. By the end of 1453, the Brescian governor had in fact sent Nogarola twenty long letters,[4] at least two a month—an unheard of correspondence between a man and a woman who were not married to one another. Disturbing to the clerical ear, surely, was the portrait of Foscarini in the dialogue as one who declares himself ready, like Ovid's notorious *miles amoris* ("soldier of love"), to lay siege to Nogarola's "fortress" (*castra*)—a sexual reference as explicit as those contemporary humanists found in the erotic poetry of antiquity they devoured along with works of philosophy and history.

The dialogue is not, however, like Tullia d'Aragona's *Dialogue on the Infinity of Love* (written a century later), an amatory dialogue between a man and a woman, both of them (like Foscarini and Nogarola) well-known intellectuals.[5] Less about sex in the sense of sexual contest and conquest, Nogarola's dialogue concerns the essential natures of male and female, the definition of which, in the fifteenth century, was heavily loaded against the female. The legal, medical, philosophical, and theological traditions all concurred in ranking women below men in the chain of being. The narrative that summed up that cumulus of misogyny was the story of Adam and Eve related in the biblical book of Genesis: Eve, who had been created by God from Adam's rib to be his helpmate and companion, giving in to the deceptive promises of the serpent who intruded upon their paradise, herself deceitfully persuaded Adam to eat the fruit of the tree that God had forbidden. In this dialogue, while Foscarini upholds tradition, Nogarola begins to disentangle that narrative and rescue Eve from infamy.

Was Nogarola, then, the author? Bosso's report of an actual dialogue between the two interlocutors must be given due weight, although the situation

3. See Abel, 2:37–38 and above, chap. 6, 118, in which we quote the passage from Foscarini's 1453 letter to Nogarola in which he indicates that Barbaro instructed him not to see her again.

4. These letters are in Abel's edition based on Foscarini's manuscript book of his collected letters: *Epistolae. Exempla rerum bene gestarum ac prudenter dictarum, industria studioque Ludovico Fuscareni ex doctissimorum libris collecta* in Vienna, Nationalbibliothek, cod. Lat. 3424 (loc.cit. in *Tabula codicum manuscriptorum*, ed. Academia Caesarea Vindobonensis, II [Vienna, 1868]: 342, 288; see King, *Venetian Humanism*, 376).

5. See, in this series, Tullia d'Aragona, *Dialogue on the Infinity of Love*, ed. and trans. Rinaldina Russell and Bruce Merry, intro. and notes by Rinaldina Russell (Chicago: University of Chicago Press, 1997).

would certainly be unusual for 1451: it was unusual, although not unprecedented, that a woman speak in public; wholly unprecedented, however, that a woman and a man debate. If indeed the debate actually occurred, or if it was staged in a salon setting, or if it emerged from an exchange of letters, then Foscarini's intellectual contribution (and he was an author of many works) to the final product must be acknowledged. Two arguments, however, point to Nogarola's final authorship. The first rests on an analysis of the arguments presented: Nogarola is the driving force, it is she who repeatedly raises new perspectives to challenge very old perceptions. The second rests on Foscarini's words, as interlocutor, near the end of the dialogue, which invite Nogarola to compose a polished literary work based on the views the two had exchanged: his words may be obscure, but "if you who are most brilliant accept them and join them to what you and I have already written, our views will become known . . . And if what I have written is clumsy, by your skill you will make it worthy of your mind, virtue, and glory. . . ."[6]

Is the dialogue, in fact, a dialogue? Or is it a disputation, a contest of wits between learned men proving their skills in a university setting on some point of law or philosophy? It has the structure of a disputation. One speaker introduces a thesis; the opponent disputes its truth and offers a counterargument; the first speaker addresses the counterargument and presents a new thesis. It is according to this model that Foscarini and Nogarola address systematically and exhaustively a series of questions: What is woman's nature? Is it nature that causes her to sin? What is the relationship between God and nature? Do humans have free will? Is nature good or evil? Is the desire for knowledge a natural thing? Can it then be evil? Can the desire for knowledge be separated from the desire for power? Are women in general inferior to men? Nogarola argues throughout that the female is by nature more fragile, more inconstant, and more ignorant than the male and that therefore she is not responsible for her actions. Quoting Aristotle, Foscarini argues first that ignorance is no excuse and second that pride, not ignorance, was the cause of Eve's sin. God's creation of woman, he insists, as an intellectually suitable companion for Adam belies Nogarola's claims of woman's inferiority.

Yet this debate on the relative sin of Adam and Eve is not in the end a disputation. Behind the display of opinions pro and con is a struggle of personalities, a human exchange that must place this work in the genre of the humanist dialogue, despite its formal structure. It is, in the form it reaches us, a work of fiction, an experiment in form developed from Nogarola's craft

6. The text is given as part of a longer quotation in n. 18 below.

as a humanist epistolographer, in which the two speakers are fully developed literary characters. As David Marsh has noted, the dialogue, a genre already fashionable among the humanists by the 1430s and 1440s, derived from the humanist epistolary tradition in terms of its conversational tone, dramatic structure, attention to the representation of selves, and the use of imaginary, contemporary, or historical people as interlocutors.[7] Classical models for the genre range in their variety from Plato and Cicero's philosophical dialogues, Xenophon's imitation of ordinary speech and its quotidian concerns, and Lucian's comic skirmishes to Augustine's formal theological disputations. The dialogue was a way of staging, in dynamic relief, a discussion demonstrating both sides of an argument: *in utramque partem disserere,* as the humanists defined the trope.[8]

The dialogue represents the splitting, in Virginia Cox's characterization of the genre, of the author's voice into two or more speaking parts; thus, the form could encompass a variety of *mise-en-scènes* from the dramatization of a debate among several characters[9] to a "soliloquy-like interchange between the author's literary self and the Augustinian conscience."[10] Crucial here is the art of prosopopoeia: the theatrical presentation of the actions and speech of absent, imaginary, or historical characters. The genre represents above all, writes Cox, the *process* of communication, illustrating the way in which readers, speakers, and texts interact.[11] Involved are the disciplines of persuasion, teaching, and listening. As Marsh has observed, humanist discussion and debate were considered "part of the individual's formation, an essential preparation for the activity which supplements the solitary exercise of reading and study."[12] Dialogues on controversial issues might end in various ways: with a reconciliation between the opposing sides, with the simple triumph of one side over the other(s), or with an open-ended ending of the conversation in which neither contender concedes victory to the other.[13]

This is exactly what happens at the close of Nogarola's dialogue, where Foscarini and Nogarola represent the splitting into two sides of Augustine's doctrine that Adam and Eve, each of them for different reasons, bear equal

---

7. Marsh, *Quattrocento Dialogue,* 25.

8. Marsh, *Quattrocento Dialogue,* 2.

9. Virginia Cox, *The Renaissance Dialogue: Literary Dialogue in Its Social and Political Contexts, Castiglione to Galileo* (Cambridge: Cambridge University Press, 1992), 5.

10. Marsh, *Quattrocento Dialogue,* 4.

11. Cox, *Renaissance Dialogue,* 4–5.

12. Marsh, *Quattrocento Dialogue,* 12.

13. Marsh, *Quattrocento Dialogue,* 10.

responsibility for the Fall.[14] As the subtitle of Nogarola's dialogue states, this will be a "discussion of Saint Augustine's teaching, namely, that Adam and Eve sinned differently because of the inequality of the two sexes but that both sinned with equal pride": *contentio super Aureli Augustini sententiam videlicet: peccaverunt impari sexu sed pari fastu.*

Nogarola's literary debate on woman's nature and her reading of Saint Augustine's commentary on Genesis 3 in the *Dialogue on the Equal or Unequal Sin of Eve and Adam* mark a turning point in her development as a writer and thinker. Not only is the dialogue the first work, with the single exception of her consolatory letter to Damiano dal Borgo (1438),[15] in which she displays her knowledge of the early church fathers and the Scriptures. The dialogue is her most learned and at the same time her most syncretic writing to date in terms of its interweaving—so characteristic of the humanists—of Christian and pagan references, paraphrases, and quotations.[16] No doubt Nogarola had read Lorenzo Valla, whose influential dialogues *On Free Will* (1439) and *On the True and False God* (1441), were inflected both by Cicero and Saint Augustine. As if to respond to Lauro Quirini's counsel, her dialogue is rich in references to Aristotle's *Nicomachean Ethics* and his *Posterior Analytics*. And seemingly with clerics such as Bosso, Maffei, and Barbaro in mind, her work fairly bristles with reminiscences and paraphrases from Saint Ambrose's *On Paradise* and *Commentary on Luke;* Saint Gregory's *Moralia* and *Pastoral Care;* Isidore's *Etymologies;* Saint Augustine's *To Orosius, The Literal Meaning of Genesis, On Nature and Grace,* and *On Free Will;* Saint Bernard's *On Grace and Free Choice;* and Boethius's *Consolation of Philosophy.* In addition, the dialogue also contains a wealth of biblical references—to Acts, Ecclesiastes, Genesis, and all four Gospels.

The importance of this work and its place among inaugural texts in the history of the European controversy over gender and nature cannot be overstated. It confronts squarely the prevalent assumptions about female inferiority attached to the reading of a canonical text. It challenges those

---

14. On the doctrine that Adam and Eve sinned differently but are equally responsible for the Fall and must be equally faulted see Saint Augustine, *The City of God,* trans. John O'Meara (New York: Penguin, 1984), 14.14: "the pride of the transgressor was worse than the sin itself" and both Adam and Eve were guilty of pride (chaps. 11–14, 568–74). See also Saint Augustine, *De Genesi ad litteram,* 12.11.35 (PL 34:449); *The Literal Meaning of Genesis,* trans. John Hammond Taylor, in *Ancient Christian Writers* (New York: Newman Press, 1982), 42:68–69.

15. See above, chap. 4, no. 16, for Nogarola's letter dated September 10, 1438, consoling dal Borgo on the deaths of his brother and daughter.

16. On the characteristic syncretism of the humanists see Rice, "The Renaissance Idea of Christian Antiquity," and Rice, *Saint Jerome.*

assumptions, although, given still potent cultural limits, it cannot annul them. It showcases, finally, the potential for a real equality of man and woman in the relationship between the characters of Ludovico and Isotta. The verbal exchanges between thse interlocutors in themselves testify to the equality of the sexes in terms of the capacity of each to reason, sense, think, learn, and articulate. Both Ludovico and Isotta are portrayed as showing profound respect for one another throughout the debate; and each offers arguments, sometimes clever, sometimes wise, which are listened to and taken seriously by the other. In the concluding speech of the dialogue, Ludovico leaves his audience with the knowledge that he believes Isotta is endowed with both literary skill and intellectual capacity and is every bit his equal:

> Although others may find that my writings suffer from the defect of obscurity, if you who are most brilliant accept them and join them to what you and I have already written, our views will become known and will sparkle and shine amid the shadows. And if what I have written is clumsy, by your skill you will make it worthy of your mind, virtue, and glory, you who march forward to new battles to the sound of sacred eloquence, as do soldiers to the clamor of trumpets, always more learned and more ready. And you march forward against me, one who has applied the whole of my thought to my reading and likewise to my writing, that I might present my case and defend myself against yours, although the many storms and floods of my obligations toss me about at whim.[17]

SYNOPSIS OF THE DIALOGUE

The arguments in the dialogue fall into four general topics: first, the argument on nature versus free will (Isotta defends Eve's action because woman is morally and intellectually weaker by nature; Ludovico condemns her because she freely chooses to do wrong); second, the argument on the relative severity of Adam and Eve's sins (Isotta and Ludovico champion, respectively, Eve and Adam, as having committed the lesser sin); third, the argument on

---

17. Abel, 2:215–16: "et quamquam apud alios haec me dicta obscuritatis vitio laborarent, si apud te clarissimam accedent et prioribus tuis ac meis scriptis iungentur, apertissima fient, illustrabuntur et radiabunt in tenebris. Atque ea si ineptissima erunt, tuo studio facies ingenio, virtute, gloria tua esse dignissima, quae te semper veluti milites tubarum clangoribus sic sacris eloquiis ad nova proelia instructiorem paratioremque offers, contra me quidem, qui omnem mearum cogitationum summam legendo et eodem, ut aiunt, spiritu scribendo converti, ut ostendam quod sentio et defendam quod scribis, licet pluribus negotiarum tempestatibus et fluctibus undique iacter. Vale."

the significance of Christ's redemption of Adam (Isotta and Ludovico argue over whether Christ's redemption of "man" and not "woman" proves that Adam's sin was greater or lesser than Eve's); and fourth, the argument over the relative severity and significance of the punishments given to the first man and woman (Isotta and Ludovico debate the question of whose punishment was greater, Adam's or Eve's).

Ludovico opens the debate by stating but not defending his position that Eve was more guilty because she received a harsher punishment, was motivated by pride, and was the cause of Adam's sin. Isotta responds that Eve could not be more guilty than Adam because Eve was weaker, lacking in constancy. It was because of her weakness, not her pride, that she ate of the fruit of the tree. Moreover, when God placed the two in Eden, he directed his command alone to Adam, and not to Eve, not to eat of the fruit of the tree of knowledge. Finally, Isotta argues, Eve was not given a harsher punishment. She was told that she would deliver children in pain; Adam, however, was punished with lifelong toil and death.

Ludovico responds that Eve did not sin from ignorance or, if she did, she is still responsible for her sin. If she was inconstant, she is responsible for that as well. Her sin was not ignorance (since God gave her knowledge) but pride. Adam's punishment was not more severe than Eve's since Eve became subject to toil and death as much as Adam did, in addition to which she was punished with bearing children in pain. Turning next from the refutation of Isotta's arguments to his own position, Ludovico contends that Eve sinned more greatly because it was on her account that Adam sinned. She set the example for Adam and he, out of love for her, followed it.

To this, Isotta responds that Eve's ignorance was not crass or affected but implanted by God, and ignorance of this kind certainly excuses sin. Her inconstancy, then, derives from the fact that she was created an imperfect creature to begin with. Adam, on the other hand, was created perfect. It was to Adam that God gave dominion over the earth. Even Adam's body was more perfect, since God created Adam's body himself, but he created Eve's body from Adam's. Further, even if Eve sinned out of pride (the desire to know good and evil), her sin was less than Adam's, who transgressed a divine commandment. So slight was Eve's sin, in fact, that no reference was made to her redemption. Her crime was not great enough to require redemption. Thus if man merited redemption, woman did all the more because her sin was less.

That Adam's sin was greater than Eve's can be proved, Isotta continues, by the fact that it required Christ's suffering to redeem it. Furthermore, it cannot be argued that Eve is more guilty because she caused Adam to sin by her example. Eve was inferior to Adam, therefore she could not constrain his free will. If he had free will, he is more guilty; if he did not, it was God who took it from him, not Eve. What is more, since Eve was weaker than Adam, she sinned less in following the serpent than Adam did in following her. The fact that Eve sinned before Adam is of no consequence, since Eve was weaker. It was not the case of sin among equals. Finally, Eve's example does not make her guilty. The Jews, who were not ignorant of God's laws, prophets, and the signs concerning Christ, were condemned more harshly than Pilate, who was.

Ludovico responds that Eve's inconstancy was not innate but a moral choice. Even if Eve were inferior to Adam, nonetheless God implanted reason in her insufficient for the health of her soul. If she were created to console Adam, she failed and instead brought him sorrow. The argument that Adam broke a divine commandment does not acquit Eve, since she did not keep the commandment either. Finally, as if to foreclose further debate, Ludovico offers two barbs conventionally used to indict women: the first, that there is no plague more deadly than an enemy in one's own household; the second, that the first mother kindled a conflagration yet to be extinguished.

XXVIII

Dialogue on the Equal or Unequal Sin of Adam and Eve: Verona, 1451[18]

*A*n honorable debate between the illustrious lord Ludovico Foscarini, Venetian doctor of the arts and civil and canon law,[19] and the noble and learned and divine lady Isotta Nogarola of Verona, regarding this judgment of Aurelius Augustine: They sinned unequally according to their sexes, but equally in pride.[20]

---

18. The present translation is based on the translation and notes originally published in King and Rabil, *Her Immaculate Hand*, no. 10.

19. Note Foscarini's designation as "doctor of both laws [canon and civil]," signifying his completion of a university education, in Nogarola's title: "Inter clarissimum D.D. Lodovicum Foscarenum Venetum Artium Utriusque Iuris Doctorem . . ." See King, *Venetian Humanist*, 41.

20. See above, n. 14.

LUDOVICO BEGINS: If it is in any way possible to measure the gravity of human sinfulness, then we should see Eve's sin as more to be condemned than Adam's because she was assigned by a just judge to a harsher punishment than was Adam; because she believed that she could become like God, which is considered an unforgivable sin against the Holy Spirit; because she provoked, and thus was the cause of Adam's sin—not he of hers; and because, finally, since it is an excuse, although a shameful one, if one is led into sin by a friend, yet she is not to be excused, since she is the one who enticed Adam to do wrong.

ISOTTA: But I see things—since you move me to reply—from quite another and contrary viewpoint. For where there is less intellect and less constancy, there there is less sin; and Eve lacked sense and constancy and therefore sinned less. Knowing her weakness, that crafty serpent began by tempting the woman, thinking the man perhaps invulnerable because of his constancy. For it says in *Sentences* 2,[21] Standing in the woman's presence, the ancient foe did not boldly persuade but approached her with a question: "Why did God bid you not to eat of the tree of paradise?" She responded, "Lest we should die." But seeing that she doubted the words of the Lord, the devil said, "You shall not die," but "you will be like gods, knowing good and evil."[22]

Adam must also be judged more guilty than Eve, second, because of his greater contempt for God's command. For in Genesis 2 it appears that the Lord commanded Adam, not Eve, where it says, "The Lord God took the man and placed him in the paradise of Eden to till it and to keep it" (and he did not say, "that they might care for and protect it"), " . . . and the Lord God commanded the man" (and not "them"): "From every tree of the garden you (singular) may eat and not "you" (plural), for the day you (singular) eat of it, you (singular) and not "you" (plural) will die."[23] God directed his command to Adam alone because he esteemed the man more highly than the woman.

Moreover, the woman did not eat from the forbidden tree because she believed she would become like God, but rather because she was weak and inclined to pleasure. It is written, "Now the woman saw that the tree was good for food and pleasing to the eyes. . . . She took of its fruit and ate it, and also gave some to her husband and he ate,"[24] and it does not say that she did so in order to be like God. And if Adam had not eaten, her sin would have had no consequences. For it does not say, "If Eve had not sinned

---

21. Peter Lombard *Sententiae in IV Libros Distinctae* 2.21.5.2 (PL 192:696).

22. Gn 3:4, 5.

23. Gn 2:15–17.

24. Gn 3:6.

Christ would not have been made incarnate," but "If Adam had not sinned," etc.[25] Thus the woman, but only because she had been first deceived by the serpent's evil persuasion, did indulge in the delights of paradise; but she would have harmed only herself and in no way endangered human posterity if the consent of the first-born man had not been offered. Therefore, Eve was no danger to posterity but *only* to herself; but the man Adam spread the infection of sin to himself and to all future generations. Thus Adam, being the author of all humans yet to be born, was also the first cause for their perdition. For this reason, the healing of humankind was celebrated first in the male and thereafter in the female sex of the human species; likewise, after Christ expelled the unclean spirit from the man, he went up from the synagogue and came to the woman to heal her.[26]

As for the argument that Eve was condemned by a just judge to a harsher punishment, it is evidently false, for God said to the woman, "I will greatly increase your pangs in childbearing; in pain shall you bring forth children; yet your desire shall be for your husband, and he shall rule over you."[27] But to Adam he said, "Because you have listened to your wife and have eaten of the tree of which I have commanded you (singular) not to eat (notice what is said, that God commanded Adam alone, and not Eve), cursed be the ground because of you; in toil shall you eat of it all the days of your life; thorns and thistles shall it bring forth to you, and you shall eat the plants of the field. In the sweat of your brow you shall eat bread till you return to the ground, since out of it you were taken; for dust you are and unto dust you shall return."[28] Here it is seen that Adam's punishment is harsher than Eve's; for God said to Adam, "To dust you shall return," and not to Eve, and death is the most terrible punishment that could be assigned. Therefore, it is established that Adam's punishment was greater than Eve's.

I have written this because you wished me to. Yet I have done so with trepidation, since this is not a woman's task. But you are kind, and if you find any part of my writing poorly done, you will correct it.

LUCOVICO: You defend the cause of Eve most subtly, and indeed defend it so well that, if I had not been born a man, you would have made me your

25. A variation on 1 Cor 15:22: "For as in Adam all die, even so in Christ shall all be made alive" (AV).

26. Abel, 2.190:15–19: "quamobrem prius in viro deinde in femina generis humani est celebrata curata, cum post expulsionem immundi spiritus a viro de sinagoga surgens persanando accessit ad feminam." Nogarola alludes to 1:23–28.

27. Gn 3:16.

28. Gn 3:17–19.

champion. But sticking fast to the truth, which is firmly rooted, I have set out to assault your fortress with your own weapons and shall now attack its foundations, which can be destroyed by the testimony of sacred Scripture, so there will be no lack of material for my refutation.

Eve sinned from ignorance and inconstancy, from which you conclude that she sinned less seriously. But ignorance—especially of those things that we are obligated to know—does not excuse us. For it is written, "But if any man be ignorant, let him be ignorant."[29] The eyes that guilt makes blind, punishment opens. He who has been foolish in guilt will be wise in punishment, especially when the sinner's mistake occurs through negligence. For the woman's ignorance, born of arrogance, does not excuse her. In the same way, Aristotle and the legal experts, who teach a true philosophy, find the drunk and ignorant deserving of a double punishment.[30] Nor do I understand how in the world you, who are so many ages distant from Eve, fault her intellect, when her knowledge had been divinely created by the supreme artisan of all things, and who, as you wrote, daunted that clever serpent lurking in paradise who was not bold enough to speak to her directly but approached her with a question.

Acts due to inconstancy, moreover, are even more blameworthy than those due to ignorance. For to the same degree that the acts issuing from a solid and constant mental attitude are more worthy and distinct from the preceding ones, so should those issuing from inconstancy be punished more severely, since inconstancy is an evil in itself and when paired with an evil sin makes the sin worse. Nor is Adam's companion excused because Adam was appointed to protect her, contrary to your contention that thieves who have been trustingly employed by a householder are not punished with the most severe punishment like strangers or those in whom no confidence has been placed. For the woman's frailty was not the cause of sin, as you write, but her pride, since the demon promised her knowledge, which leads to arrogance and inflates with pride, according to the apostle.[31] For it says in Ecclesiastes, "Pride was the beginning of every sin."[32]

And although the other women followed, yet she was the first since, when man existed in a state of innocence, his flesh was obedient to him and did not struggle against reason. The first impulse of sin, therefore, was an inordinate appetite for seeking that which was not suited to its own nature,

---

29. See 1 Cor 14:38 (AV).
30. Aristotle *Nicomachean Ethics* 3.5.1113b.30–33.
31. See 1 Cor 1:27–29; 8:1.
32. Eccl 10:13.

as Augustine wrote to Orosius, "Swollen by pride, man obeyed the serpent's persuasion and disdained God's commands."[33] For that adversary said to Eve "Your eyes will be opened and you will be like God, knowing good and evil."[34] Nor would the woman have believed the demon's persuasive words, as Augustine says in his commentary on Genesis, unless a love of her own power had overcome her, which love is a stream sprung from the well of pride.[35] I shall continue to follow Augustine in his view that at the moment when Eve desired to capture divinity she lost happiness. And those words, "If Adam had not sinned, etc." confirm me in my view. For Eve may have sinned in such a way that, just as the demons did not merit redemption, neither perhaps did she. I speak only in jest, but Adam's sin was fortunate since it warranted such a redeemer.[36]

And lest I finally stray too far from what you have written, I shall turn to your argument that Adam's punishment was more severe than Eve's and his sin, accordingly, greater. But the woman suffers all the penalties inflicted on the man, and since her sorrows are greater than his, not only is she doomed to death, condemned to eat at the cost of sweat, denied entry into paradise by the cherubim and flaming swords, but in addition to all these things that are common to both, she alone must give birth in pain and be subjected to her husband.

But because in such a matter it is not sufficient to have refuted your arguments without also putting forward my own, I shall do so now. Eve believed that she was made similar to God, and, out of envy, desired that which wounds the Holy Spirit. Moreover, she must bear responsibility for every fault of Adam because, as Aristotle testifies, the cause of a cause is the cause of that which is caused.[37] Indeed, every prior cause influences an

---

33. Augustine *Ad Orosium contra Priscillianistas et Origenistas liber unus* (PL 42:669–78), 671. Nogarola also seems to be acquainted with Augustine's *On Free Will* 3:25.76, where Augustine cites Ecclesiastes 10:13 (as Nogarola does here; see previous note) and comments, "To the devil's pride was added malevolent envy, so that he persuaded man to show the same pride as had proved the devil's damnation" (PL 32:1308); *Augustine: Earlier Writings,* Library of Christian Classics 6, trans. J. H. S. Burleigh (Philadelphia: Westminster Press, 1953), 216.

34. Gn 3:5.

35. The argument that Eve's pride led her to sin is in *De Genesi ad litteram* 11.30 (PL 34:445): *The Literal Meaning of Genesis* 42:162.

36. That Adam's sin was "fortunate" because it required for its expiation the life and death of Christ has its roots in the thought of Saint Paul, esp. Romans, and is a continuous thread in Christian theology. The "demons" Nogarola mentions are the fallen angels, expelled from heaven according to legend because they had rebelled against God; Lucifer, their leader, and the most brilliant of the angels, became the Devil, the prince of hell.

37. See Aristotle *Posterior Analytics* 2.11–12.94a20–96a19.

outcome more than a secondary cause, and the principle of any genus, according to the same Aristotle, is seen as its greatest component. In fact, it is considered to be more than half the whole.[38] And in the *Posterior Analytics* he writes, "That on account of which any thing exists is that thing and more greatly so."[39] now since Adam sinned on account of Eve, it follows that Eve sinned much more than Adam. Similarly, just as it is better to treat others well than to be well treated, so it is worse to persuade another to evil than to be persuaded to evil. For he sins less who sins by another's example, inasmuch as what is done by example can be said to be done according to a kind of law. For this reason it is commonly said that "the sins that many commit are without fault." Thus Eve, who persuaded her husband to commit an evil act, sinned more greatly than Adam, who merely consented to her example.

And if Adam and Eve both had thought that they were worthy of the same glory, Eve, who was inferior by nature, more greatly departed from the mean and consequently sinned more greatly. Moreover, as a beloved companion she could deceive her husband, vulnerable because of his love for her, more easily than the shameful serpent could deceive the woman. And she persevered longer in sin than Adam because she began first and offenses are that much more serious (according to Gregory's decree) in relation to the length of time they hold the unhappy soul in bondage.[40] Finally, to bring my discourse to a close, Eve was the cause and the example of sin, and Gregory greatly increases the guilt in the case of the example.[41] And Christ, who could not err, condemned more severely the pretext of the ignorant Jews, because it came first, than he did the sentence of the learned Pilate, when he said, "They who have betrayed me to you have greater sin, etc."[42] All who wish to be called Christians have always agreed with this judgment, and you, above all most Christian, will approve and defend it. Farewell, and do not fear, but dare to do much, because you understand so many things so well and write so learnedly.

ISOTTA: I had decided that I would not enter further into a contest with you because, as you say, you assault my fortress with my own weapons. The

---

38. *Posterior Analytics*, 2.13.96a24–96b24.

39. A paraphrase of the line of thought expressed in the previous passage; see previous note.

40. Saint Gregory *Liber regulae pastoralis* 3.32 (PL 77:115); *St. Gregory's Pastoral Rule*, in *Nicene and Post-Nicene Fathers*, ed. Philip Schaff and Henry Waceser (Peabody, Mass.: Hendrickson Publishers, 1994; orig. 1890), ser. 2, 12:65.

41. Gregory *Liber* 1.2 (PL 77.15–16; NPNF, ser. 2, 12:2).

42. Nogarola is reading into the text of the Gospels here; there is no recorded exchange between Jesus and Pilate that says exactly this, although this meaning could have been elicited from the text in contemporary (and probably anti-Semitic) sermons.

propositions you have presented me were so perfectly and diligently defended that it would be difficult not merely for me, but for the most learned men, to oppose them. But since I recognize that this contest is useful for me, I have decided to obey your honest wish. Even though I know I struggle in vain, yet I will earn the highest praise if I am defeated by so mighty a man as you.

Eve sinned out of ignorance and inconstancy, and hence you contend that she sinned more gravely because the ignorance of those things which we are obligated to know does not excuse us, since it is written, "But if any man be ignorant, let him be ignorant."[43] I would concede your point if that ignorance were crude or affected. But Eve's ignorance was implanted by nature, of which nature God himself is the author and founder. In many people it is seen that he who knows less sins less, like a boy who sins less than an old man or a peasant less than a noble. Such a person does not need to know explicitly what is required for salvation, but implicitly, because for him faith alone suffices. The question of inconstancy proceeds similarly. For when it is said that the acts that proceed from inconstancy are more blameworthy, what kind of inconstancy is understood that is not innate but that is the product of a vicious character.

The same is true of imperfection. For when gifts increase, greater responsibility is imposed. When God created man, from the beginning he created him perfect and the powers of his soul perfect and gave him a greater understanding and knowledge of truth as well as a greater depth of wisdom. Thus it was that the Lord led to Adam all the animals of the earth and the birds of heaven so that Adam could call them by their names. For God said, "Let us make humankind in our image, according to our likeness; and let them have dominion over the fish of the sea, and over the birds of the air, and over the cattle, and over all the wild animals of the earth, and over every creeping thing that creeps upon the earth."[44] making clear how great was the man's perfection. But of the woman he said, "It is not good that the man is alone; I will make him a helper like himself."[45] And since consolation and joy are required for happiness, and since no one can have solace and joy when alone, it is seen that God created woman for man's consolation; for the good diffuses, and the greater it is the more it radiates from itself. Therefore, it appears that

43. 1 Cor 14.38A.
44. Gn 1:26 (NRSV).
45. Gn 2:18.

Adam's sin was greater than Eve's. As Ambrose says, "In him to whom a more indulgent liberality has been shown, insolence is more inexcusable."[46]

"But Adam's companion," you argue, "is not excused because Adam was appointed to protect her, because thieves who have been trustingly employed by a householder are not punished with the most severe punishments like strangers or those in whom the householder placed no confidence." This is true, however, in temporal law, but not in divine law, for divine justice proceeds differently from temporal justice in punishing sin.

You argue further that "the fragility of the woman was not the cause of sin, but rather her inordinate appetite for seeking that which was not suited to her nature," which appetite is the consequence, as you write, of pride. Yet it is clearly less a sin to desire the knowledge of good and evil than to transgress against a divine commandment, since the desire for knowledge is a natural thing and all men by nature desire to know.[47] And even if the first impulse of sin were this inordinate appetite, which cannot be without sin, yet it is more tolerable than the sin of transgression, for the observance of the commandments is the road that leads to the homeland of salvation. It is written, "But if thou wilt enter into life, keep the commandments;[48] and likewise, "What shall I do to gain eternal life? Keep the commandments."[49] And transgression is particularly born of pride, because pride is nothing other than rebellion against divine rule, exalting oneself above what is permitted according to divine rule by disdaining the will of God and displacing it with one's own. Thus Augustine writes in *On Nature and Grace*, "Sin is the will to pursue or retain what justice forbids, that is, to deny what God wishes."[50] Ambrose agrees with him in his *On Paradise*: "Sin is the transgression against divine law and disobedience to the heavenly commandments."[51] Behold! It is clear that the greatest sin is the transgression against and disobedience to the heavenly commandments; whereas you have thus defined sin: "Sin is the inordinate desire to know." But it is evident that the sin of transgression against a command is greater than the sin of desiring the knowledge of good and evil. So even if inordinate desire be a sin, as with Eve, yet she did not

---

46. Ambrose *Expositio in Lucam* 9:23 (PL 15:1891).

47. "All men by nature desire to know" is the opening sentence of Aristotle's *Metaphysics*.

48. Mt 19:17.

49. Mk 10:17ff.; Mt 19:16–17; Lk 18:18ff.

50. This idea is pervasive in Augustine's *On Nature and Grace*: a close parallel is found in chap. 67 (PL 44:286–88; NPNF, ser. 1, 5:145).

51. Ambrose *De paradiso* 8.39 (PL 14:309); *Hexameron, Paradise, and Cain and Abel*, trans. John J. Savage, Fathers of the Church 42 (Washington, D.C.: Catholic University Press, 1977; orig. 1961), 316–18.

desire to be like God in power but only in the knowledge of good and evil, which by nature she was actually inclined to desire.

Next, as to your statement that those words, "if Adam had not sinned," confirm you in your view, since Eve may have so sinned that, like the demons, she did not merit redemption, I reply that she also was redeemed with Adam, because she was "bone of my bone and flesh of my flesh."[52] And it seems that if God did not redeem her, this was undoubtedly because God held her sin as negligible. For if man deserved redemption, the woman deserved it much more because of the slightness of the crime. For the rebellious angel cannot claim to be excused by ignorance, as can Eve. For the angel understands without investigation or discussion and has an intellect more in the likeness of God's—to which it seems Eve desired to be similar—than does man. Hence the angel is called intellectual and the man rational. So where Eve sinned from her desire for knowledge, the angel sinned from a desire for power. While knowledge of an appearance in some small way can be partaken of by the creature, in no way can it partake in the power of God and of the soul of Christ. Moreover, Eve in sinning thought she would receive mercy, believing certainly that she was committing a sin, but not one so great as to warrant God's inflicting such a sentence and punishment. But the angel did not think of mercy. Hence Gregory says in the fourth book of the *Moralia,* "The first parents were needed for this, that the sin that they committed by transgressing they might purge by confessing."[53] But that persuasive serpent was never punished for his sin, for he was never to be recalled to grace. It is evident, then, that Eve merited redemption more than the angels.

As to your argument that Eve is made to suffer all the penalties inflicted on Adam, and beyond those that are common to both, since she alone gives birth in sorrow and has been subjected to man, this also reinforces my earlier point. As I said, the good is diffused, and the greater it is the more it radiates from itself. So also evil: the greater it is the more it radiates from itself, and the more it is diffused the more harmful it is, and the more harmful it is the greater it is. Furthermore, the severity of the punishment is proportional to the gravity of the sin. Hence, Christ chose to die on the cross, although this was the most shameful and horrible kind of death, and on the cross he endured the culmination of every kind of suffering. Hence Isidore writes concerning the trinity, "The only-born Son of God is executing the sacrament of his death, in himself bears witness that he consummated every kind

52. Gn 2:23.
53. Gregory *Moralium libri* 4.36.62 (PL 75:670–71); *Morals on the Book of Job,* 3 vols., trans. J. Bliss (Oxford: J. H. Parker, 1844–50).

of suffering when, with lowered head, he gave up his spirit."[54] The reason was that the punishment had to correspond to the guilt. Adam took the fruit of the forbidden tree; Christ suffered on the tree and so made satisfaction for Adam's sin. As Augustine writes, "Adam disdained God's command (and he does not say Eve), accepting the fruit from the tree, but whatever Adam lost Christ restored."[55] As it says in Psalm 64, "For what I have not taken, then I atoned."[56] Therefore, Adam's sin was the greatest possible, because the punishment corresponding to his fault was the greatest possible and was general in all men. As the apostle Paul says, "All sinned in Adam."[57]

"Eve," you say, "must bear responsibility for every fault of Adam because as Aristotle shows, whatever is the cause of the cause is the cause of the thing caused." This is true in the case of things that are, as you know better than I, in themselves the causes of other things, which is the case for the first cause, the first principle, and "that on account of which anything is what it is." But clearly this was not the case with Eve, because Adam either had free will or he did not. If he did not have it, he did not sin; if he had it, then Eve forced the sin upon him, which is impossible. For as Bernard says, "Free will, because of its inborn nobility, is forced by no necessity,"[58] not even by God, because if that were the case it would be to concede that two contradictories are true at the same time. God cannot do, therefore, what would cause an act proceeding from free will and remaining free to be not free but coerced. As Augustine writes in his commentary on Genesis, "God cannot act against that nature which he created with a good will."[59] God could himself, however, remove that condition of liberty from any person and bestow some other condition on him. In the same way fire cannot, while it remains fire, not burn, unless its nature is changed and suspended for a time by divine force. No other creature, such as a good angel or devil, can do this, since they are less than God; much less a woman, since she is less perfect

---

54. Isidore did not write a book on the Trinity, and he does not make statements similar to these in his discussion of the Trinity in *Etymologiae* 7.1–4 (PL 82:259–72).

55. *De Genesi ad litteram* 8:17–19 (PL 34:387); *The Literal Meaning of Genesis* 42:58–60.

56. Ps 69:4. That is, Christ paid the penalty for sin he had not committed, as if saying, "The crimes I did not commit, for these I have atoned."

57. Rom 5:12: "Therefore as through one man sin entered into the world and through sin death, and thus death has passed unto all men because all have sinned . . ."

58. Similar although not identical statements in Bernard's *On Grace and Free Choice* 1.2 and 4.9 (PL 182:1002, 1006–7); *The Works of Bernard of Clairvaux*, vol. 7, *On Grace and Free Choice*, trans. D. O'Donovan, intro. B. McGinn (Kalamazoo, Mich.: Cistercian Publications, 1971), 55–56, 65.

59. Augustine *De Genesi ad litteram* 11.9–16 (PL 34:434–58); *The Literal Meaning of Genesis* 42: 141–48.

and weaker than they. Augustine clarifies this principle saying, "Above our mind is nothing besides God, nor is there anything intermediary between God and our mind."[60] Yet only something that is superior to something else can coerce it; but Eve was inferior to Adam, therefore she was not herself the cause of sin. In Ecclesiastes 15 it says, "God from the beginning created man and placed him in the palm of his counsel and made clear his commandments and precepts. If you wish to preserve the commandments, they will preserve you and create in you pleasing faith."[61] Thus Adam appeared to accuse God rather than excuse himself when he said, "The woman you gave me made me sin."[62]

Next you argue that the beloved companion could have more easily deceived the man than the shameful serpent the woman. To this I reply that Eve, weak and ignorant by nature, sinned much less by assenting to that astute serpent, who was called "wise," than Adam—created by God with perfect knowledge and understanding—in listening to the persuasive words and voice of the imperfect woman.

Further, you say that Eve persevered in her sin a longer time and therefore sinned more, because crimes are that much more serious according to the length of time they hold the unhappy soul in bondage. This is no doubt true, when two sins are equal, and in the same person or in two similar persons. But Adam and Eve were not equals, because Adam was a perfect animal and Eve imperfect and ignorant.

Finally, if I may quote you, "The woman was the example and the cause of sin, and Gregory emphatically extends the burden of guilt to the person who provided an example, and Christ condemned the cause of the ignorant Jews, because it was first, more than the learned Pilate's sentence when he said, 'Therefore he who betrayed me to you has greater sin.'" I reply that Christ did not condemn the cause of the ignorant Jews because it was first, but because it was vicious and devilish because of their native malice and obstinacy. For they did not sin from ignorance. The gentile Pilate was more ignorant about these things than the Jews, who had the law and the prophets and read them and daily saw signs concerning Christ. For John 15 says, "If I had not come and spoken to them, they would have no sin. But now they

---

60. Although an exact source cannot be identified, this concept is pervasive in Augustine's works (*Confessions, On True Religion,* and others) and in medieval Augustinianism.

61. Eccl 15:14–15: "It was he who created man in the beginning, and he left him in the power of his own inclination. If you will, you can keep the commandments, and to act faithfully is a matter of your own choice."

62. Gn 3:12. Or, "placed at my side gave me fruit from the tree and I ate it."

have no excuse for their sin."[63] Thus they themselves said, "What are we doing? For this man is working signs."[64] And, "Art thou the Christ, the Son of the Blessed One?"[65] For the Jewish people was special to God, and Christ himself said, "I was not sent except to the lost sheep of the house of Israel. It is not fair to take the children's bread and cast it to the dogs."[66] Therefore, the Jews sinned more, because Jesus loved them more. Let these words be enough for me, an unarmed and poor little woman.

LUDOVICO: So divinely have you encompassed the whole of this problem that your words seem to have been drawn not from the fonts of philosophy and theology but from heaven itself. Hence they are worthy of praise rather than contradiction. Yet, lest you be cheated of the utility you may experience from this debate, attend to these brief arguments that can be posed for the opposite view, that you may sow the honey-sweet seeds of paradise that will delight readers and surround you with glory.

Eve's ignorance was very base because she chose to put faith in a demon rather than in the Creator. This ignorance actually is due to her sin, as sacred writings attest, and certainly does not excuse her sin. Indeed, if the truth be plainly told, it was sheer stupidity not to remain within the boundaries that the excellent God had set for her, but to fall prey to vain hope and lose what she had possessed and what she aspired to.

The issues that you have clearly joined I shall not divide. The inconstancy of Eve that has been condemned was not an inconstancy of nature but of habit. For those qualities that are in us by nature we are neither praised nor blamed, according to the judgment of the wisest philosophers. Actually, Eve's nature was excellent and concordant with reason, her sex, and her age. For just as teeth were given to wild beasts, horns to oxen, feathers to birds for their survival, to the woman mental capacity was given sufficient for the preservation and pursuit of the health of her soul.

If, as you argue, Eve was naturally created to aid, perfect, console, and gladden man, she conducted herself contrary to the laws of her nature, providing him with toil, imperfection, sadness, and sorrow, which the holy decrees had ordained would be serious crimes. And human laws, too, ordered through long ages by the minds of great men, by sure reasoning have established that the seizure of someone else's goods merits the more serious punishment the more it injures the owner.

---

63. Jn 15:22.
64. Jn 11:47.
65. Mk 14:61; Mt 26:63; Lk 22:67, 70.
66. Mt 15:24, 26.

Your argument about Adam's transgression of God's commandments does not acquit Eve of responsibility because she did not keep them either. As to your distinction between the sin of the angel and of man, that is a huge issue, and although it provides worthy food for your brilliant mind, it is too abundant to consider in this brief space. And how you can consider it to be concordant with the principle of the highest God's goodness that greater punishments are poured out upon those who have sinned less, I cannot understand.

You push too far Aristotle's views on first causes. You agree that every cause of a cause is a cause of the thing caused. But since Adam had free will, I do not consider him free from sin, and even though I have assigned Adam's whole fault in some degree to Eve, yet I do not contend that Adam's sin was entirely and in every way caused by Eve.

I agree with what you say concerning free will and the essential goodness of human nature.

As to the ease of the man's consent to the woman's words, I want, since I am writing to you, to pass by in silence the matter of the deceitfulness of the female sex. But this ancient proverb stands: "There is no plague more deadly than an intimate enemy."[67] The first mother kindled a great fire, which to our ruin has not yet been extinguished.[68] This demonstrates the extreme seriousness of her sin: for just as those sicknesses of the body are more serious that are less curable, so also are the diseases of the soul.

Although I have spoken, you may not hear. You may spurn and disdain my words if you agree with Augustine's conclusion that they were equally guilty: "The principle of how much longer, etc." Let us read the history of the Passion and the dreams of the wife, the words of Pilate, the washing of hands, the avoidance of judgment, and we shall confess that he understood better than the Jews that the sentence was unjust.[69] These things make it quite clear that the force of my arguments has not been weakened.

I have explained my views with these few words, both because I was ordered not to exceed the paper sent me[70] and because I speak to you who are most learned. For you do not need me to guide you, for whom, because of

---

67. Boethius *De consolatione philosophiae* 3.5 (PL 63:743); *The Consolation of Philosophy,* trans. Richard Green (New York: Macmillan, 1962), 52.

68. Echoes Catiline's statement *incendium meum ruina restinguam,* reported by Sallust *Catiline* 31.9, and Cicero *Pro Murena* 25.51.

69. Passing references to the scene of Pilate's interview with Jesus and related events; based on passages in Matthew 27; Mark 15; Luke 23; John 18, 19; see also Acts 3:13, 4:27, 13:28.

70. A conventional statement; Foscarini alludes to the guidelines of length agreed upon by the two disputants.

your great goodness, the path ahead is perfectly bright and clear. I am only one who has pointed a finger, so to speak, in the direction of the sources—a reflection on earth of the celestial life; and although others may find that my writings suffer from the defect of obscurity, if you, who are most brilliant, accept them and join them to what you and I have already written, our views will become known and will sparkle and shine amid the shadows. And if what I have written is clumsy, by your skill you will make it worthy of your mind, virtue, and glory, you who march forward ever to new battles to the sound of sacred eloquence (as do soldiers to the clamor of trumpets), always more learned and more ready. And you march forward against me, who has applied the whole sum of my thinking to my reading and in the same spirit to my writing, that I might present my case and defend myself against yours, although the many storms and floods of my obligations toss me about at whim. Farewell.

VIII

THE BLACK SWAN: TWO ORATIONS
FOR ERMOLAO BARBARO (1453)

In 1434, when Nogarola's brother Antonio was studying for his doctorate at Padua, he urged her to write his friend Ermolao Barbaro, the nephew of the eminent Venetian statesman and humanist Francesco Barbaro. Ermolao, then twenty-four and full of promise, already held the title apostolic protonotary. In this first overture, Nogarola sent the young cleric a polished Latin letter in which she extravagantly sang his praises.[1] This early eulogy has two main focal points: the first, Nogarola's fear of "going public" and thus exposing her style to the scrutiny of the Venetian literati, who would talk. The second is her portrait of Barbaro, who represents a mirror of all the virtues. He is endowed with the gift of eloquence, the quality most essential to good statesmanship in the republic. He is learned in canon as well as civil law, he possesses greatness of mind, gravity, magnanimity, prudence, fairness, and all the other character traits exemplified by his distinguished patrician clan. He is, she writes, quoting the Roman satirist Juvenal verbatim, "a bird as rare as a black swan." Isotta at sixteen may have been unaware that Juvenal used the phrase to comment on the sort of woman who is so proud of her virtues that she is insufferable.[2] Certainly, in her later years she made the conscious decision in collecting her correspondence for a letterbook to keep the mocking reference to Juvenal's *Sixth Satire.*

Nogarola certainly had reason to resent Barbaro in 1453. When Ludovico Foscarini came to Verona in 1451 as the Venetian governor of the city, a growing intimacy quickly developed between Nogarola and the governor, as chapters 6 and 7 have shown. But when Foscarini's compatriot Ermolao

---

1. See above, chap. 1, no. 1.
2. Abel, 1.10: "O rara avis in terris nigroque simillima cygno," quoting Juvenal 6.162–66.

Barbaro came to Verona as the city's new bishop in 1453, Barbaro intervened decisively to put an end to the visits between the forty-four-year-old career diplomat Foscarini, who at the time was married and serving as the Venetian governor of Brescia,[3] and the thirty-five-year-old unmarried Veronese woman. Foscarini wrote Nogarola elliptically, probably in January of that year, that Barbaro had warned him of the impropriety of such visits and he told Isotta of his feelings:

> I am in torment, because now I must either fail the bishop with regard to the promises that were made at your house or deny myself the pleasure I was so much anticipating; especially since you had promised me you would be even sweeter and more generous when I return to you and that you would remember and tell me, step by step, everything that you hear and read in your holy days. It is painful to betray a promise, painful to forego those most totally honest, most fruitful, and most avidly awaited desires. I know what I should do; what I shall do I do not know.[4]

It was with this emotional struggle in the background that Nogarola dedicated two orations to Barbaro when he came to Verona as the city's bishop in 1453, the first of these an encomium congratulating him on his new appointment. This eulogy of Barbaro is very different from the one she wrote twenty years earlier. Although she again pays tribute to his full panoply of Roman virtues—his *gravitas, prudentia, magnanimitas, iustitia* (gravity, prudence, magnanimity, justice)—what she now emphasizes is the forty-three-year-old cleric's severity and his extraordinary and, she implies, joyless diligence in his studies. Barbaro would publish in 1455 two *Orationes contra poetas*, companion works attacking the study of ancient poetry on the grounds that poetry did not contribute to civic life and did not assist in the search for truth.[5] He would be scorned for these views by contemporary connoisseurs of frankly sensual Latin poetry. It is perhaps in the same vein that Nogarola here compares him to two famous ascetics in antiquity: Demosthenes who, writes Nogarola, "consumed more lamp oil than wine," and Archimedes who was

---

3. Foscarini was the governor (Podesta) of Verona 1450–51; Provveditore of Brescia 1451–52; Podesta of Brescia 1453–54; see King, *Venetian Humanism*, 375.

4. The letter at Abel, 2:37–38 is dated "principo anni 1453." The Latin text is given above, chap. 6 at n. 9.

5. For Barbaro's *Orationes contra poetas*, see King, *Venetian Humanism*, 157–61; and Frank, *Le insidie dell'allegoria*.

"so absorbed in the study of mathematics that he did not see the food on his plate."[6]

The change in tone that can be noted in this oration is paralleled by a shift in the spectrum of sources that Nogarola utilizes. Whereas her adolescent encomium to the apostolic protonotary had been laced with showy allusions to classical references including Petronius's *Satyricon*, Plautus's *Aulularia*, Cicero's *Brutus*, Plutarch's *Moralia* (*De Garrulitate*), and Juvenal's *Satires* but no biblical references, this mature oration of hers displays a subtle interweaving of classical and scriptural texts. In this second eulogy of Barbaro, Nogarola mingles texts from Exodus, Jeremiah, the Song of Solomon, and a reference to John Chrysostom's commentary on Matthew with Anecdotes and phrases from Aulus Gellius' *Attic Nights*, Cicero's *Defense of Cluentius*, Plutarch's *Lives of Cicero* and *Demosthenes*, the Elder Seneca's *Controversiae*, Statius' *Silvae*, and a lengthy quotation from Ennius's *Annales.*[7]

Although Isotta does not explicitly hail the citizens of Verona in this encomium to Barbaro of 1453, the work gives evidence of having been a delivered oration. Her numerous analogies between her own nervousness about public speaking and that of the famous orators of antiquity—Demosthenes, Theophrastus, Cicero, and Marcus Geminus—suggest that she had in mind either a public audience or a smaller gathering of friends as her audience when she composed this work. More respectful than deferential to Barbaro in this later work, she ends the letter with a promise of support from her influential family.

The second oration, in praise of Saint Jerome, explicitly addresses the citizens of Verona and is clearly a public oration delivered in Verona in 1453 shortly after Barbaro took office. In 1453, he asked Nogarola, in his role as the new bishop of Verona, to deliver a public oration on the life of Saint Jerome before the people of Verona. Did Barbaro invite Nogarola to write this oration on the life of the Church's most brilliant and learned ascetic as an act of obedience or as a lesson in renunciation after he had intervened to end

---

6. Abel, 2:270: "Nam legisse memini Demosthenem tantam in exercitatione dicendi operam posuisse, ut longe plus olei ut videret, quam ut biberet vini consumpserit." And Abel, 2:271 "testes sunt qui tecum vitam agunt, ut de te affirment quod de Archimede legitur, qui tanta mathematicarum artium abstractione detineri solitus sit, ut plerumque appositas non videret escas."

7. Recondite because Ennius's (b. 239 B.C.E. in Calabria) massive historical work in dactylic hexameter entitled *Annales*, which had eighteen books, is largely lost and already had survived only in fragments by the time of the Renaissance. Most of these fragments have come down in Cicero and Lactantius. Ennius also wrote tragedies, comedies, and several books of mixed verse.

her relationship with the former governor of Verona, Foscarini? Certainly, in the first third of the oration she stresses two qualities of her own—obedience and humility—as her motivation in accepting Barbaro's charge. She lauds the exceptional virtue of "true humility, which is obedient not to its own but another's will."[8]

The humanists often measured the corruption and faults of the established church against the lives and ideals of the early church fathers. They saw a combination of Christian piety and learned study of the ancients as a model. Key among the early fathers to be imitated in classical and biblical scholarship was the early and most authoritative translator of the Bible, Saint Jerome.[9] Four themes characterize Nogarola's portrait of Saint Jerome in her eulogy of him: the depth of his learning, from the ancient texts of Greece and Rome to those of the Near and Middle East; the syncretism of his study in the evolution of his ideas; his rejection of the established church; and his willing embrace of the desert and the abyss, or the unknown, in his search for God.

Jerome's early education in the grammar, rhetoric, history, and philosophy of the ancient Greeks and Romans was not an end in itself but formed the foundation for all his future travels, studies, and translations as he journeyed eastward, mastered new languages, and sought new knowledge. He understood that only through studying other cultures could he attain knowledge of divine truth. Just as Moses and Daniel had to embrace the teachings of the Egyptians and Babylonians to find God, so Jerome traveled eastward to the Holy Land in search of God. Having absorbed the wisdom of the East, he was at last ready to undertake his crowning achievement, the translation of the Old and New Testaments from Hebrew and Greek into what we now know as the Latin Vulgate. At last made a cardinal by the pope, Jerome refused the pomp, wealth, and corruption of the church to find his own way to Christ in the desert and through mortification of the flesh and abstention from every ordinary comfort—shelter from the heat and cold, cooked food, and clothing. Quoting at length Jerome's famous letter to his young female disciple, Eustochium "On Virginity," Nogarola emphasizes Jerome's rejection of the creature comforts of the world, passing over quickly his vow of chastity. She does, however, praise the saint's lifelong commitment to virginity in a later passage.

8. Abel, 2:278: "Et illa vera humilitas est, quae non suae sed alienae optat reverenter obtemperare voluntati."

9. For Jerome, see Rice, "The Renaissance Idea of Christian Antiquity"; and Rice, *Saint Jerome.*

By emphasizing Jerome's role as a tireless seeker of knowledge and heroically austere philosopher, Nogarola understates that message of Jerome that, in the fifteenth century generally, was understood to be paramount: his elevation of the virtue of virginity. So in a sense, Nogarola, who was meant by Barbaro to propound holy virginity, and perhaps meditate upon her own commitment to that pattern of life, here reverses roles and uses the oration to reproach Barbaro. She delivers a moral lesson to him, the epitome of the established cleric complacently enjoying the daily benefits of the established church, by placing before his eyes the image of the ascetic and learned Jerome.

With the exception of the consolatory letter she wrote for Damiano dal Borgo and her *Dialogue* on Adam and Eve, Nogarola's works before 1451 contain no biblical or Christian references. In the syncretic humanism of her later works, Nogarola seems intent on striking a balance between Christian and classical references. In this oration, while she pays tribute to the classical masters of oratory, Cicero and Quintilian; while she repeats her favorite anecdote about the Greek Euclides' determination to hear the wisdom of Socrates firsthand; while she speaks of Aristotle and Donatus and quotes from Aulus Gellius and Statius; at the same time she celebrates Jerome's translations of Isaiah, Jeremiah, Ezekiel, Daniel, the Psalms, Ecclesiastes, and the Song of Solomon and his commentaries to the New Testament.

XXIX

Oration to the Very Reverend Lord Ermolao Barbaro, Bishop of Verona, 1453

In this oration, Nogarola addresses the nephew of the Venetian statesman and humanist Francesco Barbaro on his appointment to the bishopric of Verona in 1453. Quoting a passage from Exodus and casting herself in the role of the prophet Miriam, she greets Barbaro on behalf of her city with the stock inaugural formula for such an occasion: "Let us celebrate and rejoice this day. For since God is compassionate, you are the holy high priest he has given us."

I do not doubt that there will be a good many men who will marvel at me and who will continue to accuse me of effrontery because I have seized the opportunity to write to you, although I am a woman who has neither natural talent nor skill in oratory, since they know many of the most erudite men both of our own and former times were terrified and overcome with shyness when they were about to deliver a eulogy. Among them, we have read about Demosthenes, who, for all his great eloquence, almost died from shyness when he was about to present an oration at the court of King Philip.[10] It was the same for the philosopher Theophrastus and Cicero, the prince of eloquence, so the ancient histories testify. And so I must agree with those men: I have indeed taken on a most daunting burden and one deeply alien to me.[11] Still, when I hear of your mercy, kindness, and gentleness, my fear fades and I recover. I summon new powers for my trembling mind when I think of the orator Marcus Geminus who, when he approached Caesar and was about to deliver his speech, said, "Whoever dares to speak in your presence, Caesar, is unaware of your greatness, and whoever does not dare, of your kindness."[12] Therefore, moved by your kindness, compassion, and singular piety, it pleases me—and I am overcome with joy—with the prophetess Miriam[13] and our whole republic to greet you with this festive and joyous hymn of celebration from the bottom of my heart.

For who is so hard-hearted, so lacking in gentility and piety, that he is not moved by such joy and does not give thanks to divine providence that compassion, having banished the clouds with its rays, lighted the way and led this people, who had lost their shepherd and wandered away in darkness, back to the right road? For this is the day the Lord has appointed. Let us celebrate and rejoice in this day. For, since God is compassionate, you are the holy high priest he has given us: elected not by fortune or misfortune but by divine auspices; and not undeservedly, since praise and honor are the just deserts of virtue. As to how much toil and sweat you put into your work to achieve this, I have considered it better to say nothing, since there is no power of speech, no capacity for eloquence so great that it could describe

---

10. On the extreme nervousness of Demosthenes and Theophrastus in presenting their orations in public, see Aulus Gellius 8.9; on Cicero's performance anxiety, see Plutarch *Cicero* 35.

11. "Onus et penitus a me *alienum*" (my italics): note Nogarola's use of one of the key terms that marks her discourse on gender, nature, and intellectual and literary talent (*ingenium*). What is woman's nature, she asks repeatedly, and what is *alienum* to it? Along with this question comes her query about external vs. internal goods. See, for example, her conclusion to the *consolatio* for Marcello.

12. Seneca *Excerpta Controversiarum* 6.8 (L. Annaeus Seneca Maior, *Oratorum et Rhetorum Sententiae, Divisiones, Colores*, ed. Lennart Hakanson [Leipsig: Teubner, 1989]): "Varius Geminum apud Caesarem dixit: Caesar, qui apud te audent dicere, magnitudinem tuam ignorant, qui non audent, humanitatem." Cf. Nogarola: "Qui apud te, inquit, Caesar, dicere audet, magnitudinem tuam nescit, qui vero non audet, humanitatem."

13. In Exodus 15:20, 21, the prophetess Miriam is the icon for joyous hymns of celebration; she led the women in triumphal dances after Moses led the children of Israel across the Red Sea and delivered them from the Pharaoh's oppression.

the many refinements of nature, humanity, and virtue you have attained, with nature as your guide and diligence as your companion.

For who does not know how much effort and delight you have put in mastering, from earliest childhood on, as it were, to this day, the art of oratory under Guarino, the prince of eloquence, so that it could be rightly said of you what antiquity used to say of Cicero, Demosthenes, and innumerable others? For I remember reading that Demosthenes put so much work in the practice of speaking that he consumed far more lamp oil than he did wine.[14] The discipline of rhetoric gripped him with such a fervor, he testified, that he appeared to be reduced to skin and bones from his excessive efforts.[15] You have taken care to imitate such men throughout your whole career because you know that a man who fills himself up on vice cannot acquire this ability, and you are also aware that the person who attains, as they say, the name of a "good man" applies himself to the great challenge and intensity[16] of eloquence. And my witness, lest I should appear to be spinning lies in the manner of a flatterer, is Guarino himself, in whose house you lived in such a way that he did not hesitate during that period to call you his favorite.

However, not content with the art of rhetoric alone but moved by the spirit of God, you have gathered all the other virtues together that could adorn and be useful to you, whatever post you might occupy. You studied the precepts and teachings of the philosophers, and as the companion of this pursuit you undertook the study of both civil and canon law, and you willingly perfected much in both systems, which together provide the foundations of the catholic faith. Finally, you sought the contemplation of the divine and knowledge of God the omnipotent, preferring to all else these and everything that sacred theology teaches us to know. For through study we come to know, love, enjoy, and possess God. As to how much time you have spent on this, witnesses who live with you can say of you what we read about Archimedes: he was often so absorbed in the study of mathematics that for the most part he did not see the food on his plate.[17]

---

14. "Ut longe plus olei ut videret quam ut biberet vini consumpserit": Plutarch *Demosthenes* 8 comments on the midnight lamp oil (*oleum*) Demosthenes burned in his striving for the perfect phrases and the perfect delivery. A rival even taunted him with the remark that his arguments stank of lampwick.

15. Note the Virgilian diction: "ut nimio labore vix ossibus haerere videretur": denoting emaciation as in *Eclogues* 3.102: "hi . . . vix ossibus haerent,"

16. "ad eloquentiae magnitudinem": one word does not capture the sense of *magnitudo* in this context. It denotes here more a combination of range, breadth, importance, crucial discipline, and maybe largeness.

17. We cannot identify a source for this anecdote about Archimedes, which does not appear in Plutarch's *Lives*

You knew, however, that this learning is necessary not only for men in private life but also for princes themselves and especially for those on whom the people's safety apparently depends. Jerome argues that a priest's duty is to answer questions about the law; Paul urges a bishop to pursue, among other virtues, knowledge of the Holy Scriptures; and Daniel says that just and knowledgeable men, the learned, that is, shine like stars in the firmament. Therefore, because you are graced with so great and distinguished a garland of virtues and knowledge, when you fled to the arms of the Roman Church she[18] adorned you with many honors, like the just judge who gives to each his just deserts. As to the generosity, humaneness, compassion, justice, and gravity that have characterized your life, I have decided to be silent rather than speak inelegantly or even waste your time on a subject that is very familiar. For your judgments are so illustrious and well known that they lack no eloquent eulogists, much less my own approbation or praises. But let the consequences and the outcome of things speak for themselves.

I exult therefore and I raise my hands to heaven for joy. I shed tears for piety when I look at you as our high priest, since I have no doubt that with your work, diligence, protection, and support this city of ours will be sanctified and blessed. For every evil custom will be eradicated, vices will be destroyed, virtues will be exalted, and religion, pure and incorruptible, will be preserved. As it says in Jeremiah, "Behold, I set you above all nations and kingdoms to root out and destroy, to build and to plant."[19] Now this city, its boys and unmarried girls will sing, "I sat down under the shade of that man whom I desired, and his fruit was sweet to my taste. His left hand will be under my head, his right hand will embrace me."[20] Therefore, make me immortal, most reverend father and high priest, with the splendor of your glory, and lift me up not as a lord but as a father, and cherish and embrace me. For thus you will acquire glory, praise, and the rewards of everlasting life.

We, however, will cherish your gifts and honor your attainments and your memory with as much love as Pompilius Numa and Romulus were

18. "Te igitur, hac tanta tamque insigni virtutum et scientiarum corona, ad Romanam *ecclesiam* veluti ad matrem confugientem, **ea**, temquam iustus iudex qui reddit unicuique iusta opera sua, multis dignatibus **decoravit**" (italics and bolds are ours): This a murderously Ciceronian sentence. We have repunctuated it, setting off all the prepositional phrases and subordinate clauses from the main clause; the main clause consists simply in the following: *ea* (subject nominative feminine singular) *decoravit* (verb) *te* (direct object accusative). The rest is not a problem. But what is *ea*? We are taking *ecclesiam* as its antecedent.

19. See chap. 9, n. 26, for her quotation of this same passage from Jeremiah 1:10 in her letter to Pope Pius II.

20. Sg 2:3, 6.

shown by the Roman people, who grieved for the father they had lost with these words: "O Romulus, Romulus, tell what a great defender of your city the gods bore in you! You brought us forth between shores of light. O father, O founder of our country, O blood sprung from the gods!"[21]

But what am I doing, an inept woman, who has not yet stopped troubling you with my feminine loquaciousness? I will put an end to this nonsense of mine if I can first ask you, most compassionate lord, not to be surprised or angry with me because I have been so bold as to dare, as I have said, to undertake so great a charge (and one greater than my abilities)—to write to you, I mean, and then not to have been able in any sense to compose an oration equal to the greatness of your achievements. Allow me then to put the blame on your kindness, which has given me the audacity not to hesitate in presenting and commending myself and the whole Nogarola family to you, begging you to judge us worthy of your favor and to love us with the same esteem and goodwill with which you have always cherished your most faithful friends. And I, who have always thought that something divine accompanies the friendship of such companions, promise that we will follow you most joyously and happily with as much concern, diligence, and enthusiasm as will please you.

XXX

Oration in Praise of Saint Jerome: Verona, 1453

In 1453, Ermolao Barbaro, the newly appointed bishop of Verona, asked Nogarola to deliver a public oration on the life on Saint Jerome before the people of Verona. In the preface to the oration, Nogarola addresses Barbaro directly, demurring because she lacks the power and skill needed to compose such a work. But it is a request she cannot refuse, she writes, because Barbaro has been so kind to her. The second part of the oration tells the story of Saint Jerome's life and its significance for the contemporary church.

Nogarola's panegyric for Saint Jerome, in which she addresses the citizens of Verona in her second public appearance in a year, clearly antedates the Turkish conquest of Constan-

---

21. O Romule, Romule, dic,
    qualem te patriae custodem dii genuerunt!
    Tu produxisti nos inter luminis oras.
    O pater, o genitor patriae, o sanguen diis oriundum
Ennius's *Annals* 117–21; also quoted by Cicero *De republica* 1.41.61, which cannot have been her source since she follows the early medieval textual commentator Lactantius in two places against Cicero's reading: 118 *dis* for *die*; 120–21 reversed order.

tinople and the demise of eastern Christendom the same year since it contains no hint of the
coming catastrophe. F. A. Wright has remarked that there are four important letter collections
in Latin literature, those of Cicero, Seneca, Pliny, and Jerome. Those of Cicero and Jerome,
both in terms of their substance and size, he ranks as the most significant of the group. Renais-
sance writers concurred, and foremost among those was Nogarola. This translation attempts
to capture the formality, complexity, and erudition of Nogarola's language in the opening
two paragraphs of this Ciceronian showpiece. In contrast, the rest of the letter, her Vita
Hieronymi, *imitates the diction of the gospels and Jerome's epistolary style in its artful*
artlessness and its stripped-down-to-essentials quality.

I would have thought that I should be absolutely terrified, most pious father and all you noble citizens, since I, a weak and unworthy
woman who knows she has neither virtue nor excellence, have boldly undertaken this great and awesome task: that of presenting, like a goose among
swans, an encomium of the most blessed Saint Jerome and an oration about
those qualities whose delineation exhausted, as we know, the talents of even
the most eloquent men. These would be my thoughts, were I not to trust
that I shall have the help and favor of that man who opens the eyes of the
blind and makes eloquent the tongues of the mute.[22] And I might have been
all the more frightened, since I have taken up this grave task not of my
own accord—neither from pride nor contempt, nor claiming any skills as
an orator—but in hopes that he may know[23] that I am compelled to do so
by your request and my own obedience and so that he may recognize that I
am overcome with such distress and anxiety that you could not have asked
me to do anything weightier or more daunting.

And if anyone else had spoken to me about this oration, I would have
thought he was making fun of me. But since I have experienced your goodwill and kindness to me so many times—you who, when you see me talking
nonsense, think me eloquent and articulate!—I decided, lest I should seem
ungrateful, that your commission and your request were very important to
me, however the work were to turn out. Chrysostom's writings on Matthew
also urge me to be obedient, saying, "The goodness of humility surpasses the
merits of all other virtues, since, if humility is not there, none of the other

---

22. Nogarola alludes here to the tradition that arose in the later Middle Ages that Jerome
performed miracles of healing the afflicted; see Rice, *Saint Jerome*, esp. chaps. 2 and 3.

23. "Sed tuis potius precibus, tua obedientia coactam intelligat": note the abrupt switch here
to the jussive third person present subjective. *He, Jerome,* should know that you, Barbaro, are
forcing me to write this oration regardless of my inability to do a decent job of it.

virtues will be worthy of praise. And true humility is that which is compliant not to its own but to another's will."[24]

Therefore, with your indulgence and that of the whole audience, not only will I obey your command with as short an oration as I can deliver, first so that I will not afflict everyone with disgust by speaking inelegantly and for too long, then because I know myself, the magnitude of the topic, and my weak shoulders. For I do not have Quintilian's rhetorical powers or Cicero's or Fronto's facility at oratory, so I would know or in some way could persuade myself that this is a suitable task for me. Indeed, because of your love and reverence for him, your exceptional virtue can comprehand how much toil and work it took him to order and establish all the parts of his life in the service of the greatness of his mind and the sanctity of his life, so that with divine help he was able to reach such a culmination of affairs that there was no region on earth that was not full of this holy man's name. For who does not know how he visited new peoples, surveyed provinces, and crossed seas so that he might follow the trail of fugitive letters all over the world?[25]

Having left the town of Strido as a boy, Jerome went with his parents to Rome to acquire the first rudiments of letters and grammar from the pre-eminent teacher Donatus. His parents took care to imitate King Philip of Macedonia, who wanted Alexander to begin his studies with Aristotle, thinking it useful for boys to receive their first instruction in letters from the best teachers. And that boy, being wholly devoted to his teacher, ascribed so much of his achievement to him that everyone admired him as though he were a divine being.[26] For he understood that this study, with the inspiration

---

24. See Chrysostom, *The Homilies of St. John Chrysostom on the Gospel of St. Matthew*, Homily 15, par. 3: "For this [humility] being fixed as a base, the builder in security lays on it all the rest. But if this be taken away, though a man reach to the Heavens in his course of life, it is all easily undermined, and issues in a grievous end. Though fasting, prayer, almsgiving, temperance, any other good thing whatever, be gathered together in thee; without humility all fall away and perish." The translation is that of George Prevost, revised by M.B. Riddle, in *The Nicene and Post-Nicene Fathers*, ed. Philip Schaff, 1st ser., vol. 10 (Grand Rapids, Mich.: Eerdmans, 1956), 92, column 2.

25. "Ut litteras toto orbe fugientes persequeretur": what a fascinating image is *litteras fugientes*. Fugitive letters? Elusive or escaping letters? Letters and books that seem to travel under their own steam and wind up hidden away in every corner of the earth? Cf. Statius *Silvae* 1.25 in the prose preface addressed to Statius's friend Stella ("Manlius certe Vopiscus vir eruditissimus et qui praecipue vindicat a situ litteras iam paene fugientes . . .") J.H. Mozeley in the 1982 Loeb edition renders this "Manlius, a man . . . who . . . rescu[es] from decay our almost vanishing literature" (5).

26. " . . . cui devotissimus ille puer tantum operis tribuit . . .": It's not clear here in this abrupt relative clause to whom the *cui* or the *ille puer* (which is omitted in MS G) refers to. It could be

of a divine spirit, was necessary for the stimulation and instruction of the intellect; and to this he added a sweet and eloquent companion: the art of discipline of public speaking, which I call rhetoric.[27] He undertook this study with such ardor, such delight, that he spent a great part of his life and energy in this way; and in this study, it is generally agreed that he worked with such extraordinary energy that he focused all his attention on obtaining for his own use all the works, in Greek as well as Latin, worthy of an eloquent and learned man.

He acquired a knowledge of almost all the Greek philosophers, nor is there any teaching of these men of which he was either ignorant or unfamiliar. He studied the Hebrew, Chaldaean,[28] and Syrian writers assiduously, and, finally, he embraced every field in the sciences with a kind of intimate knowledge. He published innumerable books and collected a great many beautifully written books and translated them into Latin; and that divine man lectured on these books so elegantly, so brilliantly, and his speeches shone with such richness and eloquence that an oration from his mouth was said to radiate more brilliantly than gold. He spoke with such sweetness in the languages of the Jews, the Greeks, the Chaldaeans, the Persians, the Medes, and the Egyptians that he seemed to have been born among those peoples, and it appeared that his linguistic talents were inborn and not acquired.

Finally, since he knew that wisdom of this sort was foolishness to God, with whom he had chosen to ally himself, taking the Holy Spirit as his guide, he cast aside secular books and abandoned the books of the pagans. On the command of God, he turned to the Holy Scriptures in order to read them with greater zeal than he had ever before devoted to books by mortal men. In doing so, he imitated Moses who did not come to the contemplation of God until he discovered his purpose in the teachings of the Egyptians. He also imitated Daniel, who, they say, only attained a knowledge of things divine after he had absorbed the wisdom of the Chaldaeans through the teachings of the Babylonians.

Thus it was that Jerome headed for Constantinople so that he could study sacred scripture with Gregory of Nazianzen. He entered Antioch to hear Apollinaris lecturing. In Alexandria, he heard Didymus. Among the

---

either Alexander's teacher or Jerome's, the latter making more sense because *ille puer* (denoting the former [boy]) would make both more grammatical as well as contextual sense here.

27. "dicendi rationem ac disciplinam, rhetoricam dico": note the ellipsis of the relative pronoun *quam*, which we would expect in classical Latin.

28. The Chaldaeans were, according to Cicero, Pliny, and Juvenal, a people of southern Assyria whose capital was Babylon (Pliny *Nat.* 6.121). See also Rice, *St. Jerome*, 237 n. 61.

Hebrews, he testifies that he bought the release of a Lydian as his teacher in exchange for a large payment.[29] After having toured these places with much toil, he returned to Jerusalem and Bethlehem where as an old man he heard Baramus, but since he feared the Jews, he went to him at night and gave him as payment the money he had reserved for his own familiars,[30] so desirous of knowledge was he. He recalled the story of Euclides the philosopher, whose desire for knowledge was so great that when the Athenians warned by decree that if any citizen from Megara was caught setting foot in Athens he would be put to death, he managed to journey to Athens by night without incident. Before evening came, Euclides donned a woman's long tunic, wrapped himself in a shawl of many colors, and veiled his head. He then went from his own house in Megara to Socrates' so that he could partake of the talk and wisdom of the philosopher. Before dawn he made the twenty-mile trip back home again disguised in the same clothing.[31]

At the summit of his eminence, the pinnacle of his holiness, and the grace of his revelations, this very saintly man did not want anything to elude his grasp. He found something to learn everywhere, and wherever he went he always became a better man. He spent his life pleasurably and piously by reading, speaking, debating, writing, and he never relinquished his work or study. For this servant of God understood that nothing is sweeter than leisure time spent with literature: with that liturature, I say, in which we come to know the infinity of things and nature, and in this world, the heavens, the earth, the seas, and finally God himself. For he read so much that we are amazed that he found time to write; and he wrote so many things that there could scarcely have been time for anyone to read them. For he translated all the volumes of the Old Testament from Greek and Hebrew into Latin. He made accessible the prophets, Isaiah, Jeremiah, Ezekiel, Daniel, and the twelve minor prophets. He translated the Psalms, Ecclesiastes, and the Song of Solomon with extraordinary elegance. He wrote commentaries to the New Testament, the Epistles of the Apostle Paul, Revelations of John in which he explicated disputed passages. He put in order the Divine Office.

29. "Lydium praeceptorem *magnis copiis* se redimisse testatur" (our italics on the problem phrase): Did he himself have to spend *magnis copiis* (a lot of money or wealth) to buy this teacher? Or did he purchase the *Lydium praeceptorem* because the *praeceptor* himself was endowed with *magnis copiis* (a lot of power, resources, knowledges)? It is not clear which.

30. "reservatas sibi in nessarios usus pecunias": the "necesarios" can refer to his family members or household servants or both.

31. On Euclides of Megara, Socrates' pupil, see Aulus Gellius 7.10.2–4. Nogarola also retells the same anecdote without naming her source in her letters to Niccolò Venerio (see above, chap. 3, no. 12) and Eusebio dal Borgo (see chap. 4, no. 22).

He also translated Origen's Homilies into Latin. Days would not be sufficient for me to enumerate all the volumes that were produced by him.

In the course of his career, Pope Liberius[32] was so moved by the fame and works of this worthy and very holy man that after Jerome had progressed through the *cursus honorum* of the church he made him a cardinal. Once he was established in this office he practiced such modesty, kindness, prudence, and compassion that his celebrated virtue and sanctity led everyone to admire, adore, and marvel at him. And when he saw the holy Roman church falling into corruption and ruin, what labors did he undertake, what glorious trials did he undergo! What numerous and varied discourses did he enter into to free the holy faith from the hands of the evil heretics who were viciously attacking it. He did everything, attempted everything in order that the prostrate, dying church might rise again and live. Finally, after many revolutions of the seasons, after night watches, labors, fasts, orations, and toil, he strengthened the temple of the Lord and put an end to the heretics from east to west. He burned their swords and shields with fire, and he brought back the trophy of victory from his vanquished enemies.

Then realizing that this office would be a heavy burden for one who wished to serve Christ, he lay down his cardinal's hat, abandoned the values of his age, and scorned its honors. He went into the desert exalting that religion that was judged the most ascetic and believed to be the most difficult to sustain. And he kept writing about his life and how hard and rough the road was that he took to follow Christ, and his testimony is true. Writing to Eustochium[33] he said, "I was living in the desert, in the lonely wilderness itself, which, burned by the heat of the sun, offered a terrible

---

32. Liberius supposedly was pope 352–366 C.E., although whether he ever occupied this office is a matter of dispute, as are many of the "facts" Nogarola lists about Jerome. Certainly Jerome was never a cardinal, as Nogarola claims in the next sentence.

33. See Jerome's letter to Eustochium, Ep. 22.7 (c. 384 C.E.) in *Select Letters of St. Jerome*, ed. and trans. F.A. Wright (London: Heinemann, 1933), 66: O quotiens in heremo constituus et in illa vasta solitudine, quae exusta solis ardoribus horridum monachis praestat habitaculum . . . Horrebam sacco membra deformis, squalida cutis situm Aethiopicae carnis adduxerat. Cotidie lacrimae, cotidie gemitus et, si quando repugnantem somnus imminens oppressisset, nuda humo vix ossa haerentia conlidebam . . . cum etiam languentes aqua frigida utantur et coctum aliquid accepisse luxuriae sit. Nogarola quotes the letter with some variations: Stabam, inquit, in heremo constitutus et in ipsa vasta solitudine, quae exusta solis ardore monachis horridum praestat habitaculum, quotidie gemitus, quotidie lacrimae et si quando me somnus oppressisset repugnantem, nuda humo vix ossa haerentia collidebam. Horrebant sacco membra deformia, aqua frigida etiam langens utebar et coctum accepisse luxuria sit. Cutis mea propter incommoda squalida carnis Aethyopicae situm obduxerat . . ." (Abel, 2:286) The letter to Eustochium is the classic diatribe against the perils of the flesh, praising virginity.

dwelling place to the monks. With daily groans, daily tears, and if sleep ever overcame me and I fought against it, I crushed my bones down onto the bare ground, though they barely remained still. My withered limbs bristled in the sackcloth I wore, and even in my feeble state I consumed cold water; for to receive anything cooked was a luxury. Because of the rough discomforts, my skin took on the look of Ethiopian flesh. I wept continuously and mortified my uncompliant flesh with a lack of edible foods."

But why am I swept away with so many words? Why do I exhaust myself by continuing the story? Since even if I had a hundred tongues, a hundred mouths, and a voice of iron, I could not tell all his virtues and the glorious events of his most holy life. What should I say about his continence, his virginity, and how he saved the unstained world with so much labor, austerity, and humility that here was an Israelite in whom no treachery was found? He could worthily be compared to John the Baptist since he remained a virgin throughout his life and overcame all temptations. Victorious to the very end of his life, he survived every privation with patience and love. And in the eighty-eighth year of his life, with his disciples around him, whom, purged of their sins with his help, advice, and example he had imbued with all the virtues, he departed to the Lord in his sanctified old age.

The omnipotent God honored his death with so many glorious miracles—by helping the sick, raising the dead, liberating those oppressed by the devil, consoling the infirm—that in recollecting the life of this father so praised and honored I am overwhelmed and cannot keep from bursting into tears. Who will then deny that the prophecy of the Tiburtine Sibyl about him has been fulfilled?[34] For she said, "There will rise a wondrous star having the image of four animals, and there will be a wondrous image on a trumpet. It will shine on the Greeks, and the name of the lamb will lead all the way to the end, to the virtue of God. It will liberate those conquered by the devil; and in dying, it will be illuminated, and its end will be glorious."[35]

Therefore we must always praise divine providence, which fortifies its church militant and graces its royal halls with such an angelic spirit. We should therefore celebrate this man with the highest accolades and every form of reverence, for he is glorified, pious, and shining with love, so that he will live with God as the everlasting intercessor for our sins and will be

34. Collections of alleged oracles of ancient sibyls, interpreted as "proof" of the triumph of Christianity over paganism, were in circulation since the early church and were printed many times in the Renaissance as *Oracoli sibillini* ("sibylline prophecies").

35. We can find no source for this sibylline prophecy.

worthy to govern and direct our wills in this age. And then, after a happy departure from this life, with his prayers and service, may we deservedly be enrolled in the company of the most blessed spirits in heaven because of the grace and piety of our Lord Jesus Christ, whose honor, glory, and power is with the Father and the Holy Ghost for ever and ever. Amen

IX

POPE PIUS II AND THE CONGRESS
OF MANTUA (1459)

When Pope Pius II (r. 1458–61) summoned the leading statesmen and church prelates in Europe to Mantua in July 1459 to discuss the mounting of a crusade to free Constantinople from Turkish domination, Nogarola was already something of a veteran speaker at official occasions. As was seen in chapter 6, in the jubilee year of 1450 she had delivered what Foscarini described as a brilliant oration before the pope and his entire court: "When you went to Rome on that holiest of pilgrimages, you spoke with such great authority, wisdom, and elegance—and with such admiration from the Pope and his cardinals."[1] In 1453, she had presented public orations on two separate occasions: the first to commemorate Barbaro's entrance into Verona as the city's new bishop,[2] and the second to deliver an oration on the life of Saint Jerome before the assembled Veronese citizens. Nogarola's next major oration, dated August 1, 1459, was dedicated to Pius II, still the hope of the humanists, although he had done little to foster the *studia humanitatis* since his accession to the papal throne.[3] The work was clearly written for presentation at the Congress of Mantua even though, so far as we know, Nogarola never went to the Congress to read it herself.[4]

1. See above chap. 6, no. 17; Abel, 2:50: "Cum . . . Romam piissimae peregrinationis causa petiisti, quo consilio, qua auctoritate, qua dicendi copia, quanta cum pontificis et fratrum [?] admiratione locuta es!" (The square brackets after "fratrum" are Abel's.) See chap. 6, n. 71, for this event.

2. As argued in chap. 8, although we have no testimony indicating that this piece was presented publicly, the language suggests that it was written expressly for the occasion of the bishop's inauguration.

3. *Studia humanitatis*: the standard Latin phrase coined by fifteenth-century intellectuals to designate the humanist curriculum, studies, that is, in ancient Greek and Roman literature, history, and moral philosophy.

4. In n. 61 to the introduction, Abel reports that according to Filippo da Bergamo, Nogarola delivered orations both before Niccolo V in Rome and in 1459 before Pope Pius II at the

Before coming to the papacy, the Sienese humanist Enea Silvio Piccolomini had written a number of major works in Latin including a popular novel about an adulterous love affair (*Duo amantes*, 1441),[5] a commentary on the proceedings of the Council of Basel (*De gestis concilii Basiliensis*, 1449), and a voluminous memoir on his career (*Commentarii*, written sometime 1458–64). Once he became pope, he became preoccupied not with literature but with the mounting of a military expedition to retake Constantinople for Christendom. His Congress drew pro-crusade orations and letters as well as denunciations of the Turks from the leading humanists, Nogarola among them, who hoped to win grants or pensions from the pope to support their own literary agendas. While many states sent ambassadors to the Congress, few heads of state came themselves. Venice simply refused Pius's demands for a tithe to fund his crusade against the Turks, while Florence and Milan each pledged substantial subsidies.[6] The Milanese delegation included the duke of the principality, Francesco Sforza, his eldest son Galeazzo Maria, his teenage daughter Ippolita, who delivered her own Latin oration at the Congress,[7] and the famous Hellenist in the duke's employ Francesco Filelfo. Given the date of her oration and its subject matter, it is clear that Nogarola intended her speech for the occasion of the Congress; either she would present it herself or someone else would read it for her.

This is a powerful oration, and easily the most evangelical of her works. Filled with a syncretic weaving of classical and biblical allusions, her speech is a call to arms against the Turks whom she does not name but condemns in turn as "this evil generation," "a savage nation," "infidels," and "blasphemers of the Lord." Her speech is a call both for unity among the faithful and, ultimately, blood sacrifice. In it humble apologies alternate with hymns of jubilation and praise, righteous anger with rallying cries to violence.

The oration begins tentatively, with an apology for her poor skills as a speaker couched in a series of references to the great classical orators Demosthenes, Theophrastus, and Cicero, all of whom suffered from the same

---

Congress at Mantua; and at 1.lxviii–lxix; nn. 80, 81, he notes that although Voigt and others reported that Nogarola delivered this oration at Mantua, all these reports, in the absence of contemporary testimony, are probably false, and that Nogarola probably did not attend the Congress of Mantua in 1459.

5. Now in English: Aeneas Silvius Piccolomini, *The Two Lovers: The Goodly History of Lady Lucrece and Her Lover Euralius*, ed. Emily O'Brien and Kenneth R. Bartlett (Ottawa: Dovehouse Editions, 1999).

6. On Venice, Milan, and Florence's response to Pius's call for a crusade against the Turks at Mantua, see esp. Robert Black, *Benedetto Accolti and the Florentine Renaissance* (Cambridge: Cambridge University Press, 1985), 235–54.

7. A translation of Ippolita Sforza's oration is in King and Rabil, *Her Immaculate Hand*, no. 6.

stage fright as she, she confesses: a clear signal that she conceived the work as a public oration. She next moves on, still in a subdued key, to praise the gentle nature of the pope—his mercy, clemency, kindness, gratitude, and appreciation of his lowliest subjects. Pius's magnanimity suggests to her a favorite anecdote from Plutarch's *Life of Artaxerxes* about the lowly peasant who delighted his king with a gift of river water. The theme of gratitude provides a segue into a hymn of praise and thanksgiving, which she uses to build a sense of unity among the assembled congregation. "How magnificent are your works, Lord," she intones. "Let us exalt and rejoice in this day which the Lord has made." Borrowing the imagery not only from the Psalms but the Song of Solomon, she draws an analogy between the pope as bridegroom, in his role as Christ's surrogate, and the church as bride.

Next, gradually building to a crescendo, Nogarola recalls King Nebuchadnezzar's righteous proclamation against blasphemers in the book of Daniel; she calls on the assembled host to defend the holy church as the "bride of Christ" and Pius to "gird yourself most powerfully with your sword" and "take up arms" to support the church against the infidel. Becoming more impassioned, she confronts Pius and the rest of the congregation with the same battery of questions Saint Paul put to his followers:

> What does Christ have to do with Belial? What does the faithful member have in common with the infidel? What agreement does the temple of God have with idols?[8]

She moves to a series of paraphrases and quotations from Isaiah, Jeremiah, and Ezekiel, which she uses to validate her characterization of Pius's complex role as prophet, judge, and avenger. God has sent Pius as the instrument of his righteousness not only against individuals but entire clans and peoples such as the Turks (Is 66:18–19). He is the angel of the Lord set over all nations to root and destroy, to build and to plant (Jer 1:10). He is the sentinel of God appointed to exact a blood sacrifice in recompense for the wrongs committed against his people (Ez 3:17–18). Interestingly, Nogarola concludes her call to battle by returning to a classical text: Anchises' admonition to his son in the *Aeneid*—the pope's namesake, Aeneas. She exhorts Pius "to crush the proud and show mercy to the humble" (Virgil *Aeneid* 6.852–53).

Nogarola follows her battle cry with an explicit address to "the Very Reverend Cardinals of the Church" to confess that Pius alone is their leader, and she calls on the whole assembled host to sing a hymn in praise of his

---

8. See 2 Cor 6.14–17.

name and glory. The oration comes to a quiet end with Nogarola's reiteration of her own unworthiness and God's divine mercy. She reminds her audience once again that God takes pleasure not in the offering but in the giver's intent, and she pledges her own support and that of the whole Nogarola family to Pius.

XXXI

Isotta Nogarola to Pope Pius II at the Congress of Mantua: Verona, August 1, 1459

O prince, preeminent light and honor of our age and vicar of our king Jesus Christ! I have no doubt that most people will be amazed and will blame me, because I, a woman unknown to you, have dared to address you, most holy father, stuttering rather than speaking eloquently, like someone whistling on a straw in the wind,[9] since many men situated in more honorable positions than I, and those possessed of the highest eloquence, were often overcome with fear at the beginning of their speeches. Antiquity testifies that this happened to orators in the courts of the most famous kings—to Theophrastus the philosopher and Demosthenes,[10] whose speech was sweeter than honey, and to Cicero, whose eloquence the whole world celebrates. Indeed, said Cicero, "I always being to speak with great trepidation, and as many times as I speak, I always feel I am on trial."[11] As for

---

9. "Sicut stipula ante faciem venti balbutiens": this is vividly uncharacteristic imagery for Nogarola. We have been unable to locate an exact source, although it is reminiscent of Virgil *Eclogues* 3.27: "Stridenti miserum stipula disperdere carmen," in which Menalcas accuses his friend of killing his own tune by delivering it on a creaking stalk ("stridenti stipula"). But "ut stipula . . . balbutiens" is more like "whistling in the wind."

10. Aulus Gellius 8.9 writes about how the most eloquent orators of antiquity Theophrastus and Demosthenes tended to be disturbed at the beginning of their speeches ("Theophrastus, philosophus omnis suae aetatis facundissimus, verba pauca . . . facturus deturbatus verecundia obticuerit"). Nogarola paraphrases Gellius: "multi . . . summa eloquentia praediti initio dicendi animo commoveri soleant." Plutarch *Demosthenes* 6.3–4 also talks of the Greek orator's visible discomfort at speaking publicly.

11. Cicero *Pro Cluentio* 51: "Semper equidem magno metu incipio dicere:quotienscumque dico, totiens mihi videor in iudicium venire." Nogarola quotes verbatim: "Semper equidem," inquit Cicero, "magno cum metu dicere incipio, quotienscunque dico, totiens mihi videor in iudicium venire." Plutarch in his *Cicero* 35 speaks at length of Cicero's fear and trepidation at the beginning of all his trial speeches.

me, most holy father, although I see the magnitude and splendor of your holiness, a divine compassion lifts me up, which is always there for those who have hope: it strengthens my weakness and inexperience and is the source of my enlightenment. This compassion has taught and will continue to teach this hand of mine to write; and it will direct my tongue, as it directed a certain Balaam to speak to his ass.[12]

Your extraordinary clemency, which is almost divine, your kindness and your gentleness, which the whole church hymns, summon me. They urge me to undertake this heavy burden with a happy heart, although my strength is not equal to it. It is therefore the quality of your mercy and kindness that offers me an opportunity to speak boldly in this poor and unsophisticated letter burnished with humility.[13] Indeed, it allows me to conduct myself in a kindly manner and to come to the aid of those in need with a generous hand, lest you should cast aside my natural feelings of piety and compassion. Rather, since your name has grown in dignity and magnanimity and you are also becoming a greater man each day, it occasions your hearing this hymn of exultation intoned from the depths of our hearts in this so happy, festive, and celebrated display.[14]

We read that Artaxerxes, the King of the Persians, thought it was a no less royal and humane thing to receive small gifts quickly and with kindness than it was to give large gifts.[15] When he was out for a walk on horseback, a poor and humble man encountered him on the road, and when the man offered him water from the river with both his hands—for it was the custom of the Persians to greet the king with a gift—the king received the gift with pleasure and smiled because he valued the spontaneity of the giver more than the worth of the gift.

12. See Numbers 22 (and the commentary on the story in 2 Peter 2:15, 16), a story in which God reveals his purpose to Balaam, a man who has gone astray, by speaking through the mouth of the ass Balaam is riding. Here Nogarola will attempt to speak eloquently, with God's help, even as God enabled Balaam's ass to speak.

13. "litterulas . . . verecundia dealbatas" (whitened or whitewashed with respect, modesty, diffidence, or humility): the verb *dealbare* (to whiten) and its participle are scarcely attested in classical Latin. Since the English verb "whitewash" would suggest hypocrisy, which is not intended here, we have used the verb "burnish" to indicate that humility lends embellishment to her words.

14. We have taken all of the accusative objects and the infinitives that follow "praebet" (*praebere*: "to supply," "offer," "give cause to," or "occasion")—*suscipere, subvenire, audire*—as complementary or epexegetic infinitives with "praebet." It is Pope Pius's qualities of "clementiae," etc. that enable or occasion this string of results.

15. The anecdote about Artaxerxes receiving a gift of water from a peasant is repeated verbatim from Nogarola's letter to Jacopo Foscari (see chap. 2, no. 5). The source is Plutarch *Artaxerxes* 5.1.

Since no man is so iron-hearted or so distant from himself that he is unmoved and does not thank the omnipotent God from the depths of his being and does not pronounce the words of the Psalm of David in complete awe, "How magnificent are your works, Lord,"[16] let us exult and rejoice in this day which the Lord has made. No one separates himself from taking part in God's greatness. All men are joined in a common joy. Behold, the time is at hand, the day of gladness and jubilation is at hand, the greatest of all the days of our life, on which the Lord who is steadfast in his words and holy in all his works opens his hand, and the whole world exults and rejoices in this assembly with hymns and song of praise. The world rejoices with worthy proclamations, and boys and unmarried girls sing sacred songs.

No one is so weak, so devoid of reason that he does not know how many abundant, happy, and rich fruits your holiness will bring forth, since the ineffable mercy of the Savior has brought together such an abundant harvest of graces in you. You have been adorned with honor before all others, distinguished by neither external nor earthly help, but, with ever-increasing glory and ascending step by step to divine providence, God has brought you to the divine pinnacle of the priesthood, so that it can be worthily said of you, "Here is a river of living water, bright as crystal, proceeding from the throne of God in the middle of the church, and on either side of it is the tree of life bearing fruit according to its time, and the leaves of the tree are for the healing of nations."[17]

This gentlest of men has appeared among the people, loved by both God and men, a beautiful vessel for the holy church adorned with every precious stone, a sublime work.[18] The church rejoices, and united by the embraces of such a bridegroom, it sings for joy: "I sat in the shade of the man I desired, and his fruit was sweet to my throat. Oh, that his left hand were under my head and that his right hand embraced me."[19] Since you have received me like a true bridegroom and not an adulterer, like a true shepherd and not a hireling, your every desire and action and finally your every effort

---

16. Ps 91.6: "quam magnificata sunt opera tua Domine nimis profundae factae sunt cogitationes tuae."

17. Rev 22:1–2: "Hic est flumen aquae vivae, splendidum tamquam cristallum, procedens de sede dei in medio ecclesiae et ex utraque parte eius lignum vitae afferens fructum tempore suo, cuius ligni folia sunt ad gentium sanitatem." Nogarola quotes almost verbatim.

18. "Opus excelsi": literally a work of sublimity.

19. Sg 2:3, 6: "Sub umbra illius quem desiderabam sedi et fructus eius dulcis gutturi meo; laeva eius sub capite meo et dextra illius amplexabitur me." Nogarola quotes almost verbatim. In this translation, the tenses are changed to conform to the New Revised Standard Version English translation, although the Vulgate's vocabulary is retained: *guttur* is throat, not taste.

and attempt have gone to guard the last battle line that stands before the apostolic throne, and because of this you have been prepared to give of your very soul, not to mention your earthly substance. This is something fittingly regal, as Saint Augustine testifies: "This," he said, "is the concern of kings: to want the church represented during their time as the mother from whom they were spiritually born."[20]

King Nebuchadnezzar, convinced by a miracle from God that the worship of idols was blasphemous, published a holy decree that whoever committed blasphemy against the God of Shadrach, Meshach, and Abednego would die together with his whole house.[21] But you, who are the true vicar of Christ, imbued with the divine spirit, take up this stuff of immortal glory with your hands open, as they say. May your sanctity rise up and extend the arm of its own power to help the bride of Christ against this adulterous and evil generation, since you see the Lord our redeemer so savagely blasphemed by those very men.[22] May your most holy purity abhor those evil and accursed men. For as the second apostle has said, "What does the fellowship of justice have to do with injustice? What does the company of light have to do with darkness? What does the assembly of Christ have to do with Belial? What does the faithful member have in common with the infidel? What agreement is there in the temple with idols? Therefore, come out from among them, and stand apart, says the Lord; touch nothing impure, and I shall receive you."[23]

20. We have been unable to locate this passage in Saint Augustine.

21. Nogarola alludes here to story of the conversation of Nebuchadnezzar, King of Babylon (d. 560 B.C.E.) in Daniel 1:1–3:30 (esp. 3:29). The king commanded three Hebrew youths, Shadrach, Meshach, and Abednego, to be thrown into a fiery furnace when they refused to worship the false god of the king. When the three emerged from the raging furnace miraculously unscathed, the king commanded all his subjects to worship the Hebrew god of the three youths and no other. The story initiates a series of biblical references in which she will build up portraits, one of Pius II as the representative of the stern, avenging God of the Old Testament and one of the Turkish sultan as the blasphemous archenemy of all Christians. The story inaugurates Nogarola's pitch for a new crusade led by Pope Pius II himself against the Turks.

22. " . . . immaniter ab ipsis blasphemari": the standard language used after the fall of Constantinople in 1453 to arouse passions against the Turks is here ambiguous, referring to both the Turkish "infidels" and those in the West unwilling to support military action against the "enemies of Christendom."

23. 2 Cor 6:14, 15, 16, 17 (AV): "What fellowship hath righteousness with unrighteousness? And what communion hath light with darkness? And what concord hath Christ with Belial? Or what part hath he that believeth with an infidel? And what agreement hath the temple of God with idols? . . . Wherefore come out from among them, and be ye separate, saith the Lord, and touch not the unclean thing; and I will receive you." Saint Jerome quotes the same passage from Corinthians in his letter to Eustochium (Ep. 22, a letter from which Nogarola quotes at

Therefore, gird yourself most powerfully, most blessed father, with your sword above your thigh, since you know that this power has been given to you from heaven so that you may punish the evil and not allow your church to sink into ruin and deformity. Take up your arms and shield and rise up for the support of a church conquered not by passion but zeal for justice. For there is a species of piety in severity. In your time you should want nothing more zealously than that the Roman Church, your bride, should rejoice in the tranquility and peace due her. "The bride entrusts to you her holy things and household gods; take these as companions of the fates; guard the city for them."[24]

May kings prostrate themselves before you, may the noblemen of the world obey you as though you were the Lord Jesus Christ himself, and may there be no one who will want to resist your will. Everything that he wishes you will do on earth, on sea, and in the abyss below, since the Lord has been made your aide and the protector of your safety. As divine Isaiah cried, "I come to gather together all nations and all tongues, and they will come and see my glory, and I shall place among them a sign, namely, that of the holy cross, and from those who will have been saved I shall send men with arrows to peoples on the sea, in Africa, in Lydia, and to those in Italy, Greece, and the islands far away, and to those who have not heard me and have not seen my glory, and even they will proclaim my glory to the nations."[25]

Remember the dictum sent from the Lord through his herald Jeremiah: "Behold, I have set you above all nations and kingdoms to root out and destroy, to build and to plant."[26] And through Ezekiel he said, "I made you a sentinel of the Lord over Israel. If you see the sword coming and you do

---

length in her eulogy of Jerome). But Jerome adds to the passage: "What has Horace to do with the Psalter, Virgil with the Gospels, and Cicero with Paul?" a passage Nogarola, interestingly, omits. (The translation of Jerome, above, is by F.A. Wright, *Jerome: Select Letters*, Loeb Classical Library [Cambridge, Mass.: Harvard University Press, 1933; reprint 1999], 125.)

24.   Sacra suosque tibi commendat sponsa penates;
       Hos cape fatorum comites, his moenia serva.
Nogarola here quotes and alters Virgil *Aen.* 2.293–94: "Sacra suosque tibi commendat Troia Penates: / hos cape fatorum comites, his moenia quaere . . ."

25. Is 66:18, 19. Nogarola quotes almost verbatim. She has translated the places from which the Lord will send archers, the biblical Tarshish, Pul, Lud, Tubal, and Javan, to Africa, Lydia, Italy, and Greece. Step by step, she uses texts from the Old Testament to validate Pius's role as the prophet of God sent as the righteous rewarder of the good and punisher of the evil clans and nations, as the instrument of God not merely against individuals but entire peoples (as for example, the Turks).

26. Jer 1:10: "Ecce constitui te super omnes gentes et regna, ut evellas et destruas et aedifices et plantes." Nogarola quotes almost verbatim. Again, as in the passage from Isaiah, Nogarola suggests an analogy between Jeremiah's role as avenger of evil and Pius's.

not blow your horn and the sword comes and carries away the lives of the people, I shall demand recompense for their blood from your hands."[27] For it must truly be said that you sit upon the throne of the apostolic kingdom so that you may care for your sheep; and when you see the wolf coming you must not flee but see to their freedom, safety, and utility.

Oh, how much grace is sent down from on high to your holiness! How great an occasion is readied for your praise and glory! Embrace it in gladness and rejoicing. Thus did all your predecessors before you make their entrance into the Roman Church with the greatest of gifts. Did prior centuries ever see or will future generations ever see anything more fortunate than this sanctified and glorious work? Anything more magnificent? Anything more useful to the Christian religion? Because of this—because of these gifts— the whole world, finally, will affirm[28] that it owes the greatest debt to your holiness. With the highest enthusiasm, they will proclaim the sanctity of your life, the ardor of your faith, and your exceeding constancy of mind with whatever encomia, since you in no way have allowed your bride to be disgraced by the foul embrace of this adulterer,[29] but with the straining shield of faith wrapped around you, you stood in the path of the sword coming to tear the seamless tunic of Christ.[30] What is more, you stood your ground courageously and were determined to keep her free from all servitude with your own inscrutable foresight and divine service and to cover her with regal adornment in her honor, after her veil of mourning was shed. What Isaiah has said has now been fulfilled: "The people who walked in darkness have now seen a great light. For those who live in the land of the shadow of death, the light has risen."[31] "For he put his tabernacle in the sun, and he himself

27. Ez 3:17, 18 (almost verbatim); Ez 33.6 (a loose paraphrase).

28. "Universus orbis affirmunt . . . plurimum debere": an unusual phrase: a singular subject with plural verb; then either an indirect statement with no subject in the subordinate clause, or "plurimum debere" has to serve as the direct object of "affirmunt."

29. "A foedo huius adulteri amplexu": *adulter, infidel, immanis, crudelis, saevus* are all standard terms in the invectives of the day describing the sack of Constantinople by the Turks and calling for its return to Christendom.

30. Everything is peculiar about this sentence: (1) The vocabulary choice of *inconsutilis* ("seamless," a reference to the legendary garment Christ wore when he was crucified and that the soldiers divided among themselves), striking in Nogarola's humanist prose because this word is unattested in classical Latin; (2) The use of *venire* in a purpose construction with an infinitive (*scindere*) instead of the *ut* + subjunctive expected in classical Latin; (3) The notion that the verb *amicire* (to clothe, cover, or wrap around with fabric, *amictus* being the passive participle) could be used with heavy metal on the battlefield: "Molienti scuto . . . amictus"; (4) The personifications of weapons themselves in "gladio venienti" and "molienti scuto" (the straining shield).

31. Is 9:2.

rejoiced, as the bridegroom rejoices coming from his chamber; thus is the giant glad to run the race, and his going out is from highest heaven; nor can anyone hide from his warmth."[32]

When the shadows and gloom of night are put to flight by your appearance, we shall bask in your rays of peace and tranquility. This will be the greatest sacrifice that you, the pope, can offer to our God. The omnipotent Lord will then allow you to increase the unity of the faith with great joy and honor and to preserve peace and security. You will crush proud peoples and savage nations, and you will establish laws and cities for men,[33] mindful of what Habakkuk sang: you will trample the land underfoot with a rumbling and stun nations with your rage.[34] You have gone forth for the safety of your people, for your safety with Christ. You will strike off the top of the house of the impious man, and you will lay bare its foundations down to the ground: "These will be your arts, to impose the standard of peace, / spare the conquered and subdue the proud."[35] They will affirm the sayings of the prophets about you and that which the Enigmas prophesied as well. This will go under the name *Virgilianus*, namely, "I am pious Aeneas, known in the heavens above, who carry with me my household gods snatched from the hands of the enemy."[36] Glory to God in the highest, and on earth peace, good will toward men.[37] Let us sing to the Lord since his works are magnificent, we shall proclaim this throughout the entire earth. Let us drink dry the waters from the fountains of the savior, since the impious have disappeared in their own thoughts and believing themselves to be wise men they have become foolish.

That assembly of very reverend cardinals knows this; the Church, the universal holy mother, knows this; and those praising your virtues and

---

32. Ps 19.4–6. Nogarola writes (Abel, 2:151–52), "Quoniam in sole posuit tabernaculum suum et ipse tanquam sponsus procedens de thalamo suo exultavit, ut Gigas ad currendam viam, a summo caelo egressio; nec est qui se abscondat a calore eius." "Gigas" [Gigans] is taken as a nominative/subject of *exultat* (understood), and "egressio" as a nominative absolute.

33. "Gentes indomitas populosque feroces contundes legesque viris et moenia pones": a reference to, but not a quote from, Anchises' famous advice to Aeneas in Virgil *Aen.* 6.851–53.

34. Hb 3:12 NRSV: "In fury you trod the earth, in anger you trampled nations."

35. Haec tibi artes, pacis imponere mores,
Parcere subiectis et debellare superbos.
Virgil *Aen.* 6.852–53. Nogarola here underlines for the second time a differential policy for enemies: clemency for those who submit and annihilation for those who, like the Turks, resist.

36. Virgil *Aen.* 1.378–89:
Sum pius Aeneas, raptos qui ex hoste Penates
Classe veho mecum fama super aethera aethera notus.

37. Lk 2:14 (AV).

adoring you like a deity on earth know this, since your extensive virtue, highest goodness, integrity, justice, compassion, piety, gentleness, and the most innocently lived life from earliest childhood to this day have always shone like a star so brightly that with one voice, one mind, one thought, and with no dissent (something that virtually never happens), they elected you as our pope, submitting their will to your yoke and confessing that you alone are the one under whose aegis everyone is protected and by whose work the good are lifted up and the wicked oppressed. And so, may the whole assembly of the faithful rejoice and sing a hymn of happiness and exultation aloud, since the name of the most glorious father and defender of this body, as with the fragrance of the sweetest rose or that of a cypress tree that raises its branches to the sky, has traveled to the very ends of the earth, and its memory and renown will endure forever. But what am I doing—that I dare to sing the praises that already fill the earth of so eminent a man whose splendor is like a light, since the sound of his name has journeyed over all the earth beside that of the Queen of Sheba?[38] For your wisdom and your works are greater than the stories we have heard about them. Therefore, most blessed father, give me your customary permission to exercise my poor skills, meager talent, and the poverty of my happy soul, as I said at the beginning. And do read patiently, since the reward is neither gold nor silver, but the donor's desire itself. Nor should one consider the gift but rather the donor's intention, spirit, and purpose.

The Holy Scriptures testify that God looked with respect at Abel and his gifts, if in fact he looked at Abel first and then his gifts, so we would understand the lesson that it was not as much the offering that pleased God as it was the intent of the one who offered the gift, since God esteems a giver who gives not from sorrow or necessity but joyously.[39] Nothing will be declared more admirable or more reverent than your humility and kindness. In this way, you will gain possession of heaven since the kingdom of

---

38. Interestingly, Nogarola compares the greatness and fame of the pope with that of a woman—Sheba or Sabba, a biblical queen in 1 Kings 10:1–13 and 2 Chronicles 9:1–12, identified with the woman in the Song of Solomon (which is moralized throughout the Middle Ages as the love song between the church and her people). Sabba is also identified as the Queen of Ethiopia and Egypt in Boccaccio *Famous Women* chap. 43. Queen Sabba's wisdom, knowledge, and brilliance were so world-renowned that she was considered an appropriate judge of King Solomon's intellectual acumen.

39. Nogarola alludes to Genesis 4:1–8: the story of the offerings of Abel and Cain and of God's pleasure at Abel's offering and his displeasure at Cain's because God saw in Abel's gift of the firstborn lambs from his flock a blood offering and thus an acknowledgment of his sin; whereas in Cain's gift, grain harvested from his field, God saw no such acknowledgment, no "sin offering." The lesson she hammers home here is that God expects and demands a sacrifice.

heaven is about such things, as the evangelical voice proclaims: "Learn from me who am gentle and humble of heart:[40] he casts down the powerful from their thrones and lifts up the lowly."[41] All that is left to say is that I beseech your holiness, as a supplicant and with the devotion of my whole heart, to cherish, with the same charity and kindness with which you are accustomed to cherish your most faithful servants, and to deem worthy both me, your unworthy maidservant, and my brothers, your most loyal servants, and the whole Nogarola family, which has wholly dedicated itself to your most holy name. And I urgently beseech the celestial King that he support our devoted and sacred desire: that is, that we may be able to do those things that are pleasing to your holiness at all times for the praise and glory of your name, whose honor and glory will live for ever and ever, amen. May your holiness be well. From Verona, August 1, 1459.

Again, the humble servant of your holiness.

Isotta Nogarola

40. Mt 11:29.
41. Lk 1:52.

X

THE CONSOLATION FOR MARCELLO
AND THE FRIULI CONNECTION (1461)

Nogarola wrote her last surviving major work, *A Consolatory Letter*, for the Venetian nobleman, soldier, and literary patron Jacopo Antonio Marcello on the death of his eight-year-old son Valerio on January 1, 1461.[1] Coming two years afer her polemic against the Turks composed for Pope Pius's Congress at Mantua and eight years after the public oration on Saint Jerome that she delivered to the Veronese citizens at the request of the city's new ecclesiastical patriarch Ermolao Barbaro, her consolatory letter for Marcello *On the Death of His Most Sweet and Noble Son*, was, like her other principal works of the 1450s, a public production and one indicative of her standing not only in Verona but also in Venice. For in writing this work, she was contributing to a volume that centered on the humanist circle of the dead child's father.

After Valerio's unexpected death, Marcello initiated plans for the assembling of an elegant funerary volume. The book would eventually contain a collection of twenty-three consolatory works by nineteen authors commemorating Valerio's life and death. With its chapter capitals trimmed in gold and illuminated with brilliant colors and its pages bordered with flora, fauna, and gems, the book comprised 426 pages.[2] Among its contributing authors were Nogarola; Francesco Filelfo, court poet to Duke Francesco Sforza of Milan; Niccolò Sagundino, the eminent humanist, papal secretary, and longtime Venetian ambassador to Greece; Pietro Perleone, public historian, humanist teacher at the state-funded Scuola di San Marco and mentor to Venice's

---

1. For the life and death of Jacopo Antonio Marcello, see King, *Death of the Child;* see the same for Nogarola's consolatory work in its literary and political context, esp. 36–37 and 70–71.

2. On the production, physical appearance, and subsequent provenance of the volume see King, *The Death of the Child,* 1–5.

future statesmen; and George of Trebizond, the famously peripatetic Greek emigré scholar.

There were many reasons why Marcello should have commissioned a consolatory work from Nogarola. First, most Venetian rulers of the terra ferma had longstanding ties of friendship with the leading families of their client cities, cemented through marriage ties and social, political, and literary networks; and if they did not already have such alliances, they took care to forge them. This, as we have seen, appears to have been the case both with Foscarini's relationship to the Nogarola family and Marcello's, whose friendship with her family Nogarola traces back for decades: "I who have loved you like a father," she writes in her consolatory letter, "from the earliest years of my childhood."[3]

Second, we must consider the ties that existed between Foscarini and Marcello. Although never close friends, the two Venetian noblemen had circled around one another for years. Marcello first met Nogarola and her family in November 1439 when he was *provveditore* (supervisor next in rank to the general) of the Venetian forces that liberated Verona from the occupying army of the Duke of Milan (then Filippo Maria Visconti).[4] That year, Foscarini, roughly ten years Marcello's junior, was serving as the Venetian governor of Feltre, a city located just northeast of Verona. In 1461–62, Foscarini served as Venice's governor of Friuli at Udine, where he played a leading role in that city's literary circle.[5] In 1462–63, Marcello, following in Foscarini's footsteps, assumed the governorship of Friuli.[6] Thus, given that Marcello and Foscarini lived in close proximity in the months that followed Valerio's death, Foscarini may have recommended Nogarola to Marcello as a potential contributor to his volume, particularly since after the death of her mother in 1461 she appears to have been living in the Foscarini household. On the other hand, it is just as likely that Isotta, who had achieved no small literary celebrity on her own during the 1450s, would have occurred to Marcello as an appropriate addition to his stable of writers, even without an outside recommendation. Moreover, Marcello might have felt that

---

3. Abel, 2:162–63: "Ego vero, quae te ab ineunte aetate mea colui ut patrem . . ."

4. Visconti's defeated Milanese forces were led by the Condottiere Niccolò Piccinino in 1439. The Venetian army at the time of the "liberation" was led by the Captains Francesco Sforza (who in 1451 became lord of Milan after Visconti's death), with whom Marcello had a very close relationship, and Gattamellata.

5. See King, *Venetian Humanism*, 7, 12, 376; and *The Death of the Child*, 301.

6. See profiles of the career moves of Ludovico Foscarini and Jacopo Antonio Marcello in King, *Venetian Humanism*, 374–75 and 393–97. See also King's chronology of the posts they held for Venice in *Death of the Child Valerio*, esp. 248–301 (chronology for 1439–61).

Nogarola, who had so recently lost her mother, Bianca Borromeo, whom he had known, would be especially sympathetic to his grief.

Funerary collections were a common species of manuscript book in the fifteenth century. Such books were circulated informally and even bought and sold, although the price was often prohibitively high and copies were rare. By the middle of the fifteenth century, the consolatory tradition was already well established as a genre for humanist books. As George McClure has shown, from Petrarch's two consolatory works, the *De remediis utriusque fortune* and the *De secreto conflictu curarum medicarum*, came new role models for humanist consolers as *medici animorum* (soul doctors).[7] In these fourteenth-century works, Petrarch combined ancient and medieval funerary tropes from the Stoicizing philosophers Cicero, Augustine, and Boethius, which would become standard in fifteenth-century consolatory works, all of which can be seen in Nogarola's *Consolatio ad Marcellum*, in particular, the themes of self-consolation, contempt for this world (*contemptu mundi*), the vanity of human life (*vanitas huius vitae*), the instability of fortune (*variabilitas fortunae*), the necessity for moderation in mourning (*de temperantia in luctu*), and the warning against the sin of despair and depression (*aegritudo or torpor animi*). At the end of the fourteenth century, in the consolatory letters and treatises of Coluccio Salutati, we see a new theme that Nogarola appropriates in her *Consolatio*: a Ciceronian emphasis on social concerns in grieving and on one's duty to serve one's family, friends, and city in the midst of death, sorrow, and mourning.

Between 1400 and 1461, however, four major humanist consolations that specifically targeted the death of a son came into circulation. These new literary works provided a template for Nogarola's *Consolatio*: Salutati's consolatory letters to Francesco Zabarella (1400–1401); Giannozzo Manetti's *Dialogus de filii sui morte consolatorius* (1438), Giovanni Conversini da Ravenna's *De consolatione de obitu filii* (1401), and Francesco Filelfo's own *Oratio consolatoria de obitu Valerii filii* (1461) for Marcello's volume, although only Filelfo's letter was a consolation for another man's son in which his grief for his own child Olimpio was simply part of the larger treatise.[8] In 1433, on the death of Cosimo de' Medici's mother, Carlo Marsuppini and Alamanno Rinuccini each wrote consolatory works for their bereaved patron: both Marsuppini's *Consolatio* and Rinuccini's translation of Pseudo-Plutarch's *Consolatio ad Apollonium*, dedicated to Cosimo, became widely known and were mined for their

7. McClure, *Sorrow and Consolation*, 18ff.

8. McClure, *Sorrow and Consolation*, 93–109.

topoi.[9] Three decades later, two further manuals for consolatio writing were added to the growing body of literature on the genre: the *De tolerandis adversis* (1462–63) by Nogarola's friend, the Veronese canon Matteo Bosso,[10] and the *De consolatione* (1464–65), written by the Dalmatian bishop Nicolaus of Modrus.[11]

Nogarola clearly drew on this rich humanist consolatory tradition from Petrarch to Marsuppini and Rinuccini. The main themes in her *Consolatio ad Marcellum* reflect her Salutatian concern for her fellow man. One's duties and responsibilities to family, friends, and city must not be neglected in the course of mourning or by giving oneself over to an excess of grief. Nogarola's sources represent again the same sort of rich mix of classical and biblical references with which she studs her major works during the last decade and a half of her life. Among the classical authors she draws from in her *Consolatio* are Virgil's *Georgics*, Ovid's *Metamorphoses*, Juvenal's *Satires*, Livy's *History of Rome*, Valerius Maximus' *Memorable Doings and Sayings*, Cicero's rhetorical and philosophical works, Plutarch's *Lives of Pericles, Alexander, Aemilius Paulus, Cicero, Cato the Younger, Tiberius Gracchus*, and *Gaius Gracchus*, Plutarch's *Ancient Customs of the Spartans*, the Pseudo-Plutarch's *Consolatio ad Apollonium*, and Seneca's *On Providence*. Among her biblical sources in this oration are Kings, Job, Isaiah, Ecclesiastes, Luke, John, Acts, Romans, Corinthians, Philippians, James, and Peter.

XXXII

Isotta Nogarola to Jacopo Antonio Marcello: Verona, August 9, 1461

To the Illustrious and Magnificent Soldier, the Venetian Patrician Lord Iacopo Antonio Marcello on the Death of His Most Sweet and Noble Son Valerio Marcello, a Consolatory Letter from Isotta Nogarola.

I remember that I read in Plutarch, magnanimous and most illustrious lord and father, that when a certain philosopher attempted to console Queen Arsinoe who was suffering grievously over the death of her son, he began to tell her the following story:

9. McClure, *Sorrow and Consolation*, 134–35.

10. On Bosso's letters to Nogarola see chaps. 5 and 7.

11. McClure, *Sorrow and Consolation*, 118–20.

Once upon a time, O queen, Jupiter distributed honor to all the gods according to the particular dignity of each one of them. At that time Mourning was away, and when he returned to find that the honors had been distributed, he asked Jove to venerate him also with some honor. Since all the honors had already been distributed, Jupiter hesitated for a long time. Finally, he gave Mourning the honor he had given to the dead so that humans would sacrifice to him with sorrow and tears, and, just as the rest of the gods love those who worship them and sacrifice to them, thus it became the custom of Mourning to come to those who made sacrifices to him. Therefore, woman, if you grant him no honors he will never come to you. But if you honor him diligently with mourning and tears, he will love you, embrace you, never abandon you, and he will always offer something to you with which you will be able to honor him perpetually.[12]

When the philosopher told her this, they say the queen put away all her grief, which she now understood was also what great men must do, lest they should spend their lives mourning and weeping like wretches, although the wisest philosophers and holiest men never censured the man who grieved, only the one who exceeded moderation in his grieving.

Therefore, on learning from your own pious writings and the reports of many other people that you were sunk in grief and mourning for your sweetest little boy far longer than is right, I who have loved you as though you were my own father from the earliest years of my childhood, who have cherished you as my lord and master, and who hoped you would always be happy, decided, as if by some guiding principle, to try to soothe, in so far as I could, this sorrow of yours, in which I cannot but grieve myself, and to call you back to reason, lest we appear, though we are humans, to be engaged like the Giants in a battle with the gods.[13] Still, I am afraid I might appear impudent to many people since I dare to thrust myself in the midst of the fray amid the ranks of so many orators and philosophers who have attempted to console you with their most elegant writings and weighty sentiments.

Perhaps these inelegant writings I have dedicated to you will do more,

12. Abel errs in not capitalizing the noun *luctus* (mourning, sorrow), here personified as the mythological character Luctus (Mourning) in Nogarola's almost verbatim translation from the tale of *To Penthos* (mourning or sorrow in Greek; personified and capitalized in Plutarch's *Consolatio ad Apollonium* 111F–112A (from the *Moralia*).

13. Sons of Coelus and Terra (Uranus and Ge) who were defeated in their war with Jupiter and the Olympic gods after Jupiter's victory over the Titans. The story is ubiquitous in classical literature from Hesiod on: Homer *Od.* 7 and 10; Virgil *Georgics* 1.280; Ovid *Met.* 1.151.

however, to assuage this bitterest sorrow of yours, since your excellency will consider that I have performed the duty of a true daughter in preferring to be thought audacious and impudent by everyone but you, the kindest father, and those who know from your extraordinary affection for me and the Nogarola family and my respect for you that I have been judged from my earliest years on (as I said) your caring daughter. For the goodness of humility exceeds the worth of all the other virtues. But how shall I console you when I am in need of this consolation myself, when I have seemed to retreat, forgetful of all philosophy and religion, a prisoner of the sorrow and mourning that overwhelmed me when my dearest and most pious mother died, since which time I have suffered incredible sorrow, more profound than any I ever imagined?[14]

But since in order to be strong I strive to be a Christian in both fact and deed, I have decided to write you, although in words perhaps awkward and ill composed, so that we might both embrace moderation.[15] And since we are dealing with two spheres—the mind and the emotions—and since the emotions have been satisfactorily treated, let us call on the mind and on reason, since the sacred histories testify that our Christ and all the saints always adhered to moderation. For I agree not with the poets who claim we originated from stone or hard oak, but with the satirist who says nature gave humans the softest hearts: "What tears he gave. The emotions are our best part. We sigh at the power of nature, when the death of a maiden occurs or an infant is enclosed in the earth."[16]

They say that Horatius, when he was officiating as the priest in the dedication of the temple of Jupiter and heard that his son was dead, did not remove his hand from the temple doorpost that he was holding, nor did he turn his face away from the public ritual to mourn privately, lest the duties

---

14. Abel, 2:164: "Sed quo modo te consolabor, cum ipsa eadem consolatione egeam et omnis philosophiae ac religionis oblita terga dare visa sim, meque dolor et moeror, quem ex morte sanctissimae ac dulcissimae matris meae cepi, captivam ducant, ex qua incredibilem ac graviorem quam unquam existimassem concepi dolorem?" It is this statement that permits Abel and us to establish the year of Bianca Borromeo's death (1461), important for constructing Nogarola's last years. It was later this same year that she joined the household of Foscarini.

15. ". . . decrevi . . . scribere ut mediocritatem simul amplexemur": could there be a pun in this *ut* clause, so that the meaning might be, "when you read this ineptly written letter, then we will both be embracing mediocrity together?"

16. Juvenal 15.133, 138–39 (our translation):
Quae lacrimae dedit. Haec nostri pars optima sensus;
naturae imperio gemimus, cum funus adultae
virginis occurrit, vel terrae clauditur infans.

of the father should appear to take precedence over those of the priest.[17] They say that when the co-consul of Cato the Elder, Quintus Martius, lost his son—a man of the finest character, the source of all his father's hopes, and his only son, this being no small addition to the tragedy—he bore his death with such constancy and moderation of mind that when he left his son's funeral pyre he went to the curia and convened the Senate, since it was supposed to meet on that day.[18] They praise Xenophon because, when he was conducting a solemn sacrifice and learned that his son was dead in the city of Mantinea, not thinking that the worship of the gods ought to be disrupted, he was content only to remove the garland he wore. And having waited to hear how it happened, when he learned that his son had fought back with great courage, he put the garland back on his head and swore to the deities he had honored that he felt greater pleasure from his son's virtue than bitterness from his death.[19]

They praise Pericles, the leader of the Athenians—on whose lips the goddess of persuasion lived, called Suada by the Latins[20]—whose divine eloquence the Greek comic writers did not hesitate to compare to thunder and lightning,[21] who in the space of four or eight days, if we believe Stesimbrotus, saw death steal two adolescent sons from him, Xanthippus and Paralus. Pericles also lost in those days his sister and the majority of the friends who were his chief supporters in the republic. During these days they say his constancy was so great that he kept his face dry and shed no tears, but that immediately after the death of his sons, garlanded and dressed in a white robe as was the custom in his city, he held a meeting to incite the Athenians to go to war.[22] Lucius Aemilius Paullus[23] is rightly exalted to the

---

17. The source is Livy 2.8.6–8; a capsule version is given in Val. Max. 5.10. Nogarola's vocabulary here bears resemblances to both classical texts. Her exemplar is Horatius Pulvillus, co-consul with P. Valerius in 509 B.C.E.

18. Val. Max. 5.10. Nogarola's paraphrase uses the same vocabulary.

19. Val. Max. 5.10. Nogarola's paraphrase is again almost verbatim.

20. This phrase about Pericles' lips comes from Cicero *De oratore* 3.138.

21. The phrase about thunder and lightning is in Plutarch *Pericles* 8.3. The details of Pericles' self-control on hearing the news of his son's death are in Plutarch *Pericles* 36 and *Moralia, Ad Apollonium* 118E–F.

22. The details about the white funeral garb and Pericles inciting the Athenians to go to war are in Plutarch *Ad Apollonium* 118F.

23. Lucius Aemilius Paullus Macedonicus, father of Scipio Africanus the Younger; consul in 182 B.C.E.; conquered King Perseus at Pydna in 168; lost his two younger sons soon after that victory; he is referred to also as Aemilius Paulus, Lucius Paulus, or Paulus. The story of the loss

skies with glorious praise, for when he returned victorious to Rome he conducted funeral rites for his two sons whose lives he had saved. The one son
he buried four days before his triumphal parade; the other, three days after
his victorious ride through the city. Yet Lucius Paullus bore this tragedy with
the highest constancy, the highest magnitude of mind, and finally with the
greatest strength; and he delivered this great oration to the Roman people:

> I have always feared, citizens, that Fortuna, who is usually envious
> when things go well in my observation, would strike back with some
> evil. Therefore, I prayed to almighty Jupiter, Queen Juno, and Minerva
> that they would cause any evil that ever menaced the Roman people to
> fall wholly on my house. And so, be of good cheer, citizens. For things
> have gone well: the immortal gods have agreed to fulfill my prayers.
> For they have seen to it that you will grieve for our tragedy rather than
> that I should weep for your calamity.

People have also marveled at the constancy of the weaker sex. A Spartan
woman who had sent her son into battle, on hearing that he had been killed,
said, "I gave birth to him so that he would be a man who would not hestitate
to die for his country."[24] We are told that Cornelia, the glory of mothers,
who is said to have contributed much to the eloquence of her sons,[25] when
she tragically lost two sons who were endowed with such courage and such
eloquence, said, "Never will I, who bore the Gracchi, call myself unhappy."[26]

Ah yes, but I, who am not ashamed to be a woman, speak as a woman,
and I shall defend myself with the authority of most male pagan and Christian writers, saying that the above exempla should be compared to colossal
marble statues rather than human beings, since they inspire piety in men's
hearts.[27] And who is so desirous of glory, so hard, so ungentle, so iron-
hearted that he is not moved to tears by the death of his parents, his children, or his friends? Let them cast their eyes on our Christ who shed tears
and mourned over the death of his friend Lazarus. With the Evangelist as

---

of his two sons and even the speech after their death is close to verbatim from Val. Max. 5.10.2.
The same story is also told in Plutarch *Aemilius Paulus* 36.

24. The saying of a Laconian woman ("Lacaena," meaning Spartan woman) is a translation of
a passage from Plutarch *Moralia, Instituta Laconica* 241C–D.

25. On Cornelia as educator, see Plutarch *Tiberius Gracchus* 1.5.

26. On Cornelia's happiness, see Plutarch *Caius Gracchus* 2.1.

27. References to the colossal marble statues of Roman heroes on the Capitoline Hill and else-
where in Rome are just as ubiquitous in ancient and humanist literature as the literary exempla
themselves; the marble statues of the Gracchi are mentioned, for example, in Plutarch *Tiberius
Gracchus* 2.1.

our witness, he sighed aloud when he saw both Mary and the Jews who had come with her weeping, and he felt pity for the human condition.[28]

We also know that the same Lord wept at the destruction of Jerusalem, which would be carried out by the Roman Emperors Titus and Vespasian, and the Evangelist said, "When Jesus approached Jerusalem and saw the city, he wept over it."[29] Mary, his sweet mother, wailed bitterly over her crucified son[30] whose death was a "sword that pierced her soul."[31] The apostolic brothers wept as they departed, leaving him alone in the Acts of the Apostles,[32] and it is certain that Isaac, Jacob, Joseph, and David, a man close to the Lord's heart, shed tears.[33] Finally, even the angels wept over the passion of their Lord, as Isaiah prophesied: "The angels of peace will weep bitterly."[34]

Readers should reflect on the histories of the pagans. Cato seems to have grieved more over the death of his brother than was fitting for a philosopher.[35] Cicero says that he always inveighed against fortune and overcame it; but when he lost his beloved daughter, he confessed he was beaten by fortune.[36]

Since, therefore, moderation must be kept in all things, and since enough space, as I have said, has been devoted to the emotions, let us summon back the reins of reason and not allow ourselves to wallow any longer in sorrow. For, above all, you know this, most illustrious man, since great and admirable praise[37] comes from having borne calamities wisely, from not having been crushed by the blows of fortune, and from having maintained

---

28. Jn 11:33–38.

29. Lk 19:41; in the verses that follow, Jesus prophesies the destruction of Jerusalem.

30. Jn 20:11. This whole passage with its indirect statements all dependent on the main verb "flevit" deals with the theme of *pietas*, the deep love, compassion, and loyalty of family members for one another, particularly, as is appropriate to this consolatory letter to Marcello, the *pietas* between parents and their children, which has its origins in the love of God/Jesus for all his children.

31. Lk 2:35: it was prophesied that Mary would weep for her son Jesus and that "a sword would pierce her soul."

32. Acts 1:3–12.

33. See 1 Kgs 11:4 on David's special favor with the Lord.

34. On Christ's suffering prophetically described see Isaiah 53:2–7; 63:9; the reference to the angels (in Greek the word means messengers or envoys) of peace is Isaiah 33.7.

35. Plutarch *Cato the Younger* 9.1–3.

36. Plutarch *Cicero* 41.5 mentions Cicero's excessive grief on the death of his daughter Tullia. Cicero himself had written a self-consolation on Tullia's death, now lost; and his grief is the subject of an exchange in *Epist. ad Fam.* 4.5 and 4.6; see King, *Venetian Humanism*, 192 and n. 98.

37. *Laus* (praise, writings, eulogies, immortality, *literarisches nachleben*) not *honor* is what Nogarola, the writer and eulogist, is exalting here. Marcello may *read* the gift she gives him as honor (*honor, honestum, decus*), but what she really can give Marcello is longer lasting than mere honor.

dignity throughout the worst times; and all the more so at present, since no calamity is more tragic than this, although as Seneca writes, "As to the man who experienced no misfortune in his life, the gods ruled badly."[38]

When Philip, king of the Macedonians, received three happy messages at one time, the first that he was the victor in the four-horse chariot race at the Olympic games, the second that his general Parmenio had vanquished the Dardanians in battle, and the third that Olympias had given birth to a male child, he raised his eyes and hands to heaven and said, "O God, after these things, repay me with moderate misfortune." For he knew, since he was a wise king, that Fortune tends to envy those who achieve the greatest success.[39]

You had this son for a fitting time and, like something entrusted on loan, thus you kept him for God the lender, so that when God sought his return you would gladly restore him. He was by his very nature endowed with such gifts of mind and body that it was possible to hope for all the great things from him. His mind was so quick at understanding things and so sharp in examining them that, in speaking of his very great intellectual gifts, I do not hesitate in the least to call attention to the gravity of his opinions. He was so greatly endowed with the highest powers of reason, greatness of mind, moderation, prudence, and eloquence beyond his years that he seemed like a new and unheard of miracle to everyone who knew him. Everyone believed that he would easily attain distinction in all the virtues and every sphere of learning and that he would be a most worthy ornament and a pleasure to you, his father, wherever you might be.

Since he departed from life having accumulated so many virtues, you ought not grieve over his immature death but think instead—since the addition of a few years can in no way add to our happiness—that he has been called by God and rejoice that he has come to rest, beyond the reach of all tragedy and the sight of misery, safe and sound in a peaceful harbor. And with divine grace presiding, from death has come the day of his birth, and the end of life has granted the beginning of life, since, as Paul the Apostle has said, "Thus to live is Christ, and to die is gain,"[40] because in such a death

---

Note also that in her use of perfect tense infinitives as substantives (as opposed to present tense infinitives) she brings out the sense of action completed, not ongoing as with present infinitives.

38. Seneca *De Providentia* 3.3.5: "nihil, inquit, mihi videtur infelicius eo cui nihil umquam evenit adversi . . . , male tamen de illo dii iudicaverunt." Nogarola quotes almost verbatim: "Cui nihil evenit adversi, male de illo dii iudicaverunt."

39. The story of the three messages is in Plutarch *Alexander* 3.4–5 and the *Ad Apollonium* 105A–B. Nogarola appears to have translated the whole anecdote verbatim from the latter source.

40. Phil 1:21: "Talibus vivere Christus est et mori lucrum."

he gains eternal life.[41] This Valerio seemed to know with an old man's knowledge, since he endured death with so brave and manly a spirit that no one saw him grieve, but rather he hoped for death, to the extent that he could do so piously, with the most lofty prayers. For he knew that he was departing to a better life where there would be no death beyond this life, no mourning, and no sorrow; and since he had lived as a stranger and a sojourner in this life, he knew that he was going from exile to his fatherland, from misery to glory, and from mortality to immortality.

You, therefore, an old man, should not be ashamed to imitate this child, your son Valerio, who has shown you the way, and thus you must bear his death and those of your other loved ones. Remember, while he watched his last day pressing to a close, how expressively, eloquently, and gravely he consoled you, his father, urging you not to want to mourn him or to put on the mourning that women wear, since Valerio knew with divine inspiration that mourning and mournful lamentation are suitable for weak women, not for strong and noble-hearted men. Cast your mind back on these things, therefore, and ponder them often, lest you seem to yourself, as an elderly man now, to have failed in your duty and to be overcome by remorse.[42] You have lived your life with such wisdom, such glory in the administration of your offices, and such use of your circumstances (and with your help and advice not only many noble men but also many of the common people have flourished)[43] that no age will ever bring an end to your praises, and your fame will travel to the ends of the earth. You have displayed piety toward your city, incredible justice, and the highest gravity. You have been a refuge to those who are oppressed and the supporter of the most distinguished men; and you have exhibited loyalty, authority, and eloquence in the administration of the affairs of the republic.

I shall make no mention of the offices, magistracies, governorships, and ambassadorships that you have held with such integrity, modesty, humanity, and wisdom that you were admired and esteemed even by your enemies because of the distinction of your many virtues. All were aware that you

---

41. Nogarola's comment, or a paraphrase of Paul: see Rom 6:4, 10.

42. We are taking "provecto" ("advanced in time," usually with *aetate* meaning in years, but more rarely as here without *aetate*) as a dative passive participle from *provehere* with "tibi." In the phrase "ne tibi iam provecto defuisse . . . videaris," it is important to emphasize Nogarola's use of perfect tense infinitives. She imagines Marcello already ("iam") looking back on his duties as a father critically and finding himself deficient ("defuisse"). "Provecto" could of course also mean carried along as by emotion, but the interpretation above makes more sense.

43. Note the contrast here between "homines" and "populi," which have been translated as "leading men" and "the populace," respectively.

undertook not utility or private advantages from the offices you held but rather the defense of the poor, the promotion of the good, the eradication of evil, and the health and well-being of the whole populace.[44]

A witness is our Verona, where you achieved so much that was remarkable that at the most critical moment in the city's worst disaster you were chosen as commander-in-chief from among so many vigorous leaders. At the same time, the illustrious Venetian Senate confirmed the appointment and entrusted the highest command over the whole war to you. For they hoped that with such a leader they would be the victors, and they were not disappointed in their hopes. For you distinguished yourself with such wisdom, loyalty, eloquence, and experience in war that after you had put the enemy to flight, you brought not only victory but admirable counsel about peace and war. You also brought greatness of mind, toil in official transactions, bravery in the face of danger, energy and speed in the execution of assignments, and consultation in taking precautionary measures: all that was fitting to a commander in chief. In you they came to recognize the highest level of expertise as a soldier and an administrator.

Powerful in arms and rich in farmland, Brescia too is a witness, for there your virtue shone in an almost godlike manner, and under your leadership and auspices so many campaigns were conducted that everyone there calls you the champion, the defender and protector, as though you were sent down from heaven.

Finally, all Italy bears witness. For you have preserved her power with your extraordinary virtue and magnanimity, dignity, and majesty, and you have restored peace and tranquility to her, and thus glory, honor, and liberty. Instead of bitter bereavement, the slaughter of citizens, the burning of homes, the rape of virgins,[45] the pillaging of cities, and every form of atrocity and enslavement of citizens, Italy has enjoyed harmony, well-being, and happiness.

Many other memorable things I shall pass over; this is not the place either for remembering or writing about them,[46] since in my condition I must judge these things as foreign to me: that is, my form of life and my

---

44. Again, *populi* in the phrase *totius populi correctionem* has been translated "populace" to distinguish it from the *bonorum* in the phrase *sublevationem bonorum*, since the *boni* in humanist vocabulary generally refer to the noblemen or men of rank in the city.

45. "Pro vexationibus virginum": a classical euphemism for rape; cf. Cicero *Catil.* 4.2.

46. "Quoniam non est hic commemorandi neque scribendi locus": perhaps her meaning is, as becomes clear at the end of this paragraph, that this is not the place to praise material achievements, especially not Marcello's; this is a consolation not an encomium.

sex dictate that I value other kinds of things.[47] Such accomplishments are glorious and highly acclaimed, but in them either an external virtue or the power of fortune is being praised, since, as that man[48] has said, fortune, as though subject only to its own laws, appropriates the greatest share of things for its own use, and almost everything that comes from prosperity it calls its own. Such praise, whose companionship you have, I think is neither your own nor internal to you, since neither lineage nor ancestors, offspring, sacred offices, thrones, agility of the body, military campaigns or the triumphs brought back from an enemy or any of those things that are commonly regarded as goods are the internal goods of persons.[49] But fearing God, overcoming desire, constraining wrongdoing, using the virtues to strengthen justice, constancy, gentleness, sanctity of character, integrity of life, goodness, pity, piety—and all the goods that proceed from reason and the deep-seated counsels of the mind[50] and those that teach us to bear misfortune lightly and luck with self-discipline—these are the goods we call our own.

Come therefore, illustrious man, let us cast out the works of darkness and put on the armor of light, knowing that we humans are born under the condition that we must die and whoever attempts to resist death strives to fight against divine will,[51] which we cannot nor should we resist. But let us instead give thanks with blessed Job to our creator, who corrects and

---

47. Again, as often in Nogarola's letters, there is an oscillation between the explicit "loquor *ut femina*," the less explicit "*nostra* conditione," on the one hand, and, on the other, her elision of her femaleness and her identification with the men. This constant uncertainty as to how to represent herself sexually calls for further investigation. What is intended by "other kinds of things" (*haec vita, hic sexus alios mores postulet*) is also tantalizing—otherworldly things, perhaps, rather than the this-worldly glory she has just been celebrating?

48. "Ille inquit": the identity of "ille" is unclear. Perhaps Aristotle, of *ipse dixit* fame, is intended.

49. Nogarola's opposition here between *aliena* and *propria bona* (translated as "external" and "internal" goods, respectively) is clearly her adaptation of Aristotle's *bonum per aliud* and *bonum per se*.

50. " . . . ratione et intimo mentis ductu." Interesting formulation; *ratio* is usually the *dux* or the *ductus* (fourth declension noun: leadership, usually military leadership in classical literature).

51. "cogitantes nos natos esse . . . et nititur": double indirect statement; we would expect "eum niti" (an infinitive instead of the indicative "nitiur"). On the statement that we are born under the condition that we must die, see Cicero *Letters to Atticus* 15.1.1: "sed ad haec omnia una consolatio est quod ea condicione nati sumus ut nihil quod homini accidere possit recusare debeamus" ("the condition to which we are born is such that we must not rebel against any part of the human lot.") The translation is that of D.R. Shackleton Bailey in *Cicero: Letters to Atticus*, vol. 4 (Cambridge, MA.: Harvard University Press, 1999), 217. The source of this statement is Cicero *Epistolae Ad familiares* 5.16.2: "Homines nos ut esse meminerimus ea lege natos, ut omnibus telis fortunae proposita sit vita nostra, neque recusandum, quominus ea, qua nati sumus, conditione vivamus . . ."; or perhaps *Epist. ad Att.* 15.1.2: "sed ad haec omnia una consolatio est quod ea conditione nati sumus ut nihil quod homini accidere possit recusare debeamus." The same theme appears in chap. 4 at n. 29.

castigates us with a father's affection, saying with him, "The Lord gave, the Lord has taken away, and as it has pleased the Lord, so it has been done."[52]

And if we accept the good from the Lord's hand, why then should we not endure the bad? Accordingly, nothing we receive from him should seem evil, but instead, like children of the best father, we should endure all things patiently and moderately, thinking of all things, as the Apostle said, as filth,[53] to the end that we make Christ our gain.[54] We should say with Ecclesiastes, "I have seen all things under the sun, and behold, all is vanity."[55] And else-where, "I have seen vanity and vexation of the mind in all things, and there is nothing lasting under the sun."[56] And Peter the Apostle calls this life brief, wretched, and unstable: "All flesh is grass and all glory like the flower of grass; the grass withers and the flowers falls away."[57] And James the Apostle says, "Our life is wholly vapor; it shall be exterminated, root and branch."[58] And Paul says,

> Thus I say this, brothers, time is brief; in short: those who have a wife should be as though they had none, and those who weep as though they do not weep; and those who rejoice should be as though they did not rejoice; and those who sell should be as though they had no possessions; and those who made use of this age should be as though they had not. For the phantom of this world passes by; I, however, want us to be without care.[59]

We should therefore obey these most holy writings; you in turn con-sole me with your words, but let us not mourn the mortal bodies that have slipped away,[60] for we know that in a short time we shall see them, as long as

---

52. Job 1.21: "Dominus dedit, dominus abstulit, sicut domino placuit ita factum est."

53. 1 Cor 4.13; Jas 1.21.

54. A reference to Philippians 1:21, which Nogarola quoted earlier.

55. Eccl 1.14: "Vidi cuncta quae fiunt sub sole, et ecce universa vanitas."

56. Eccl 2.11: "Vidi in omnibus vanitatem et afflictionem animi et nihil permanere sub sole."

57. 1 Pt 1.24: "Omnis caro fenum et omnis gloria tamquam flos feni; exaruit fenum et flos eius decidit."

58. Jas 4.14: "Vita nostra vapor est admodum; parens et deinceps exterminabitur."

59. 1 Cor 7.29–32: "Hoc itaque dico, fratres, tempus breve est; reliquuum est, ut qui habent uxorem tanquam non habentes sint, et qui flent tanquam non flentes, et qui gaudent tanquam non gaudentes, et qui emunt tanquam non possidentes, et qui utuntur hoc seculo tanquam non utamur; praeterit enim figura mundi huius, volo autem nos sine sollicidutine esse."

60. The clause, "caduca mortalium corpuscula . . . brevi" is loaded with resonances that Noga-rola's fifteenth-century audience would have recognized immediately, especially the phrase "ca-duca mortalia" or its variations, which is found in Cicero, Virgil, and Ovid. Nogarola's use of the

we are good. In this way, wisdom—the moderator of all things, honor, and peace will return those things to you, believe me, and praise will flow. Armed with so grandiose and ornate a spectacle of knowledge and fortified with a garrison of virtues,[61] you will fall victim to no calamities, but with patience as your guide you will rejoice that you have entered that battle that offers you the highest praise and glory, since virtue is honed by tribulation. Those who live in our era will praise you, posterity will venerate you, and you will be heir to everlasting life, won through hard labor and nightlong vigils. Vale Verona. August 9, 1461.

---

highly graphic image *caduca*—"falling," "slipping," or "drooping" is an image the ancient poets and philosophers employed to convey the ephemerality and mortality of flowers, vines, crops, humans, and all things in nature.

61. "ornato . . . spectaculo . . . praesidio munitus . . . duce . . . certamen": note the imagery of military games and martial pageantry.

APPENDIX A
CONCORDANCE BETWEEN ABEL EDITION
AND THE KING/ROBIN TRANSLATION

King/Robin no.	Abel no.	Vol:Pages	To	Date
1	2	1:6–11	Ermolao Barbaro	1434?
2	6	1:36–38	Giorgio Bevilacqua	July 1437 [1436?]
3	7	1:39–41	Giorgio Bevilacqua	July 1437 [1436?]
4	8	1:42–45	Antonio Borromeo	1436? 1437?
5	9	1:46–54	Jacopo Foscari	Sept. 1436
6	12	1:65–78	Guarino Veronese	After 11 Oct. 1436
7	13	1:79–82	Guarino Veronese	Before 10 Apr. 1437
8	16	1:103–8	Girolamo Guarini	Early 1438
9	18	1:116–20	Ludovico Cendrata	Early 1438
10	20	1:129–36	Tobia dal Borgo	Jan. or Feb. 1438
11	22	1:146–57	Cardinal Giuliano Cesarini	29 Mar. 1438
12	23a	1:164–69	Niccolo Venier	After 8 June 1438?
13	24	1:170–76	Feltrino Boiardo	1438?
14	26	1:186–91	Niccolo Barbo	9 Dec. 1438/25 Jan. 1439
15	28	1:199–205	Cardinal Francesco Condulmer	1439
16	30	1:210–14	Damiano dal Borgo	10 Sept. 1438
17	33	1:219–20	Damiano dal Borgo	Jan. 1439
18	35	1:222–23	Eusebio dal Borgo	Jan. 1439
19	37	1:227–28	Damiano dal Borgo	Feb. or Mar. 1439
20	39	1:231–32	Damiano dal Borgo	Apr. 1439
21	41	1:240–41	Damiano dal Borgo	5 May/10 Sept. 1439
22	45	1:249–51	Eusebio dal Borgo	Late Nov. 1439
23	46	1:252–53	Damiano dal Borgo	3 Dec. 1439
24	47	1:254–58	Damiano dal Borgo	1439–40
25	53	2:9–22	Isotta Nogarola, from Lauro Quirini	1445–48/51/52?
26	55	2:28–34	Ludovico Foscarini	1451
27	57	2:39–51	Isotta Nogarola, from Ludovico Foscarini	1453
28	86	2:187–216	Dialogue: Adam and Eve*	1451

King/Robin no.	Abel no.	Vol:Pages	To	Date
29	89	2:267–75	Oratio to Ermolao Barbaro*	1453a
30	90	2:276–89	Oratio in praise of Saint Jerome*	1453b
31	79	2:143–56	Pope Pius II	1 Aug. 1459
32	82	2:161–78	Jacopo Antonio Marcello*	9 Aug. 1461

Note: Asterisked entries are not letters. All entries refer to works written by Isotta Nogarola unless specified.

APPENDIX B
A CHRONOLOGICAL LIST OF SOURCES
CITED BY ISOTTA NOGAROLA

I sotta Nogarola's references to the works she studied, borrowed, and owned in the course of her twenty-seven-year career as a writer and orator provide a clear index to the course her literary and religious studies took. As the list below shows, Nogarola's intellectual development falls into three discrete periods: 1434–40, her early letters, which, with the exception of her consolatory letter to Damiano dal Borgo, contain references only to classical works and not to biblical or patristic works; 1441–49, the formative middle years, which represent a period of intense study and intellectual awakening but from which no writings survive; and 1450–61, the rich late period, during which Nogarola experimented with new humanist genres and produced in her writings a mature syncretism of classical and humanistic, biblical, and patristic learning and thought.

PRE–1451

1434: Letter to Ermolao Barbaro

Petronius *Satyricon* 118
Plautus *Aulularia* 124
Cicero *Brutus* 45
Juvenal *Satires* 6.165
Plutarch *Moralia, De Garrulitate*
No biblical references

1436: Letter to Jacopo Foscari

Plutarch *Life of Artaxerxes* 5.1 (anecdote about the poor man who gave the gift of
    water); 4.3–4 (anecdote about a peasant's gift of a pomegranate)
Cicero *De amicitia* 15.55 (allusion)
Valerius Maximus *Factorum et dictorum memorabilium* 8.7.2
Philostratus *Life of Apollonius of Tyana* (Neo-Pythagorean philosopher, 1st c. B.C.E.):
    2.33; 2.24; 2.43
Cicero *De officiis* 1.6.18
Philostratus *Apollonius of Tyana* 1.2

Diogenes Laertius *Lives of the Philosophers, Socrates*
Cicero *Epistolae ad Familiares* 9.14.4
Virgil *Aeneid* 1.607–9
No biblical references

1436: Letter to Guarino (Abel 12)

She thanks the Lord Jesus for having brought Guarino to the study of letters
No biblical references

1437 (or 1436): Letter to Giorgio Bevilacqua (Abel 7; 1:39–41)

Bevilacqua has sent Nogarola a book on the death of Saint Jerome

1438: Letter to Ludovico Cendrata

Plutarch *Life of Alexander, Life of Aristides* 6
Virgil *Eclogues* 10.73–74
Cicero *Pro Roscio* 111
Virgil *Eclogues* 6.69–71, 5.46–48
No biblical references

1438: Letter to Damiano dal Borgo (Abel 30)

Nogarola's letter of consolation to dal Borgo contains her only references to the bible
   in her works prior to 1451
Job
John 11:17–44
Saint Jerome's *Letter to Tyasius, Letter to Heliodorus*
Cicero *Epistolae ad Familiares* 5.16.2
Virgil *Eclogues* 10.73–74, 1.61–63
Romans 5:14
Resonances from 2 Corinthians 5:1
and 2 Peter 1:12, 13

1438: Letter to Niccolo Venier

Plutarch *Life of Demetrius* 9.5–6 (anecdote on the Greek philosopher Stilpo)
References on "virtutum studiis" (studies in the virtues) from Cicero's *De inventione, De
   officiis, De partitione oratoria*
Aulus Gellius *Attic Nights* 7.19.2–4 (Euclides of Megara anecdote)
Valerius Maximus 8.7.4 (on Demetrius's donation of his patrimony to his patria) Fac-
   torum et dictorum memorabilium
No biblical references

*1439 or 1440: Letter to Damiano dal Borgo (in defense of women to dal Borgo's charge of women's
loquacity)*

Plautus *Aulularia* 124
Valerius Maximus 4.4. (on Cornelia, Gracchi mother)

Valerius Maximus 8.3.1 (on Amesia or Maesia oratrix) 8.3.2 (on Affrania or Afrania oratrix) 8.3.3 (Hortensia oratrix)

Aulus Gellius *Attic Nights* 19.9.4 (on Sappho)

Valerius Maximus 8.2.3. (on Fannia's courage)

Virgil *Aeneid* 11 (on Camilla); see also Boccaccio *Famous Women* 39

Valerius Maximus 3.2.25 (Portia, Brutus's wife)

Boccaccio *Famous Women* 49 (on Queen Thomyris); see also Valerius Maximus 9.10. ext.1

Boccaccio *Famous Women* 11–12; 19–20 (on the Amazon queens)

Virgil *Aeneid* 1.491

No biblical references

POST–1450s

New classical texts referred to after 1451 and not mentioned prior to the 1450s are marked with an asterisk (*).

1445–52

A letter from Lauro Quirini to Nogarola advises her, following the example of the late fourth-century C.E. Neoplatonic philosopher Hypatia (flor. 390–415) to read and study Aristotle's *Moralia, Physics, Metaphysics, De interpretatione,* and the *Categories* and to also read the commentaries of Averroes, Avicenna, Boethius, and Aquinas. He also recommends that she read Cicero and Livy.

1451–53: The Dialogue

The *Dialogue* is the most syncretic work of Nogarola's to date: a stitching together of classical and Christian references. Moreover, it is the first of her works to cite biblical and patristic sources at length with the exception of her letter of consolation to Damiano dal Borgo.

Her *Dialogue* includes references to Augustine, passages from the Old and New Testament, Aristotle's *Nicomachean Ethics** and *Posterior Analytics,* Boethius, Cicero, and Sallust.*

A More Precise List of Classical and Christian References in Nogarola's Dialogue

Genesis, books 2 and 3, esp. 2:15–17 and 3:16–19

Lorenzo Valla and Cicero *Dialogues* (resonances only; influence assumed*)

Saint Augustine (*Civitas Dei*) *The City of God, De Genesi ad litteram* (*The Literal Meaning of Genesis*)

Peter Lombard *Sententiae in IV Libris Distinctae* 2.21.5.2

1 Corinthians 14:38; 1:27–29

Aristotle, *Nicomachean Ethics** 3.5.1113b

Saint Augustine *Ad Orosium contra Prisc. et Origen. liber unus.* Also *On Free Will, On Nature and Grace* (see the passage in Patrologia latina 44:286–88)

Aristotle, *Posterior Analytics** 2.11–13.96a. 20–96a 19

Saint Gregory *Liber regulae pastoralis;* also *Moralium libri* 4.36)

Saint Ambrose *Expositio in Lucam;* Saint Bernard *On Grace and Free Choice* 1.2; 4.9

Matthew 19.17; 15:24, 26; 26:63; 27
Mark 10.17 ff.; 14.61; 15
Psalms 69.4
Romans 5.12
John 15:22; 11:47; 18, 19
Luke 22:67, 22:70; 23
Boethius, *The Consolation of Philosophy*
Luke 18:18ff.

1451: Letter to Ludovico Foscarini (Abel 55)

Saint Augustine
Cicero *Pro Plancio**
Plato *Republic* (philosopher kings general reference)
Plutarch, Lucullus* (88–59 B.C.E., general in Third War against Mithradates; lover of
    literature and the arts, generous patron)
Cicero *Epistolae ad Quintum Fratrem* 1.1.29
Plutarch *Timoleon of Corinth** (d. 334 B.C.E. Liberated Greek Sicily from Carthaginian
    domination; credited with reconstruction of Sicily)
Pliny *Naturalis historiae** 2.53; and Livy* 37, 38, 40, 46, 57 (on Paulus and especially the
    Roman victory at Pydna in the Third Macedonian War and his military tribune
    and astronomer Gaius Sulpicius Gallus, who predicted an eclipse of the moon
    on 168 B.C.E. before the battle of Pydna; there are no references to Livy prior
    to 1451 except for a request for a manuscript of the *Decades*)
Plutarch,* lost life of Epaminondas (362 B.C.E. Neo-Pythagorean) as excerpted in Pau-
    sanias 9.31 Foscarini praised for his knowledge of scriptures in general
But no references to specific biblical or patristic works in this letter to Foscarini

1453: Letter to Ermolao Barbaro

Aulus Gellius *Attic Nights* 8.9 (on Demosthenes' and Theophrastus's nervousness be-
    fore public speaking)
Cicero *Pro Cluentio**
Plutarch *Lives of Cicero** 35 and *Demosthenes** 6.3–4
Seneca *Excerpta Controversiarum** 6.8
Virgil, echoes from *Eclogues* 3.102
Ennius *Annals** 117–21 (as quoted by Lactantius and Cicero *De republica* 1.41.61)
Exodus 15:20, 21
Jeremiah 1:10
Song of Solomon 2:3, 6

1453: Oration for Ermolao Barbaro: In Praise of Jerome

Passing reference to John Chrysostom on Matthew
Statius *Silvae** 1.25
Aulus Gellius *Attic Nights* 7.10.2–4 (Euclides of Megara anecdote)
Jerome *Letter to Eustochium*
Passing references (some new*) to Quintilian, Cicero, and Fronto and their skill as
    orators, the great fourth-century C.E. classical scholar and Virgil commentator

Donatus (Jerome's teacher); Philip of Macedonia sending his son Alexander to
Aristotle

1461: Consolatio for Jacopo Antonio Marcello

Plutarch *Moralia**, *Consolatio ad Apollonium** (on the story of the Goddess Luctus)
Allusions to Hesiod, Homer, Virgil, and Ovid on the battle of the Giants with the
    gods
Juvenal 15.133*
Livy 2.8.6–8*
Valerius Maximus 5.10:3* citations
Cicero *De oratore** 3.128
Plutarch *Life of Pericles** 8.3, *Moralia**, *Consolatio ad Apollonium** 118 E–F
Valerius Maximus 5.10.2
Plutarch *Life of Aemilius Paulus** 36, *Moralia**, *Instituta Laconica** 241 C–D, *Life of Tiberius
    Sempronius Gracchus** 1.5, *Life of Gaius Sempronius Gracchus** 2.1
John 11
Luke 19
John 20
Luke 2
Acts 4; 1
Isaiah 53; 63; 33
Plutarch *Life of Cato the Younger** 9, *Life of Cicero* 41.5
Seneca *De Providentia** 3.3.5
Plutarch *Life of Alexander* 3.4–5, *Consolatio ad Apollonium* 105 A–B
Philippians 1
Romans 6:4
Job 1:21
1 Corinthians 4:13
James 1:21
Ecclesiastes 1; 2
1 Peter 1:24
James 4:14
1 Corinthians 7:29

SERIES EDITORS'
BIBLIOGRAPHY

Note: Titles cited in the volume editors' list are not repeated here.

PRIMARY SOURCES

Alberti, Leon Battista. *The Family in Renaissance Florence.* Translated by Renée Neu Watkins. Columbia, S.C.: University of South Carolina Press, 1969.

Arenal, Electa, and Stacey Schlau, eds. *Untold Sisters: Hispanic Nuns in Their Own Works.* Translated by Amanda Powell. Albuquerque, N.M.: University of New Mexico Press, 1989.

Astell, Mary. *The First English Feminist: Reflections on Marriage and Other Writings.* Edited and with an introduction by Bridget Hill. New York: St. Martin's Press, 1986.

Atherton, Margaret, ed. *Women Philosophers of the Early Modern Period.* Indianapolis, Ind.: Hackett Publishing Co., 1994.

Aughterson, Kate, ed. *Renaissance Woman: Constructions of Femininity in England. A Source Book.* London & New York: Routledge, 1995.

Barbaro, Francesco. *On Wifely Duties.* Translated by Benjamin Kohl. In *The Earthly Republic,* edited by Benjamin Kohl and R.G. Witt, 179–228. Philadelphia: University of Pennsylvania Press, 1978, 179–228.

Behn, Aphra. *The Works of Aphra Behn.* 7 vols. Edited by Janet Todd. Columbus, Ohio: Ohio State University Press, 1992–96.

Boccaccio, Giovanni. *Corbaccio or the Labyrinth of Love.* Translated by Anthony K. Cassell. 2d Rev. Ed. Binghamton, N.Y.: Medieval and Renaissance Texts and Studies, 1993.

Bruni, Leonardo. "On the Study of Literature (1405) to Lady Battista Malatesta of Moltefeltro." In *The Humanism of Leonardo Bruni: Selected Texts.* Translated and with an introduction by Gordon Griffiths, James Hankins, and David Thompson, 240–51. Binghamton, N.Y.: Medieval and Renaissance Studies and Texts, 1987.

Castiglione, Baldassare. *The Book of the Courtier.* Translated by George Bull. New York: Penguin, 1967.

Cerasano, S. P., and Marion Wynne-Davies, eds. *Readings in Renaissance Women's Drama: Criticism, History, and Performance 1594–1998.* London & New York: Routledge, 1998.

Clarke, Daniel, ed. *Isabella Whitney, Mary Sidney and Aemilia Lanyer: Renaissance Women Poets.* New York: Penguin Books, 2000.

Crawford, Patricia, and Laura Gowing, eds. *Women's Worlds in Seventeenth-Century England: A Source Book.* London & New York: Routledge, 2000.

Daybell, James, ed. *Early Modern Women's Letter Writing, 1450–1700.* Houndmills, England & New York: Palgrave, 2001.

Elizabeth I: Collected Works. Edited by Leah S. Marcus, Janel Mueller, and Mary Beth Rose. Chicago: University of Chicago Press, 2000.

Elyot, Thomas. *Defence of Good Women: The Feminist Controversy of the Renaissance.* Facsimile Reproductions. Edited by Diane Bornstein. New York: Delmar, 1980.

Erasmus, Desiderius. *Erasmus on Women.* Edited by Erika Rummel. Toronto: University of Toronto Press, 1996.

Female and Male Voices in Early Modern England: An Anthology of Renaissance Writing. Edited by Betty S. Travitsky and Anne Lake Prescott. New York: Columbia University Press, 2000.

Ferguson, Moira, ed. *First Feminists: British Women Writers 1578–1799.* Bloomington, Ind.: Indiana University Press, 1985.

Galilei, Maria Celeste. *Sister Maria Celeste's Letters to Her Father, Galileo.* Edited and translated by Rinaldina Russell. Lincoln, Neb., & New York: Writers Club Press of Universe.com, 2000.

Gethner, Perry, ed. *The Lunatic Lover and Other Plays by French Women of the 17th and 18th Centuries.* Portsmouth, N.H.: Heinemann, 1994.

Glückel of Hameln. *The Memoires of Glückel of Hameln.* Translated by Marvin Lowenthal. New introduction by Robert Rosen. New York: Schocken Books, 1977.

Henderson, Katherine Usher, and Barbara F. McManus, eds. *Half Humankind: Contexts and Texts of the Controversy about Women in England, 1540–1640.* Urbana, Ill.: University of Illinois Press, 1985.

Joscelin, Elizabeth. *The Mother's Legacy to Her Unborn Childe.* Edited by Jean leDrew Metcalfe. Toronto: University of Toronto Press, 2000.

Kaminsky, Amy Katz, ed. *Water Lilies, Flores del Agua: An Anthology of Spanish Women Writers from the Fifteenth Through the Nineteenth Century.* Minneapolis, Minn.: University of Minnesota Press, 1996.

Kempe, Margery. *The Book of Margery Kempe.* Translated and edited by Lynn Staley. A Norton Critical Edition. New York: W.W. Norton, 2001.

Klein, Joan Larsen, ed. *Daughters, Wives, and Widows: Writings by Men about Women and Marriage in England, 1500–1640.* Urbana, Ill.: University of Illinois Press, 1992.

Knox, John. *The Political Writings of John Knox: The First Blast of the Trumpet against the Monstrous Regiment of Women and Other Selected Works.* Edited by Marvin A. Breslow. Washington, D.C.: Folger Shakespeare Library, 1985.

Kors, Alan C., and Edward Peters, eds. *Witchcraft in Europe, 400–1700: A Documentary History.* Philadelphia: University of Pennsylvania Press, 2000.

Krämer, Heinrich, and Jacob Sprenger. *Malleus Maleficarum* (ca. 1487). Translated by Montague Summers. London: Pushkin Press, 1928. Reprint, New York: Dover, 1971.

Larsen, Anne R., and Colette H. Winn, eds. *Writings by Pre-Revolutionary French Women: From Marie de France to Elizabeth Vigée-Le Brun.* New York & London: Garland Publishing Co., 2000.

de Lorris, William, and Jean de Meun. *The Romance of the Rose.* Translated by Charles Dahlbert. Princeton: Princeton University Press, 1971.

Marguerite d'Angoulême, Queen of Navarre. *The Heptameron.* Translated by P. A. Chilton. New York: Viking Penguin, 1984.

Mary of Agreda. *The Divine Life of the Most Holy Virgin.* Abridgment of *The Mystical City of God.* Abridged by Fr. Bonaventure Amedeo de Caesarea, M.C. Translated from French by Abbé Joseph A. Boullan. Rockford, Ill.: TAN Books, 1997.

Myers, Kathleen A., and Amanda Powell, eds. *A Wild Country out in the Garden: The Spiritual Journals of a Colonial Mexican Nun.* Bloomington, Ind.: Indiana University Press, 1999.

Russell, Rinaldina, ed. *Sister Maria Celeste's Letters to Her Father, Galileo.* San Jose & New York: Writers Club Press, 2000.

Teresa of Avila, Saint. *The Life of Saint Teresa of Avila by Herself.* Translated by J. M. Cohen. New York: Viking Penguin, 1957.

Weyer, Johann. *Witches, Devils, and Doctors in the Renaissance: Johann Weyer, De praestigiis daemonum.* Edited by George Mora with Benjamin G. Kohl, Erik Midelfort, and Helen Bacon. Translated by John Shea. Binghamton, N.Y.: Medieval and Renaissance Texts and Studies, 1991.

Wilson, Katharina M., ed. *Medieval Women Writers.* Athens, Ga.: University of Georgia Press, 1984.

―――, ed. *Women Writers of the Renaissance and Reformation.* Athens, Ga.: University of Georgia Press, 1987.

Wilson, Katharina M., and Frank J. Warnke, eds. *Women Writers of the Seventeenth Century.* Athens, Ga.: University of Georgia Press, 1989.

Wollstonecraft, Mary. *A Vindication of the Rights of Men and a Vindication of the Rights of Women.* Edited by Sylvana Tomaselli. Cambridge: Cambridge University Press, 1995. Also *The Vindications of the Rights of Men, The Rights of Women.* Edited by D. L. Macdonald and Kathleen Scherf. Peterborough, Ontario: Broadview Press, 1997.

Women Critics 1600–1820: An Anthology. Edited by the Folger Collective on Early Women Critics. Bloomington, Ind.: Indiana University Press, 1995.

Women Writers in English 1350–1850; 15 volumes, published through 1999 (projected 30-volume series suspended). Oxford: Oxford University Press, 1993–99.

Wroth, Lady Mary. *The Countess of Montgomery's Urania.* 2 parts. Edited by Josephine A. Roberts. Tempe, Az.: MRTS, 1995, 1999.

―――. *Lady Mary Wroth's "Love's Victory": The Penshurst Manuscript.* Edited by Michael G. Brennan. London: The Roxburghe Club, 1988.

―――. *The Poems of Lady Mary Wroth.* Edited by Josephine A. Roberts. Baton Rouge, La.: Louisiana State University Press, 1983.

de Zayas Maria. *The Disenchantments of Love.* Translated by H. Patsy Boyer. Albany, N.Y.: State University of New York Press, 1997.

―――. *The Enchantments of Love: Amorous and Exemplary Novels.* Translated by H. Patsy Boyer. Berkeley, Calif.: University of California Press, 1990.

SECONDARY SOURCES

Akkerman, Tjitske & Siep Sturman, eds. *Feminist Thought in European History, 1400–2000.* London & New York: Routledge, 1997.

Backer, Anne Liot Backer. *Precious Women.* New York: Basic Books, 1974.

Barash, Carol. *English Women's Poetry, 1649–1714: Politics, Community, and Linguistic Author-ity.* New York & Oxford: Oxford University Press, 1996.

Battigelli, Anna. *Margaret Cavendish and the Exiles of the Mind.* Lexington, Ky.: University of Kentucky Press, 1998.

Beasley, Faith. *Revising Memory: Women's Fiction and Memoirs in Seventeenth-Century France.* New Brunswick, N.J.: Rutgers University Press, 1990.

Beilin, Elaine V. *Redeeming Eve: Women Writers of the English Renaissance.* Princeton: Prince-ton University Press, 1987.

Bissell, R. Ward. *Artemisia Gentileschi and the Authority of Art.* University Park, Penn.: Pennsylvania State University Press, 2000.

Blain, Virginia, Isobel Grundy, and Patricia Clements, eds. *The Feminist Companion to Literature in English: Women Writers from the Middle Ages to the Present.* New Haven: Yale University Press, 1990.

Bloch, R. Howard. *Medieval Misogyny and the Invention of Western Romantic Love.* Chicago: University of Chicago Press, 1991.

Bornstein, Daniel, and Roberto Rusconi, eds. *Women and Religion in Medieval and Renais-sance Italy.* Translated by Margery J. Schneider. Chicago: University of Chicago Press, 1996.

Brant, Clare, and Diane Purkiss, eds. *Women, Texts and Histories, 1575–1760.* London & New York: Routledge, 1992.

Briggs, Robin. *Witches and Neighbours: The Social and Cultural Context of European Witchcraft.* New York: HarperCollins, 1995; Viking Penguin, 1996.

Brown, Judith C. *Immodest Acts: The Life of a Lesbian Nun in Renaissance Italy.* New York: Oxford University Press, 1986.

Cervigni, Dino S., ed. *Women Mystic Writers,* Annali d'Italianistica 13 (1995) (entire issue).

Cervigni, Dino S., and Rebecca West, eds. *Women's Voices in Italian Literature.* Annali d'Italianistica 7 (1989) (entire issue).

Charlton, Kenneth. *Women, Religion and Education in Early Modern England.* London & New York: Routledge, 1999.

Cholakian, Patricia Francis. *Rape and Writing in the* Heptameron *of Marguerite de Navarre.* Carbondale and Edwardsville, Ill.: Southern Illinois University Press, 1991.

————. *Women and the Politics of Self-Representation in Seventeenth-Century France.* Newark: University of Delaware Press, 2000.

Clogan, Paul Maurice, ed. *Medievali et Humanistica: Literacy and the Lay Reader.* Lanham, Md.: Rowman & Littlefield, 2000.

Crabb, Ann. *The Strozzi of Florence: Widowhood and Family Solidarity in the Renaissance.* Ann Arbor: University of Michigan Press, 2000.

Davis, Natalie Zemon. *Society and Culture in Early Modern France.* Stanford: Stanford University Press, 1975. Especially chapters 3 and 5.

————. *Women on the Margins: Three Seventeenth-Century Lives.* Cambridge, Mass.: Har-vard University Press, 1995.

DeJean, Joan. *Ancients against Moderns: Culture Wars and the Making of a fin de Siècle.* Chi-cago: University of Chicago Press, 1997.

————. *Tender Geographies: Women and the Origins of the Novel in France.* New York: Columbia University Press, 1991.

Dixon, Laurinda S. *Perilous Chastity: Women and Illness in Pre-Enlightenment Art and Medicine.* Ithaca, N.Y.: Cornell University Press, 1995.

Dolan, Frances, E. *Whores of Babylon: Catholicism, Gender and Seventeenth-Century Print Culture.* Ithaca, N.Y.: Cornell University Press, 1999.

Donovan, Josephine. *Women and the Rise of the Novel, 1405–1726.* New York: St. Martin's Press, 1999.

De Erauso, Catalina. *Lieutenant Nun: Memoir of a Basque Transvestite in the New World.* Translated by Michele Ttepto & Gabriel Stepto; foreword by Marjorie Garber. Boston: Beacon Press, 1995.

Erickson, Amy Louise. *Women and Property in Early Modern England.* London & New York: Routledge, 1993.

Ezell, Margaret J. M. *The Patriarch's Wife: Literary Evidence and the History of the Family.* Chapel Hill: University of North Carolina Press, 1987.

————. *Social Authorship and the Advent of Print.* Baltimore: Johns Hopkins University Press, 1999.

————. *Writing Women's Literary History.* Baltimore: Johns Hopkins University Press, 1993.

Ferguson, Margaret W., Maureen Quilligan, and Nancy J. Vikers, ed. *Rewriting the Renaissance: The Discourses of Sexual Difference in Early Modern Europe.* Chicago: University of Chicago Press, 1987.

Fletcher, Anthony. *Gender, Sex and Subordination in England, 1500–1800.* New Haven: Yale University Press, 1995.

Frye, Susan, and Karen Robertson, eds. *Maids and Mistresses, Cousins and Queens: Women's Alliances in Early Modern England.* Oxford: Oxford University Press, 1999.

Gallagher, Catherine. *Nobody's Story: The Vanishing Acts of Women Writers in the Marketplace, 1670–1820.* Berkeley: University of California Press, 1994.

Garrard, Mary D. *Artemisia Gentileschi: The Image of the Female Hero in Italian Baroque Art.* Princeton: Princeton University Press, 1989.

Gelbart, Nina Rattner. *The King's Midwife: A History and Mystery of Madame du Coudray.* Berkeley: University of California Press, 1998.

Goldberg, Jonathan. *Desiring Women Writing: English Renaissance Examples.* Stanford: Stanford University Press, 1997.

Goldsmith, Elizabeth C. *Exclusive Conversations: The Art of Interaction in Seventeenth-Century France.* Philadelphia: University of Pennsylvania Press, 1988.

————, ed. *Writing the Female Voice.* Boston: Northeastern University Press, 1989.

Goldsmith, Elizabeth C., and Dena Goodman, eds. *Going Public: Women and Publishing in Early Modern France.* Ithaca, N.Y.: Cornell University Press, 1995.

Greer, Margaret Rich. *Maria de Zayas Tells Baroque Tales of Love and the Cruelty of Men.* University Park, Penn.: Pennsylvania State University Press, 2000.

Hackett, Helen. *Women and Romance Fiction in the English Renaissance.* Cambridge: Cambridge University Press, 2000.

Hall, Kim F. *Things of Darkness: Economies of Race and Gender in Early Modern England.* Ithaca, N.Y.: Cornell University Press, 1995.

Hampton, Timothy. *Literature and the Nation in the Sixteenth Century: Inventing Renaissance France.* Ithaca, N.Y.: Cornell University Press, 2001.

Hardwick, Julie. *The Practice of Patriarchy: Gender and the Politics of Household Authority in Early Modern France.* University Park, Penn.: Pennsylvania State University Press, 1998.

Harth, Erica. *Ideology and Culture in Seventeenth-Century France.* Ithaca, N.Y.: Cornell University Press, 1983.

————. *Cartesian Women. Versions and Subversions of Rational Discourse in the Old Regime.* Ithaca, N.Y.: Cornell University Press, 1992.

Haselkorn, Anne M., and Betty Travitsky, eds. *The Renaissance Englishwoman in Print: Counterbalancing the Canon.* Amherst: University of Massachusetts Press, 1990.

Herlihy, David. "Did Women Have a Renaissance? A Reconsideration." *Medievalia et Humanistica,* NS 13 (1985): 1–22.

Hill, Bridget. *The Republican Virago: The Life and Times of Catharine Macaulay, Historian.* New York: Oxford University Press, 1992.

A History of Women in the West.

Volume 1: *From Ancient Goddesses to Christian Saints.* Edited by Pauline Schmitt Pantel. Cambridge, Mass.: Harvard University Press, 1992.

Volume 2: *Silences of the Middle Ages.* Edited by Christiane Klapisch-Zuber. Cambridge, Mass.: Harvard University Press, 1992.

Volume 3: *Renaissance and Enlightenment Paradoxes.* Edited by Natalie Zemon Davis and Arlette Farge. Cambridge, Mass.: Harvard University Press, 1993.

Hobby, Elaine. *Virtue of Necessity: English Women's Writing 1646–1688.* London: Virago Press, 1988.

Horowitz, Maryanne Cline. "Aristotle and Women." *Journal of the History of Biology* 9 (1976): 183–213.

Hufton, Olwen H. *The Prospect before Her: A History of Women in Western Europe, 1: 1500–1800.* New York: HarperCollins, 1996.

Hunt, Lynn, ed. *The Invention of Pornography: Obscenity and the Origins of Modernity, 1500–1800.* New York: Zone Books, 1996.

Hutner, Heidi, ed. *Rereading Aphra Behn: History, Theory, and Culture.* Charlottesville, Va.: University Press of Virginia, 1993.

Hutson, Lorna, ed. *Feminism and Renaissance Studies.* New York: Oxford University Press, 1999.

James, Susan E. *Kateryn Parr: The Making of a Queen.* Aldershot and Brookfield, UK: Ashgate Publishing Co., 1999.

Jankowski, Theodora A. *Women in Power in the Early Modern Drama.* Urbana, Ill.: University of Illinois Press, 1992.

Jansen, Katherine Ludwig. *The Making of the Magdalen: Preaching and Popular Devotion in the Later Middle Ages.* Princeton: Princeton University Press, 2000.

Jed, Stephanie H. *Chaste Thinking: The Rape of Lucretia and the Birth of Humanism.* Bloomington, Ind.: Indiana University Press, 1989.

Jordan, Constance. *Renaissance Feminism: Literary Texts and Political Models.* Ithaca, N.Y.: Cornell University Press, 1990.

Kelly, Joan. "Did Women Have a Renaissance?" In Joan Kelly, *Women, History, and Theory.* Chicago: University of Chicago Press, 1984. Also in Renate Bridenthal, Claudia Koonz, and Susan M. Stuard, eds., *Becoming Visible: Women in European History.* 3d Ed. Boston: Houghton Mifflin, 1998.

————. "Early Feminist Theory and the *Querelle des Femmes.*" In *Women, History, and Theory.*

Kelso, Ruth. *Doctrine for the Lady of the Renaissance.* Foreword by Katharine M. Rogers. Urbana, Ill.: University of Illinois Press, 1956, 1978.

King, Carole. *Renaissance Women Patrons: Wives and Widows in Italy, c. 1300–1550.* New York & Manchester: Manchester University Press (distributed in the U.S. by St. Martin's Press), 1998.

Krontiris, Tina. *Oppositional Voices: Women as Writers and Translators of Literature in the English Renaissance.* London & New York: Routledge, 1992.

Kuehn, Thomas. *Law, Family, and Women: Toward a Legal Anthropology of Renaissance Italy.* Chicago: University of Chicago Press, 1991.

Kunze, Bonnelyn Young. *Margaret Fell and the Rise of Quakerism.* Stanford: Stanford University Press, 1994.

Laqueur, Thomas. *Making Sex: Body and Gender from the Greeks to Freud.* Cambridge, Mass.: Harvard University Press, 1990.

Larsen, Anne R., and Colette H. Winn, eds. *Renaissance Women Writers: French Texts/ American Contexts.* Detroit: Wayne State University Press, 1994.

Lerner, Gerda. *The Creation of Patriarchy and Creation of Feminist Consciousness, 1000–1870.* 2 Vols. New York: Oxford University Press, 1986, 1994.

Levin, Carole, and Jeanie Watson, eds. *Ambiguous Realities: Women in the Middle Ages and Renaissance.* Detroit: Wayne State University Press, 1987.

Levin, Carole, et al. *Extraordinary Women of the Medieval and Renaissance World: A Biographical Dictionary,* Westport, Conn.: Greenwood Press, 2000.

Lindsey, Karen. *Divorced Beheaded Survived: A Feminist Reinterpretation of the Wives of Henry VIII.* Reading, Mass.: Addison-Wesley Publishing Co., 1995.

Lochrie, Karma. *Margery Kempe and Translations of the Flesh.* Philadelphia: University of Pennsylvania Press, 1992.

Lougee, Carolyn C. *Le Paradis des Femmes: Women, Salons, and Social Stratification in Seventeenth-Century France.* Princeton: Princeton University Press, 1976.

Love, Harold. *The Culture and Commerce of Texts: Scribal Publication in Seventeenth-Century England.* Amherst, Mass.: University of Massachusetts Press, 1993.

MacCarthy, Bridget G. *The Female Pen: Women Writers and Novelists 1621–1818.* Preface by Janet Todd. New York: New York University Press, 1994 . . . originally published by Cork University Press, 1946–47.

Maclean, Ian. *Women Triumphant: Feminism in French Literature, 1610–1652.* Oxford: Clarendon Press, 1977.

———. *The Renaissance Notion of Women: A Study of the Fortunes of Scholasticism and Medical Science in European Intellectual Life.* Cambridge: Cambridge University Press, 1980.

Matter, E. Ann, and John Coakley, eds. *Creative Women in Medieval and Early Modern Italy.* Philadelphia: University of Pennsylvania Press, 1994 . . .

McLeod, Glenda. *Virtue and Venom: Catalogs of Women from Antiquity to the Renaissance.* Ann Arbor: University of Michigan Press, 1991.

Meek, Christine, ed. *Women in Renaissance and Early Modern Europe.* Dublin-Portland: Four Courts Press, 2000.

Mendelson, Sara, and Patricia Crawford. *Women in Early Modern England, 1550–1720.* Oxford: Clarendon Press, 1998.

Merrim, Stephanie. *Early Modern Women's Writing and Sor Juana Inés de la Cruz.* Nashville, Tenn.: Vanderbilt University Press, 1999.

Miller, Nancy K. *The Heroine's Text: Readings in the French and English Novel, 1722–1782.* New York: Columbia University Press, 1980.

Miller, Naomi J. *Changing the Subject: Mary Wroth and Figurations of Gender in Early Modern England.* Lexington, Ky.: University Press of Kentucky, 1996.

Miller, Naomi J., and Gary Waller, eds. *Reading Mary Wroth: Representing Alternatives in Early Modern England.* Knoxville, Tenn.: University of Tennessee Press, 1991.

Monson, Craig A., ed. *The Crannied Wall: Women, Religion, and the Arts in Early Modern Europe.* Ann Arbor: University of Michigan Press, 1992.

Newman, Karen. *Fashioning Femininity and English Renaissance Drama.* Chicago & London: University of Chicago Press, 1991.

Okin, Susan Moller. *Women in Western Political Thought.* Princeton: Princeton University Press, 1979.

Ozment, Steven. *The Bürgermeister's Daughter: Scandal in a Sixteenth-Century German Town.* New York: St. Martin's Press, 1995.

Pacheco, Anita, ed. *Early [English] Women Writers: 1600–1720.* New York & London: Longman, 1998.

Pagels, Elaine. *Adam, Eve, and the Serpent.* New York: HarperCollins, 1988.

Panizza, Letizia, and Sharon Wood, eds. *A History of Women's Writing In Italy.* Cambridge: University Press, 2000.

Perry, Ruth. *The Celebrated Mary Astell: An Early English Feminist.* Chicago: University of Chicago Press, 1986.

Rapley, Elizabeth. *A Social History of the Cloister: Daily Life in the Teaching Monasteries of the Old Regime.* Montreal: McGill-Queen's University Press, 2001.

Raven, James, Helen Small, and Naomi Tadmor, eds. *The Practice and Representation of Reading in England.* Cambridge: University Press, 1996.

Reardon, Colleen. *Holy Concord within Sacred Walls: Nuns and Music in Siena, 1575–1700.* Oxford: Oxford University Press, 2001.

Reiss, Sheryl E., and David G. Wilkins, ed. *Beyond Isabella: Secular Women Patrons of Art in Renaissance Italy.* Kirksville, Mo.: Truman State University Press, 2001.

Rheubottom, David. *Age, Marriage, and Politics in Fifteenth-Century Ragusa.* Oxford: Oxford University Press, 2000.

Richardson, Brian. *Printing, Writers and Readers in Renaissance Italy.* Cambridge: University Press, 1999.

Riddle, John M. *Contraception and Abortion from the Ancient World to the Renaissance.* Cambridge, Mass.: Harvard University Press, 1992.

———. *Eve's Herbs: A History of Contraception and Abortion in the West.* Cambridge, Mass.: Harvard University Press, 1997.

Rose, Mary Beth. *The Expense of Spirit: Love and Sexuality in English Renaissance Drama.* Ithaca, N.Y.: Cornell University Press, 1988.

———. *Gender and Heroism in Early Modern English Literature.* Chicago: University of Chicago Press, 2002.

———, ed. *Women in the Middle Ages and the Renaissance: Literary and Historical Perspectives.* Syracuse, N.Y.: Syracuse University Press, 1986.

Rosenthal, Margaret F. *The Honest Courtesan: Veronica Franco, Citizen and Writer in Sixteenth-Century Venice.* Foreword by Catharine R. Stimpson. Chicago: University of Chicago Press, 1992.

Sackville-West, Vita. *Daughter of France: The Life of La Grande Mademoiselle.* Garden City, N.Y.: Doubleday, 1959.

Schiebinger, Londa. *The Mind Has No Sex?: Women in the Origins of Modern Science.* Cambridge, Mass.: Harvard University Press, 1991.

———. *Nature's Body: Gender in the Making of Modern Science.* Boston: Beacon Press, 1993.

Schutte, Anne Jacobson, Thomas Kuehn, and Silvana Seidel Menchi, eds. *Time, Space, and Women's Lives in Early Modern Europe.* Kirksville, Mo.: Truman State University Press, 2001.

Shannon, Laurie. *Sovereign Amity: Figures of Friendship in Shakespearean Contexts.* Chicago: University of Chicago Press, 2002.

Shemek, Deanna. *Ladies Errant: Wayward Women and Social Order in Early Modern Italy.* Durham, N.C.: Duke University Press, 1998.

Sobel, Dava. *Galileo's Daughter: A Historical Memoir of Science, Faith, and Love.* New York: Penguin Books, 2000.

Sommerville, Margaret R. *Sex and Subjection: Attitudes to Women in Early-Modern Society.* London: Arnold, 1995.

Spencer, Jane. *The Rise of the Woman Novelist: From Aphra Behn to Jane Austen.* Oxford: Basil Blackwell, 1986.

Spender, Dale. *Mothers of the Novel: 100 Good Women Writers before Jane Austen.* London & New York: Routledge, 1986.

Sperling, Jutta Gisela. *Convents and the Body Politic in Late Renaissance Venice.* Foreword by Catharine R. Stimpson. Chicago: University of Chicago Press, 1999.

Steinbrügge, Lieselotte. *The Moral Sex: Woman's Nature in the French Enlightenment.* Translated by Pamela E. Selwyn. New York: Oxford University Press, 1995.

Stephens, Sonya, ed. *A History of Women's Writing in France.* Cambridge: Cambridge University Press, 2000.

Stuard, Susan M. "The Dominion of Gender: Women's Fortunes in the High Middle Ages." In *Becoming Visible: Women in European History* edited by Renate Bridenthal, Claudia Koonz, and Susan M. Stuard. 3d Ed. Boston: Houghton Mifflin, 1998.

Summit, Jennifer. *Lost Property: The Woman Writer and English Literary History, 1380–1589,* Chicago: University of Chicago Press, 2000.

Teague, Frances. *Bathsua Makin, Woman of Learning.* Lewisburg, Pa.: Bucknell University Press, 1999.

Todd, Janet. *The Secret Life of Aphra Behn.* London, New York, & Sydney: Pandora, 2000.
———. *The Sign of Angelica: Women, Writing and Fiction, 1660–1800.* New York: Columbia University Press, 1989.

Van Dijk, Susan, Lia van Gemert, and Sheila Ottway, eds. *Writing the History of Women's Writing: Toward an International Approach.* Proceedings of the Colloquium, Amsterdam, September 9–11. Amsterdam: Royal Netherlands Academy of Arts and Sciences, 2001.

Wall, Wendy. *The Imprint of Gender: Authorship and Publication in the English Renaissance.* Ithaca, N.Y.: Cornell University Press, 1993.

Walsh, William T. *St. Teresa of Avila: A Biography.* Rockford, Ill.: TAN Books, 1987.

Warnicke, Retha M. *The Marrying of Anne of Cleves: Royal Protocol in Tudor England.* Cambridge: Cambridge University Press, 2000.

Watt, Diane. *Secretaries of God: Women Prophets in Late Medieval and Early Modern England.* Cambridge, UK: D. S. Brewer, 1997.

Welles, Marcia L. *Persephone's Girdle: Narratives of Rape in Seventeenth-Century Spanish Literature.* Nashville, Tenn.: Vanderbilt University Press, 2000.

Wiesner, Merry E. *Women and Gender in Early Modern Europe.* Cambridge: Cambridge University Press, 1993.

Wilson, Katharina, ed. *An Encyclopedia of Continental Women Writers.* New York: Garland, 1991.

Woodbridge, Linda. *Women and the English Renaissance: Literature and the Nature of Womankind, 1540–1620.* Urbana, Ill.: University of Illinois Press, 1984.

Woods, Susanne. *Lanyer: A Renaissance Woman Poet.* New York: Oxford University Press, 1999.

Woods, Susanne, and Margaret P. Hannay, eds. *Teaching Tudor and Stuart Women Writers.* New York: MLA, 2000.

INDEX